Mastering the Microsoft Deployment Toolkit

Take a deep dive into the world of Windows desktop deployment using the Microsoft Deployment Toolkit

Jeff Stokes

Manuel Singer

BIRMINGHAM - MUMBAI

Mastering the Microsoft Deployment Toolkit

First published: May 2016

Production reference: 1260516

Published by Packt Publishing Ltd.

Livery Place

35 Livery Street

Birmingham

B3 2PB, UK.

ISBN 978-1-78217-249-9

www.packtpub.com

Credits

Authors

Jeff Stokes

Manuel Singer

Reviewers

Florian Klaffenbach

Brian Mithen

Commissioning Editor

Saleem Ahmed

Acquisition Editors

Saleem Ahmed

Prachi Bisht

Content Development Editor

Mayur Pawanikar

Technical Editor

Pranil Pathare

Copy Editor

Vibha Shukla

Project Coordinator

Nidhi Joshi

Proofreader

Safis Editing

Indexer

Mariammal Chettiyar

Graphics

Jason Monteiro

Production Coordinator

Arvindkumar Gupta

About the Authors

Jeff Stokes is a deployment and performance specialist for Windows operating systems. Jeff has a passion for the user experience in enterprise environment. As an avid public speaker, podcaster, blogger, and mentor, Jeff started his IT career at Digital in the 90s, and has been hard at work ever since. Currently, employed at Microsoft, he is expanding his horizons with projects in big data and data analytics.

When not working, he enjoys spending time with his family and friends. His hobbies are gaming, music, and writing.

I'd like to thank my wife, Ana, for her continued support. I couldn't have done this without you! I would also like to give a nod to Carl Luberti, Michael Niehaus, Aaron Margosis, Bill Curtis, and all the other deployment folks I've learned so much about deployment from over the years.

Manuel Singer works as a Premier Field Engineer for Windows Client at Microsoft and is based in Germany. He has more than 10 years of experience in system management and deployment using Microsoft technologies. He specializes in client enterprise design, deployment, performance, reliability, and Microsoft devices. Manuel works with local and international top customers from the private and public sectors, providing professional, technical, and technological support.

Additionally, he is an experienced Microsoft Certified Trainer and holds public and private Microsoft workshops across Europe. He is also a speaker and a*sk the expert* at various Microsoft premier events.

First and foremost, my thanks goes out to my wife, Renate, who allowed me to follow my dreams and make every day worth living, and my two wonderful children, Cornelius and Theresa, who constantly remind me of what's important in my life. Furthermore, I would like to thank all the people who have supported me throughout the writing of this book. Last but not least, I would like to thank the team at Packt Publishing for their support throughout the process of writing this book.

About the Reviewers

Florian Klaffenbach started his IT career in 2004 as a first and second level IT support technician and IT salesman trainee for a B2B online shop. Later, he moved to a small company, working as an IT project manager, planning, implementing, and integrating industrial plants and laundries into enterprise IT. In some time, he changed his path to Dell Germany. There, he started from scratch as an enterprise technical support analyst and later worked on a project to start Dell technical communities and support over social media in Europe and outside of the US. Currently, he is working as a solutions architect and consultant for Microsoft Infrastructure & Cloud, specializing in Microsoft Hyper-V, file services, System Center Virtual Machine Manager, and Microsoft Azure IaaS.

Additionally, he is active as a Microsoft blogger and lecturer. He blogs, for example, on his own page, `Datacenter-Flo.de`, or Azure Community Germany. Together with a very good friend, he founded the Windows Server User Group Berlin to create a network of Microsoft IT pros in Berlin. Florian maintains a very tight network with many vendors such as Cisco, Dell, and Microsoft and communities. This helps him enhance his experience and get the best solution for his customers. Since 2016, he is also the co-chairman of the Azure Community Germany. In April 2016, Microsoft awarded Florian the Microsoft Most Valuable Professional for Cloud and Datacenter Management.

Florian has worked for several companies, such as Dell Germany, CGI Germany, and his first employer, TACK GmbH. Currently, he is working at msg services ag in the role of senior consultant in Microsoft Cloud Infrastructure. He has worked on the books *Learning System Center App Controller*, *Microsoft Azure Storage Essentials*, and *Mastering Microsoft Deployment Toolkit*, all by *Packt Publishing*. He is also currently working on *Mastering Cloud Development using Microsoft Azure*, by *Packt Publishing*.

I want to thank Packt Publishing for giving me a chance to review the book. I also want to thank my employer and my girlfriend. Especially her, for not killing me because I spend so much of my spare time on the community and work.

Brian Mithen is a systems and network administrator with the Topeka & Shawnee County Public Library in Kansas. He maintains group policies and MDT deployment strategies for over 400 computers in use by the staff and public. When not at work, he breeds and shows American Bullies on the A.B.K.C. circuit with his kennel 8-Bit Bullies.

www.PacktPub.com

For support files and downloads related to your book, please visit www.PacktPub.com.

Did you know that Packt offers eBook versions of every book published, with PDF and ePub files available? You can upgrade to the eBook version at www.PacktPub.com and as a print book customer, you are entitled to a discount on the eBook copy. Get in touch with us at service@packtpub.com for more details.

At www.PacktPub.com, you can also read a collection of free technical articles, sign up for a range of free newsletters and receive exclusive discounts and offers on Packt books and eBooks.

https://www2.packtpub.com/books/subscription/packtlib

Do you need instant solutions to your IT questions? PacktLib is Packt's online digital book library. Here, you can search, access, and read Packt's entire library of books.

Why subscribe?

- Fully searchable across every book published by Packt
- Copy and paste, print, and bookmark content
- On demand and accessible via a web browser

Free access for Packt account holders

If you have an account with Packt at www.PacktPub.com, you can use this to access PacktLib today and view 9 entirely free books. Simply use your login credentials for immediate access.

Table of Contents

Preface	1
Chapter 1: Imaging Concepts and Theory	7
Imaging history	7
Imaging concepts	9
Imaging tools	11
Setup	11
Summary	12
Chapter 2: Setting Up Your Environment	13
Setting up MDT for the first time	13
Setting up the virtual machine	14
Downloading the MDT installer	15
Installing Windows ADK	17
Installing MDT	18
Setting up reference share and deployment share	18
Specifying a share name	19
Specifying a descriptive name	20
Modifying deployment options	20
Summary and confirmation	22
Exploring the completed reference share	23
Setting reference properties	25
Setting up our reference share task sequence	27
Increasing the scratch space	28
Including trace files in the boot WIM	28
Naming ISO-generated files	29
Updating up the deployment share	30
Automatic boot media creation	32
Importing an OS	34
Choosing the type of OS to add	36
Importing an OS from DVD media	37
Viewing image properties	39
Importing Hyper-V drivers	40
Importing patches	41
Downloading a hotfix	42
Setting up a packaged import	43

Updating the deployment share to include the hotfix 45
Adding applications to our reference image 46
Automating image updates 46
Finding .msi files with the ITNinja repository 47
Placing the .msi file 47
Setting up a new application 48
Specifying application details 49
Finding the .msi source directory 50
Specifying the destination directory 51
Entering command details 52
Summary 53

Chapter 3: Creating Reference Images 55

Creating a reference image in the management console 56
Specifying the general settings 56
Selecting the template and the OS 57
Specifying a product key and OS settings 58
Passwords and security 59
Summarising our entries 60
Finalising the task sequence 60
Observing the task sequence 63
Making configuration changes 64
Creating an application bundle 65
Making an application bundle object 68
Installing the bundle 70
Modifying the bundle 70
Managing updates 71
Sysprep run supportability 71
Boot media for the reference task sequence 73
Summary 74

Chapter 4: Default User Profile Customization 75

Customizing the image 75
Checking out the customization documentation 75
Accessing Windows System Information Manager 76
Adding games to our Enterprise image 78
Analyzing our changes 82
Leveraging the Audit mode 83
Local Policy Object Customizations and SCM 86
Shell customizations 88
Windows 7 Start menu and taskbar 88

Windows 7 background, logon screen, and user tiles	90
Windows 8 customizations	92
Summary	94
Chapter 5: CustomSettings.ini and Task Sequence	95
The structure of the CustomSettings.ini file	95
The Unattend.xml structure	101
The variables.dat structure	104
CustomSettings.ini and the Unattend.xml file	106
Dynamic modification	106
Task sequence structure	107
Initialization	107
Validation	108
State capture	109
Preinstall	110
Install	112
Postinstall	113
State restore	113
Logging	113
Summary	115
Chapter 6: Drivers	117
Understanding offline servicing	118
The MDT method of driver detection and injection	118
Populating the Out-of-Box Drivers node of MDT	119
Utilizing model variable to control what drivers are installed	123
Drivers as applications	126
Win PE drivers	128
Summary	132
Chapter 7: Image Deployment	133
Reference image deployment	134
Thick image	134
Thin image	135
Hybrid image	135
Virtual machine creation	136
Deployment	142
Deployment share	147
Deployment scenarios and network considerations	153
Deployment networks	153
Configuration of the deployment network	154
Geographical considerations	154

Summary	155

Chapter 8: USMT – The User State Migration Tool — 157

History	157
Supported scenarios and minimum requirements	159
What USMT will migrate and won't migrate	160
Where to download	163
How USMT works	163
USMT basics	163
The ScanState process	165
The LoadState process	167
ScanState and LoadState syntax	168
UsmtUtils tool	171
Delete hard-link migration store	171
Verify compressed migration store	171
Recover files from a compressed migration store	172
Supported cryptographic algorithms on the current system	173
Customization of XML files	173
Migrate registry keys	174
Migrate a folder from a specific drive	174
Including subdirectories	174
Excluding subdirectories	175
Migration options	176
PC Refresh scenario	176
PC Replacement scenario	177
Online versus offline migration	179
File copy versus hard-link	179
Using Windows XP with ADK 8.1	180
Best practices	181
Troubleshooting USMT	185
GUI wrappers for USMT	192
Summary	193

Chapter 9: Troubleshooting Deployment Logs — 195

Delving into Windows logs	196
Microsoft deployment toolkit logs and task sequencer logs	199
Getting CMTrace	202
Clearing a failed (dirty) MDT deployment	204
Look up error codes	206
Common errors and frequent pitfalls	208

Further help	216
User state migration tool logs	216
Summary	217
Chapter 10: Validating the Image	219
Driver Verifier	220
Windows Performance Toolkit	222
Windows Assessment Toolkit	223
Windows Assessment Toolkit example 1 – verifying drivers	225
Windows Assessment Services	232
Summary	256
Chapter 11: Database, UserExit Scripts, and Web Services	257
MDT Configuration Database step by step	257
Supported versions of SQL Server	258
Configuring the SQL Server	259
Creating a MDT database	270
Configuring permission of the MDT database	276
Using the MDT database	281
Applying customizations to individual computers	287
Applying customizations to roles	292
Applying customizations to locations	294
Applying customizations to computers based on their manufacturer and model	296
Considerations on MDT database usage	298
UserExit script	299
Web services	303
Summary	305
Appendix: Additional Enterprise Configuration Items	307
Reference VM configuration	307
Securing the MDT process	308
Windows Imaging and Configuration Designer	309
Index	313

Preface

Microsoft Deployment Toolkit (MDT) 2013 is a lightweight task sequencing environment and has a well-established community of IT professionals that use it. It's fully supported by Microsoft and is available for free.

> "Q: Why is it still "MDT 2013" when the year is almost 2016? Two primary reasons. First, we have only made minor changes to MDT which in our opinion does not constitute a major version revision. Second, per the MDT support lifecycle, a new major version will drop support for MDT 2012 Update 1 which still supports legacy platforms."
> — Aaron Czechowski, Senior Program Manager

With its support for Windows 7 and higher versions, including Windows 10 and Windows Server 2008 R2 and higher versions, it is the ideal tool for golden image creation and image deployment. This article will help you understand the important imaging techniques and build up your own MDT 2013 environment.

What this book covers

Chapter 1, *Imaging Concepts and Theory*, covers the basic terminology of imaging, when to use thick versus thin versus hybrid images, and why deployment changed in Vista and higher versions. Furthermore, the reader will learn the concepts behind reference image versus deployment image, where to integrate patches and why, and what apps and drivers are from the MDT perspective.

Chapter 2, *Setting Up Your Environment*, explains how to construct an MDT environment from scratch. This chapter will be a walkthrough of the different installation options and will explain why I recommend a particular configuration for production environments.

Chapter 3, *Creating Reference Images*, helps to understand the principles of a reference image and how it applies to the organization. Sysprep practices, patching, maintenance, and bitness will be covered in depth.

Chapter 4, *Default User Profile Customization*, covers the intricacies of customizing the default user profile from version to version of Windows. Tools and concepts available to brand the image, tweaking settings prior to deployment, and supported methods of doing so will be discussed in this chapter.

Chapter 5, *CustomSettings.ini and Task Sequence*, covers the `CustomSettings.ini` file and task sequence engine in detail and depth. Tips for customizing the deployment share, enabling logging, branding, and more will be covered here.

Chapter 6, *Drivers*, explains how driver handling can be a challenge for larger organizations. We'll cover driver concepts, when drivers are applications and when they are drivers and how to handle both scenarios, and also mandatory driver profiles.

Chapter 7, *Image Deployment*, focuses on the deployment share configuration, deployment best practices, and guidelines on securing the deployment share.

Chapter 8, *USMT - The User State Migration Tool*, covers USMT in depth, configuration of XML files, walkthroughs of the process, and troubleshooting. This also includes XML configuration and customization, USMT process top to bottom, and troubleshooting.

Chapter 9, *Troubleshooting Deployment Logs*, shows what to do when things go wrong. How to read MDT logs, which log file contains what data, how to interpret the binary error codes, and frequent pitfalls will be covered as well. We will also cover error code resolution, MDT log files, Trace32, and error messages.

Chapter 10, *Validating the Image*, covers Driver Verifier and Windows Performance Toolkit for image validation scenarios. We will talk about different tools that can be used to validate the image, check for bad drivers and poor performance, articulate the cost of purchasing lower-end hardware for management, and the operational and performance costs of anti-malware, antivirus, and other security-auditing software.

Chapter 11, *Database, UserExit Scripts, and Web Services*, explains the ability to web frontend the MDT implementation, as well as how to utilize the database capabilities of MDT for deeper deployment options. Also, we'll discuss a little about UserExit scripts. We'll get into the whys and hows of UserExit scripts, what options are available, and when to use them.

Appendix, *Additional Enterprise Configuration Items*, discusses some considerations of the Windows 10 tool set, as well as some configuration suggestions for secure environments.

What you need for this book

MDT 2013 Update 2 (6.3.8330), Windows Assessment and Deployment Kit (ADK) for Windows 10, Windows Server 2012 R2 x64 or Windows 10 installation with Hyper-V enabled, and ISOs of the OS and software you want to image/deploy will be required for this book.

Who this book is for

This book is for IT professionals who want to take a deeper look into imaging techniques and setting up a MDT 2013 environment.

Conventions

In this book, you will find a number of text styles that distinguish between different kinds of information. Here are some examples of these styles and an explanation of their meaning.

Code words in text, database table names, folder names, filenames, file extensions, pathnames, dummy URLs, user input, and Twitter handles are shown as follows: "The ADK comes as a web installer, `adksetup.exe`, by the way."

A block of code is set as follows:

```
[Default]
DeployRoot=\\mdt-share\Reference Share
UserID=< >
UserDomain=< >
UserPassword=< >
SkipBDDWelcome=YES
```

When we wish to draw your attention to a particular part of a code block, the relevant lines or items are set in bold:

```
<var name="ISDESKTOP">
  <![CDATA[ True ]]>
</var>
```

Any command-line input or output is written as follows:

```
msiexec /i EnterpriseFoxitReader605.0618_enu.msi /qn
```

New terms and **important words** are shown in bold. Words that you see on the screen, for example, in menus or dialog boxes, appear in the text like this: "The primary area we are concerned with is the **Deployment Shares** line, which we will select with the mouse, and then right-click to select **New Deployment Share**."

 Warnings or important notes appear in a box like this.

 Tips and tricks appear like this.

Reader feedback

Feedback from our readers is always welcome. Let us know what you think about this book-what you liked or disliked. Reader feedback is important for us as it helps us develop titles that you will really get the most out of.

To send us general feedback, simply e-mail `feedback@packtpub.com`, and mention the book's title in the subject of your message.

If there is a topic that you have expertise in and you are interested in either writing or contributing to a book, see our author guide at `www.packtpub.com/authors`.

Customer support

Now that you are the proud owner of a Packt book, we have a number of things to help you to get the most from your purchase.

Downloading the color images of this book

We also provide you with a PDF file that has color images of the screenshots/diagrams used in this book. The color images will help you better understand the changes in the output. You can download this file from `https://www.packtpub.com/sites/default/files/downloads/MasteringTheMicrosoftDeploymentToolkit_ColorImages.pdf`.

Errata

Although we have taken every care to ensure the accuracy of our content, mistakes do happen. If you find a mistake in one of our books-maybe a mistake in the text or the code-we would be grateful if you could report this to us. By doing so, you can save other readers from frustration and help us improve subsequent versions of this book. If you find any errata, please report them by visiting http://www.packtpub.com/submit-errata, selecting your book, clicking on the **Errata Submission Form** link, and entering the details of your errata. Once your errata are verified, your submission will be accepted and the errata will be uploaded to our website or added to any list of existing errata under the **Errata** section of that title.

To view the previously submitted errata, go to https://www.packtpub.com/books/content/support and enter the name of the book in the search field. The required information will appear under the **Errata** section.

Piracy

Piracy of copyrighted material on the Internet is an ongoing problem across all media. At Packt, we take the protection of our copyright and licenses very seriously. If you come across any illegal copies of our works in any form on the Internet, please provide us with the location address or website name immediately so that we can pursue a remedy.

Please contact us at copyright@packtpub.com with a link to the suspected pirated material.

We appreciate your help in protecting our authors and our ability to bring you valuable content.

Questions

If you have a problem with any aspect of this book, you can contact us at questions@packtpub.com, and we will do our best to address the problem.

1
Imaging Concepts and Theory

In this chapter, you'll learn the concepts and best practices of Microsoft Windows imaging techniques and in doing so learn the terminology associated with deployment. You will also become familiar with the different approaches to imaging and when each approach is generally regarded as the *best in show* for a given scenario. Finally, you'll learn some history on how things have changed in imaging from the old Windows XP style deployment to Windows 7, Windows 8, and now Windows 10. The solutions accelerator from Microsoft, the **Microsoft Deployment Toolkit** (**MDT**), is the answer to a lot of the deployment problems facing deployment projects and will be the focus of this book.

Imaging history

In the beginning there was DOS, and it was good. But then there was a need for more and Windows came into being. At first, it was *OK* to pop the floppy disks that contained Windows for Workgroups into machines one by one on each computer individually in an enterprise environment. But soon, businesses started asking for things such as configuration settings for deploying Windows en masse.

And so, `Unattend.txt` and `Sysdiff.exe` and other fun things were created, where the intrepid NT 3.5 admin could build a machine, tweak it, and run Sysdiff to create a template with which other installations could follow and be identical, more or less. Later, as things progressed, the need was strong for a way to really *clone* machines!

And so, in the distant past (10+ years ago), the world of imaging and deploying the Windows Client came to be ruled by disk sector duplication deployments. This process was fairly involved, in that a technician would install a copy of Windows XP, patch it, install updated drivers, configure Windows XP's look and feel, install applications, patch the applications and finally configure the applications. After that was done (a process that could take a day or more) it was captured with a tool in a sector-by-sector fashion into a file for later deployment over network or media, again, sector-by-sector. Thus the technician would have an image, for a single model of computer, with a single set of applications.

So imagine an enterprise-level environment with say, 10 models of computers (I've seen some with over 100 models so 10 is a good example) and 1-3 sets of applications installed per model. Now the technician (or now it's most likely technicians at this point) is patching and managing roughly 10-30 images in our conservatively estimated enterprise environment. We didn't even throw 32 bit versus 64 bit into the equation.

So this poses a few problems for deployment projects that may not be readily apparent:

- Each image is say 15-20 GB in size post-compression. Particularly in computing ages past, maintaining a library of images of this size was a daunting proposition.
- Each image needs to be updated on a semi-regular basis to take into account service packs, OS patches, application patches, driver updates, and random configuration tweaks requested by management and marketing departments. Not doing so increases the deployment time as all the work of applying updates and patches then occurs at every deployment process instead of once before capture.
- Each machine had the same **globally unique identifier** (**GUID**), because it was in fact a clone of another machine. So when you joined both to the same Windows domain (even with different names) hilarity ensued. Tools were created, such as NewSID and Sysprep's `/generalize` switch, which helped get around this.

But around 2006, with the release of Windows Vista, things changed. There was a new paradigm in image deployment that would change everything: the **Windows Imaging Format** (**WIM**) format. The WIM format is essentially a container for an image. With it, and some tools from the **Assessment and Deployment Kit** (**ADK**), one can service the Windows image offline, which allows us to add patches, drivers, and remove components such as games from our image, all without having to install it first on bare-metal hardware.

An example of this would be something like the **Deployment Image Servicing and Management** (**DISM**) command (in an elevated command prompt) to remove a hotfix from your running system:

```
DISM /online /remove-package
    /packagename:Package_for_KB2868623~31bf3856ad364e35~amd64~~6.1.1.1
```

Around this same time enters a tool known as BDD. The **Business Desktop Deployment (BDD)** toolkit was a set of scripts that could be used to customize, configure, and deploy the Windows image in the enterprise environment. BDD 2.5 was released in August 2005, prior to the RTM of Vista.

BDD had several iterations and even had a Microsoft Certified Professional Exam created for one of its versions. These iterations were each an improvement upon the last until finally, in November 2007, the MDT was released.

Fast forward to the present, and MDT 2013 Update 2 is current at the time of writing. At this point, MDT is essentially System Center Configuration Manager (SCCM) "lite". You can backend it with a database, put a web frontend on it, do dynamic actions based on hardware make and model, install previous applications, and much more.

This tool, the MDT, will be the focus of this book. There are other (typically more expensive) solutions out there to be sure, but if one is preparing to perform deployments at scale, MDT should be looked at as it can easily do a lot of manual work and, while it costs nothing, it is supported by Microsoft Support.

Imaging concepts

When we look at utilizing the WIM format and MDT, there are essentially three schools of thought in building what is commonly termed a **golden image** in deployment. These are the thick, thin, and hybrid images. They each have their merits and rather than adhere to a single one, I tend to view each as a tool in the deployment toolbox. So depending on the situation and customer needs, I would recommend one over another:

- **Thick Image**: A thick image is an image that contains a patched operating system plus all applications used in the environment. It is large, sometimes problematic to deploy, and has some interesting licensing implications as well in that every deployed system has every piece of software installed.

  Sometimes a thick image is the best option due to logistics. Imagine you need to deploy Windows to systems on a submarine or a cruise ship. Sending media containing a thick image by freight/helicopter might be an answer versus deployment from a share.

- **Thin Image**: A thin image is (as one might assume) an image that contains nothing except a patched operating system. It is quick to deploy, but customization post-deployment can take quite some time, even by automated scripts. This is a minimalist approach but has merit when you need an image of the smallest size or only a few diverging applications from a golden base image.
- **Hybrid Image**: A hybrid image is an image that contains a patched operating system and core business applications, typically applications for which the business has a site license. Typically, some limited customizations occur post deployment with these images as part of a task sequence.

Applications, drivers and packages are three components that can be included in the image, depending on type of image. These are defined clearly in the MDT documentation and UI, but need introduction here:

- **Applications**: Applications are usually software installation packages one wants to place into the image or deploy as part of the task sequence itself. Sometimes driver packages can fall into this category as well. The Hewlett-Packard ProLiant Support Pack is a great example of a bundled offering of driver and firmware updates for systems that work best when run as an installation (application in MDT) rather than as a **Plug and Play** (**PnP**) operation. Further, many Bluetooth driver stacks, network teaming software, and video graphics driver packs fall into this grouping. They may install in PnP, but do not behave properly unless run as a packaged installation. Generally, this is a result of the installer checking/updating firmware as part of the installation, and PnP just adds the driver and moves on.
- **Drivers**: Drivers are components usually provided by the hardware manufacturer (hopefully in concentrated CAB files for ease of deployment, we will discuss it later). These drivers can (and usually should) be provisioned using mandatory driver profiles, but for small scale or single model deployments, the natural PnP feature of Windows can be used to select and install drivers from MDT.
- **Packages**: Packages are updates from Microsoft to address a problem or defect in the operating system. Typically, these are pulled from the Microsoft Update Catalog and then imported into the MDT console for application to Windows PE or the image itself.

Imaging tools

The following tools are used for imaging:

- **MDT**: The toolset covered in this book. MDT is a collection of visual basic and PowerShell scripts used for different deployment tasks all wrapped together in a management console UI and sequencing engine used to call the scripts in stages for deploying Windows or performing other tasks related to Windows imaging (such as patching or servicing a current installation, capturing an image for later deployment, or modifying the image in some manner).
- **Task Sequence**: A task sequence is a series of commands executed by MDT's task sequencer. This is the heart of MDT, where the administrator can configure deployment steps, capturing the user state for later migration, servicing, and patching and other tasks.
- **Task Sequencer**: The name of the process MDT uses to manage its tasks. This is almost analogous to a computer virus in that the task sequencer, depending on the commands being performed, can modify the boot environment, boot over a network, collect additional task sequence commands from a central remote share, and boot off of media. It keeps track of a task's progress in a central store known as `variables.dat` and logs to a set of log files for troubleshooting and audit purposes.
- **variables.dat**: A flat file db format used to store data for an executing task sequence. It will contain metadata such as the chassis type of the machine the task is executing, how much RAM is installed, and many other variables that are queried to the hardware, PnP bus, and BIOS/firmware.

Setup

For most Windows users, the setup process is something of a black box. You run setup and *stuff happens* and then voilá, you have a Windows installation. For the deployment engineer however, the setup process is where the magic happens. MDT manipulates the setup by providing variables along the process, to customize the resulting image for the target machine.

MDT does this by inserting variables into the `Unattend.xml` file for Windows setup. Some of these variables can even be provided dynamically based on queries using a technique known as **UserExit scripts**. These are used to determine a variables property based on something such as the **organizational unit (OU)** of a user account, the location of the machine on the network (usually determined by what the default gateway value is), or a hardware query such as `chassis type=laptop` to specify that the machine is a laptop and therefore needs a VPN client installed.

The options available to the engineer are detailed in depth in the technical documents of the MDT word documents available on the Microsoft download site at `https://technet.mic rosoft.com/en-us/library/dn781292.aspx`. Some are documented in MSDN as well in further detail.

Troubleshooting in the setup isn't generally considered an easy thing to work on in IT. MDT makes it somewhat more straightforward for engineers by centralizing a logging directory for the administrator. A master `smsts.log` file logs the activity of the task sequencer and will indicate which sublog is needed to review for additional information if needed.

Summary

By now, you should have a grasp of what imaging is about and why it is needed. In addition, you can see the history of why we are where we are in the technology space of deployment. `Chapter 2`, *Setting Up Your Environment*, will walk you through building out your deployment system using the MDT and Windows ADK. You'll learn some best practices to set up your deployment share and imaging practices and get some configuration guidance on modifying the ADK/MDT scripts.

2
Setting Up Your Environment

In this chapter, we will cover setting up the basic environment:

- Hosting OS configuration
- Installing the Workbench
- Discussing VM creation principles
- Discussing general customizations of the share

Setting up MDT for the first time

To implement **Microsoft Deployment Toolkit** (**MDT**), one must have a properly provisioned system on which we can lay down the **Windows Assessment and Deployment Kit** (**Windows ADK**) and MDT install files. It must have space, CPUs, some amount of RAM, and most importantly, quick network links to other systems.

All the particulars around these requirements of course depend on what you are using MDT for. Are you building a golden image with which you will deploy via another deployment system? Are you implementing a deployment scenario where you need to deploy to laptops, desktops, medical imaging systems, and point-of-sale devices at multiple sites around the world, all from one infrastructure?

Setting up the virtual machine

So, for the sake of moving things along, we'll start small—with nothing. In this chapter, we'll get started with a single system. In order to illustrate, we will be using Windows Server 2012 R2, so transfers will be faster over the new **Server Message Block** (**SMB**) improvements. It's a virtual machine that is configured as shown in the following screenshot:

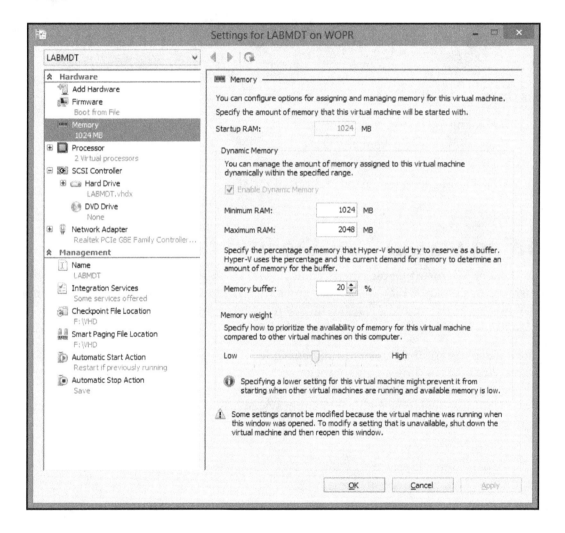

For Windows 8(.1) and Windows 10 guest

The specification settings for the virtual machine are described as follows:

- 1,024 MB of RAM as a floor, autoscaling to 2,048 MB as the OS demands it.
- 2 core—as that's my preference in a virtual machine guest for anything I want to be fairly productive from a performance perspective.
- The only real consideration for an MDT installation is disk space. I've allotted 300 GB in the example, but this number is primarily up to the deployment engineer. The number of images and applications will generally drive the need for space. Using a disk system that allows for easy growth (SAN or NAS environment) or even a RAID array of local disks would work well.

Downloading the MDT installer

I recommend, for the purpose of this book, downloading the MDT installer for 2013. As of this printing, it is located here at `https://www.microsoft.com/en-us/download/details.aspx?id=50407`.

Also, you will need the Windows ADK, which is located at `http://www.microsoft.com/en-us/download/confirmation.aspx?id=39982`.

The ADK comes as a web installer, `adksetup.exe`, by the way. For serious work, download the complete ISO by first downloading `adksetup.exe` and then selecting the **Download the Windows Assessment and Deployment Kit** option:

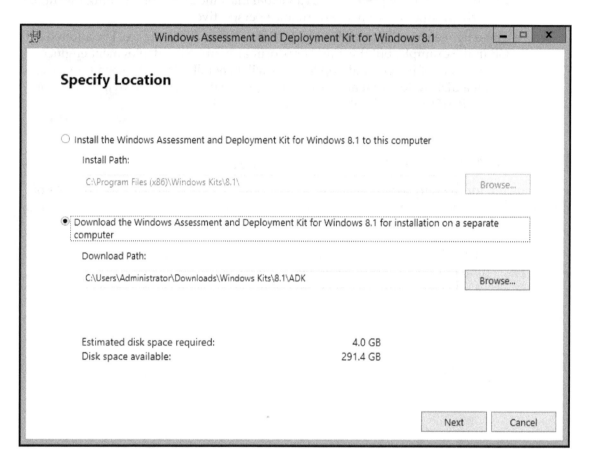

This option stores all the ADK setup files so that the following installations won't require a potentially lengthy download and can even be done on machines that don't have the Internet access going forward.

Installing Windows ADK

Once you have the files, simply run `adksetup.exe`. For the purpose of this work, you'll want to tick the following boxes in the installer:

- **Deployment Tools**
- **Windows Preinstallation Environment (Windows PE)**
- **User State Migration Tool (USMT)**
- **Volume Activation Management Tool (VAMT)**

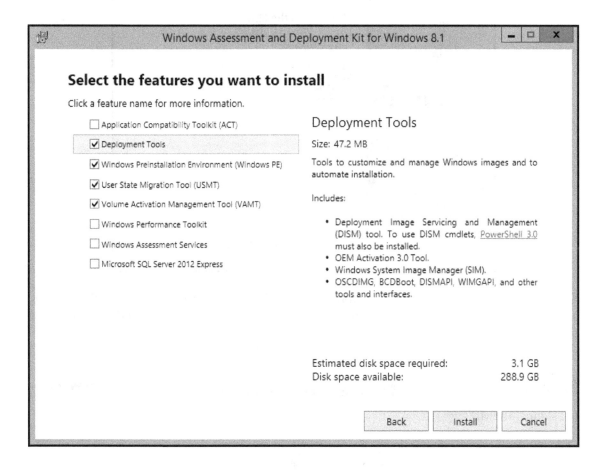

Installing MDT

After the ADK for Windows 8.1 is installed, we can get started with installing the actual MDT. As my virtual machine is Windows Server 2012 R2, it is a 64-bit machine, so I will download and install the `MicrosoftDeploymentToolkit2013_x64.msi` MDT 2013 and run it:

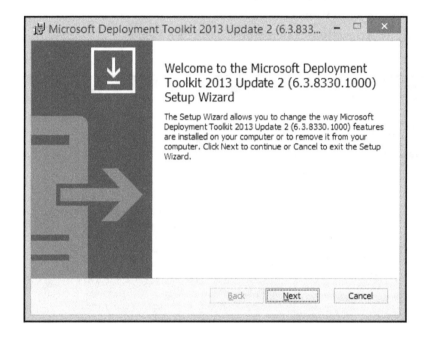

So, we're installing the **6.2.5019.0** version of MDT 2013. Install it to `C:\`, along with the ADK as done previously, and then we are ready to set up the reference share and the deployment share.

Setting up reference share and deployment share

Let'slaunchtheMDT:

We are presented with a console that should look similar to a typical **Microsoft Management Console** (**MMC**):

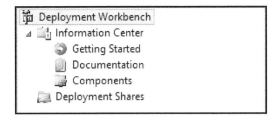

Feel free to poke at the console. The primary area we are concerned with is the **Deployment Shares** line, which we will select with the mouse, and then right-click to select **New Deployment Share**. Make sure to change the **Deployment share path** to reflect this as a reference share, not a deployment share.

In the next window, as shown in the following image, the wizard puts up a window to create the deployment share. In this case, we will name it `ReferenceShare` and place it on our `C:` drive, which has plenty of space allocated in the virtual machine:

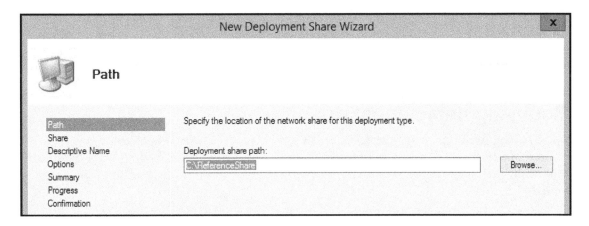

Now, keep in mind, this can be pretty much anywhere. It's a filesystem-based directory/share here. We aren't doing complex DB work like Microsoft Exchange; we are creating a file share at this point, that's it. If you have a volume for this, fine, you can put it here. No problem. Antivirus can cause some issues while hitting the **Next** button though, especially, if the filter driver is set to prevent the creation of `autorun.inf` files.

Specifying a share name

The **Share** screen is to set the actual share for the reference share that we will use to create the reference image.

Specifying a descriptive name

On the **Descriptive Name** screen, specify the reference rather than deployment in the **Deployment share description** box:

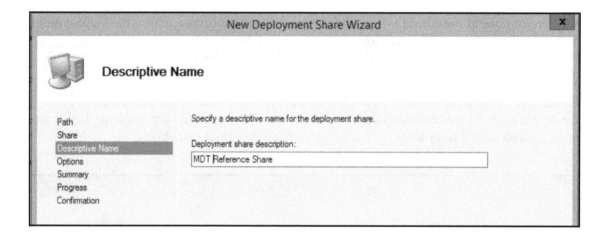

Modifying deployment options

We are going to utilize this reference share as a workshop of sorts; it isn't going to be utilized in a traditional deployment sense. As such, we don't need it to do a lot of default actions that are available on the **Options** screen, except **Ask if an image should be captured**.

What the following checkboxes are doing is setting properties in the `CustomSettings.ini` file, also known as the `Rules` section of the share:

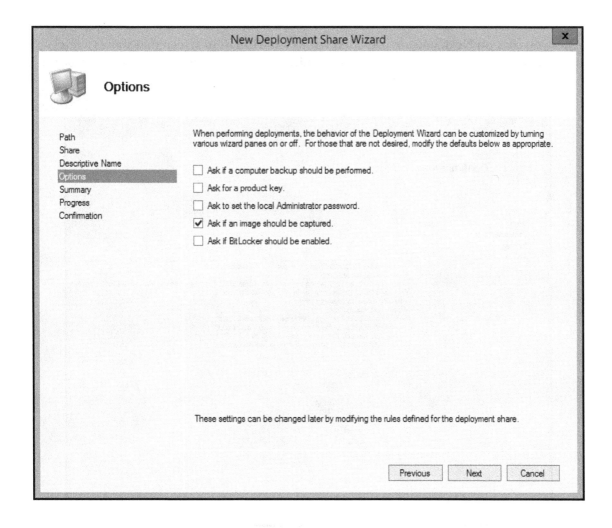

Summary and confirmation

The Summary screen shows the options that have been previously selected for confirmation.

After you click on **Next**, you are provided with a **Confirmation** screen that shows a few interesting options. The first is the **Save Output...** box, which will save the output of what was just done for logging purposes:

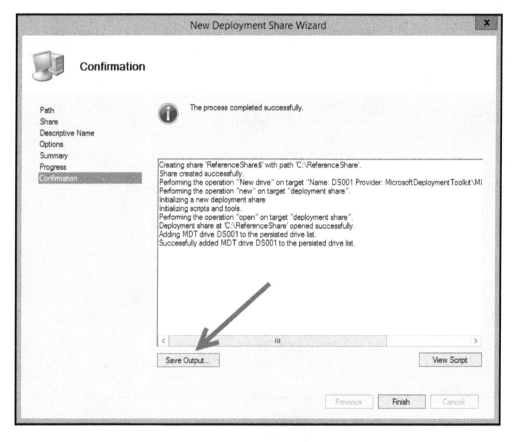

The next is the **View Script** button that does just that, reveals the PowerShell script that was run with the variables you provided. This is handy if you need to document what was done and be able to reproduce it at will for change control, versioning, disaster recovery, or any other reason.

So, once you finish running the wizard, click on the **View Script** button. It will open **Notepad**, where the script is present in raw text, as shown in the following screenshot:

Exploring the completed reference share

If we've completed the previous steps, we'll be rewarded with a reference share as shown in the following image, under **Deployment Shares**:

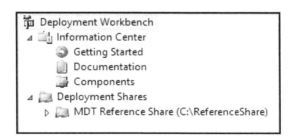

Clicking on **MDT Reference Share** will give us a view of some folders. These mirror, to some extent, is the flat filesystem that we have created:

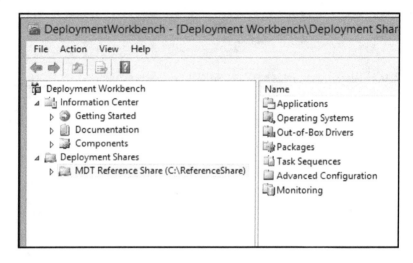

As opposed to the filesystem shown in the following screenshot:

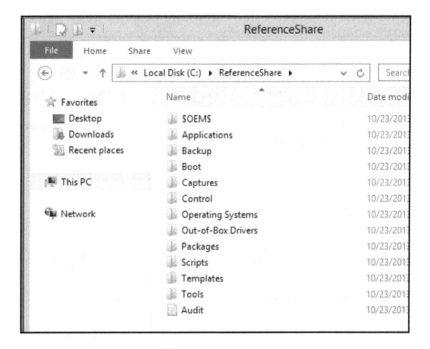

Note the presence of or absence of an attribute, depending on your scenario requirements, matching folders. MDT is keeping some records out of the **user interface** (**UI**) for us. This is quite intentional.

> For typical best practice, one does not have to go into the actual filesystem for anything. In fact, all the times I've had to modify the filesystem rather than the UI, I was doing something I either shouldn't have been doing (we'll call it experimenting) or trying to fix something someone else had done (by their experimenting).

Setting reference properties

The first thing to do with our reference share is to open the properties and set some items. Getting into the share properties is quite easy; right-click on **MDT Reference Share** and select **Properties**:

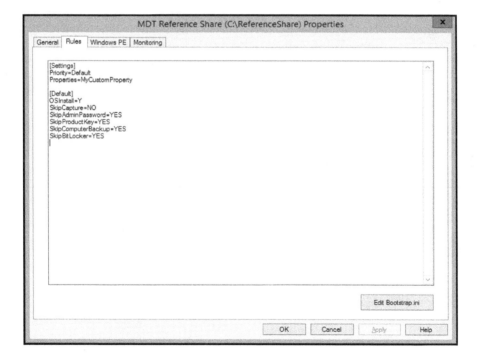

This will bring up the **MDT Reference Share Properties** window. Go to the **Rules** tab, where there are several `Skip` properties. These are used to skip past the MDT wizard that runs during a task sequence.

Think practically; what would you want to skip to make this an automated process, and what are your options? The MDT Print Ready Documentation Pack has a list of all the Skips. You will download the pack at the same location used for MDT 2013. Open the `Toolkit Reference.docx` document and use the **Navigation** pane view to search for Skips in order to find all the Skips headings in the document-simply type `Skip` in the **Search document** field:

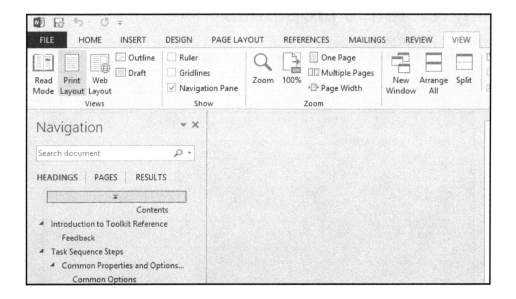

The Toolkit Reference document can also be directly accessed at `https://technet.microsoft.com/en-us/library/dn781091.aspx`

Setting up our reference share task sequence

We will want to skip things for a reference share that are different than things skipped for a deployment share. The reason for this is that in a reference share task sequence, we will typically want this to run in a fully automated fashion (Zero Touch-Lite Touch, if you will). So when we need to rerun the task sequence in the future, we can simply apply a change, fire up the virtual machine targeted to be run, run the task sequence, and off we go.

Therefore, the `Rules` section can look similar to the following code. This is properly formatted and skips many steps, which in a reference image task sequence, would be considered superfluous. Note that `UserID`, `UserDomain`, and `UserPassword` will be dependent on your configuration. In the following example, I am using a domain user account with rights to the share (read and write, as the reference image has to be written as a WIM file into this share using the ID):

```
[Settings]
Priority=Default
Properties=MyCustomProperty

[Default]
OSInstall=Y
SkipAppsOnUpgrade=YES
SkipCapture=NO
SkipAdminPassword=YES
SkipProductKey=YES
_SMSTSOrgName=MDT Reference Task Sequence
SkipBitLocker=YES
SkipDomainMembership=YES
JoinWorkgroup=Workgroup
SkipFinalSummary=YES
SkipLocaleSelection=YES
SkipSummary=YES
SkipTimeZone=YES
SkipUserData=YES
TimeZoneName=Eastern Standard Time
UserID=<account with rights to the MDT share>
UserDomain=<domain>
UserPassword=<password>
FinishAction=SHUTDOWN
```

Next, you will click on **Apply** and then click on the **Edit Bootstrap.ini** button shown in the following screenshot, as we have more customization to do:

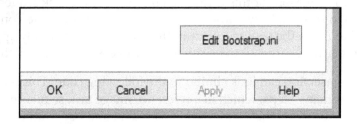

I will add some items here to speed the task sequence along. Your `UserID`, `UserDomain`, and `UserPassword` are all similar to the ones in the `Rules` section:

```
[Settings]
Priority=Default

[Default]
DeployRoot=\\mdt-share\Reference Share
UserID=< >
UserDomain=< >
UserPassword=< >
SkipBDDWelcome=YES
```

The reason for these `Skip` commands is to skip parts of the MDT wizard. As we're setting up a reference image, we don't need to be prompted for things such as time zone or fluffy welcome screens.

Increasing the scratch space

Some driver installations have a problem with low memory availability. Increasing scratch space is the best way to avoid these issues. Click on the **Windows PE** tab and then increase the scratch space to `128`.

Including trace files in the boot WIM

A general troubleshooting best practice is to include `trace32.exe` in the boot WIM. This tool is part of the **System Center Configuration Manager** (**SCCM**) tools and can be used to interpret the `.log` files that are produced by the task sequence engine in a much more legible manner.

To do this, you will install Trace32 from the SCCM tools and then copy `trace32.exe` into a directory. In this case, I have placed it in a directory named `Trace32` on the `Desktop`. Then just specify this directory for inclusion in the WinPE WIM generation.

Naming ISO-generated files

In the **Windows PE** tab, name your ISO-generated files something logical. For the purpose of this example, we'll be naming them `Reference_LiteTouchPE_x86.iso`. Right now, your **Windows PE** tab should look similar to the following image:

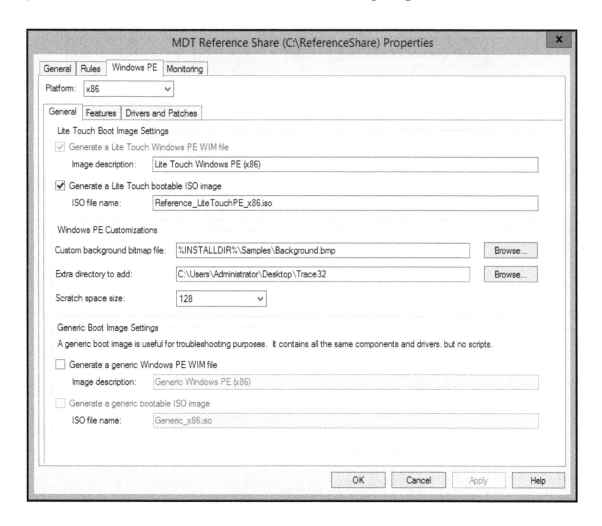

Don't forget that you must modify the x86 and x64 media separately!

Updating up the deployment share

Next we're going to walk through updating the deployment share. Right-click on the reference share that we've just set up, and select **Update Deployment Share**:

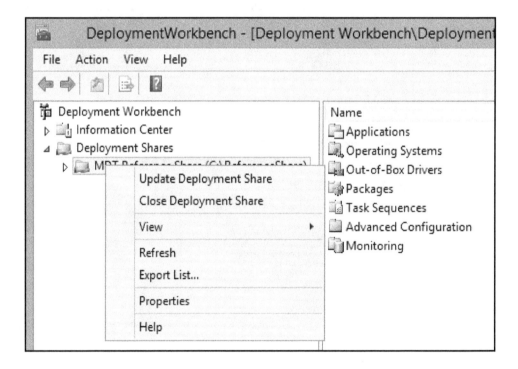

The **Update Deployment Share Wizard** dialog box will appear, as shown in the following image:

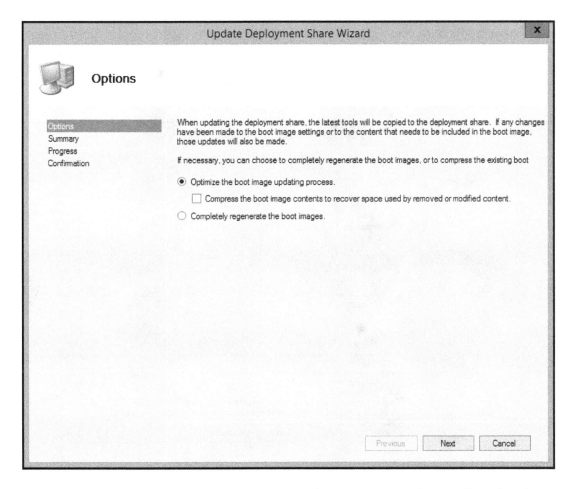

The defaults, as shown in the previous image, are fine here. You will typically only select the compress checkbox when you have retired a model of hardware and want to reclaim this driver whitespace out of the WinPE build. If you don't do this, it'll be consumed as you add newer drivers to the WinPE image. Click on **Next**.

The **Completely regenerate the boot images** option is typically used as a troubleshooting step when your boot media appears confused and it is best to rebuild from a known good set of settings rather than try to figure out what went wrong.

Automatic boot media creation

In the following screenshot of the **Progress** screen, MDT indicates that no existing boot image exists, so it is creating a new image. This is correct and expected. After you have created boot media once, and a change is made that requires a media rebuild, the verbiage will be different, but it has the same type of indication that something has changed and an update to the media is needed. Note that it is updating x86 here; it'll update x64 later. If you had unchecked one of the architectures, it would only update the one selected here:

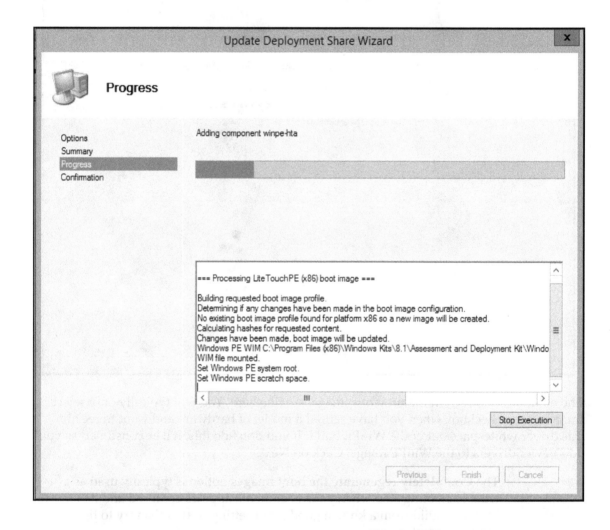

After the process is complete, you should be rewarded with boot media, as shown in the following screenshot:

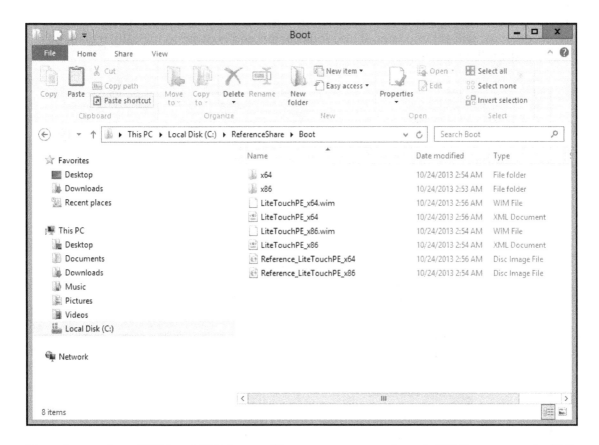

Note that we have WIM and ISO format files, so we can use these in WDS or mount the ISO to a virtual machine (which is the plan in this book), or even write the ISO to a USB stick or CD/DVD for boot media.

Importing an OS

Next we will be importing our OS. Create a folder structure in the **Operating Systems** area. This helps with the organization of selection profiles, which are a tool for driver organization we will get into later. It also looks better and is easier to logically manage, as shown in the following image:

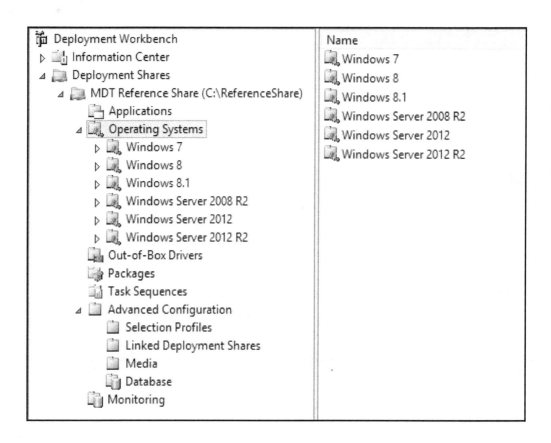

Right-click on the appropriate folder for the OS that you wish to import and click on **Import Operating System**. We need the ISO for media for this. I downloaded mine from MSDN and then mounted the ISO in Hyper-V so that it is presented to the MDT Server as a DVD:

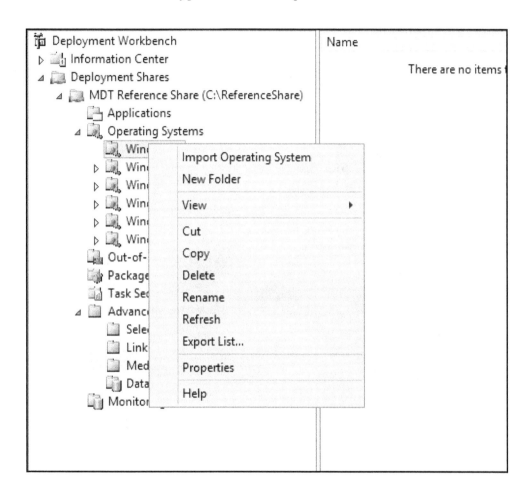

Choosing the type of OS to add

After selecting **Import Operating System**, you'll be asked something that probably doesn't make a lot of sense, **Choose the type of operating system to add**, as shown in the following screenshot:

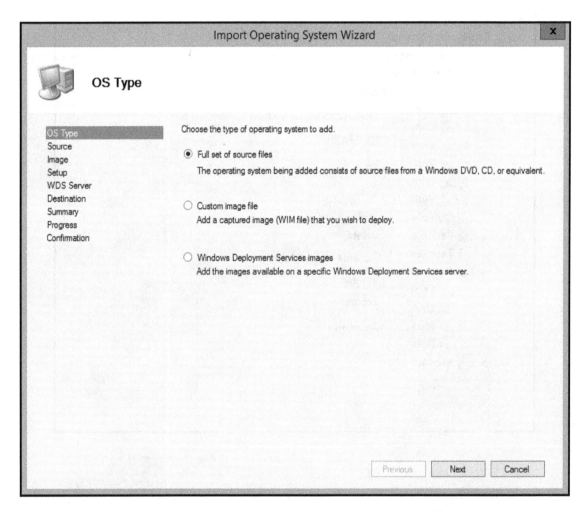

For a reference image, we'd pretty much always start with a base OS DVD and use the top radio button for **Full set of source files**. However, the options are there to import a custom WIM that is already captured, or a WDS image as well.

Importing an OS from DVD media

In the **Source** screen, which is shown in the following image, point the import wizard to the root of the DVD media:

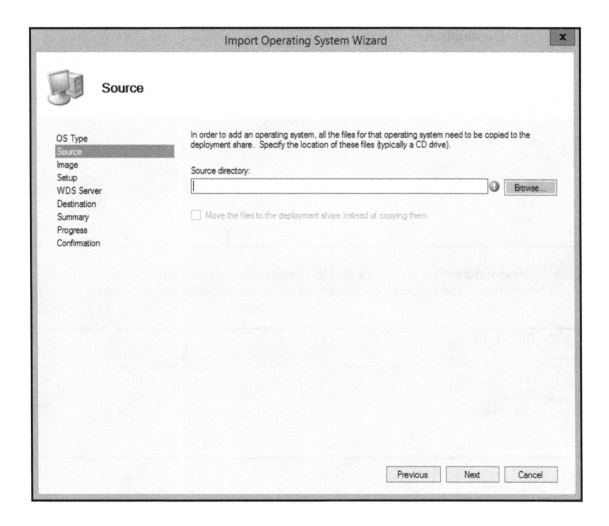

The wizard will read the media and autofills the window with the media to be imported, as shown in the following image:

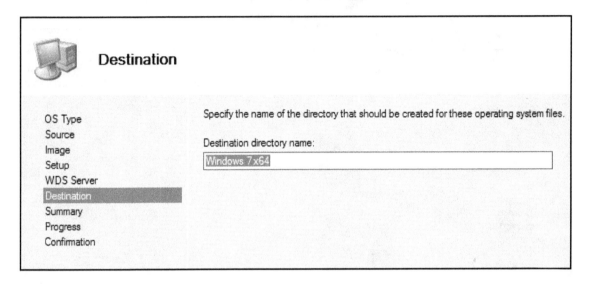

Click on **Next** and then the job will import the media files into the specified OS folder and you'll be rewarded with an OS in your share, as shown in the following screenshot:

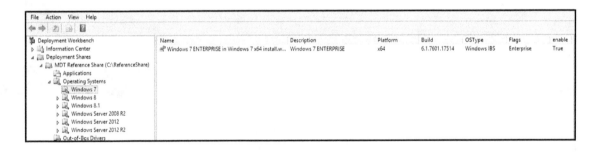

Viewing image properties

If there is ever a question on what the image is, a simple right-click and selecting **Properties** will reveal a lot of details, which we can see in the following image:

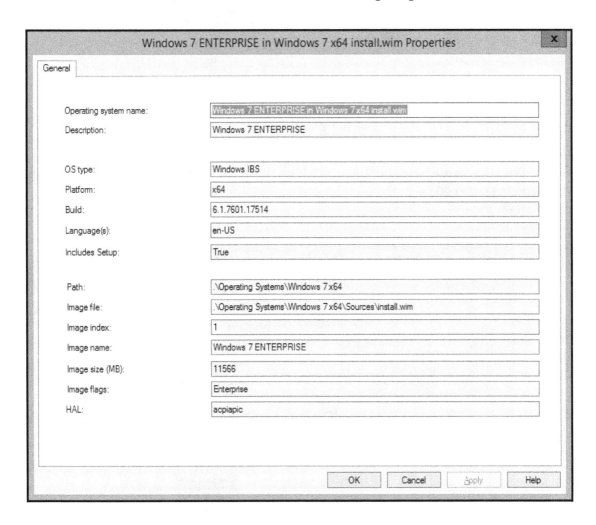

Importing Hyper-V drivers

Our next step is to include the new Hyper-V additions in WinPE and the OS.

We would use this, for example, if we are capturing and deploying Windows 7, but are using Windows Server 2012 or 2012 R2 to run the capture from. The same process applies for physical drivers, but remember that we are only capturing a reference image into a VM, not physical. The drivers for actual model numbers will come later, in our deployment share. So in the Hyper-V Virtual Machine Connection, I selected **Action** and then **Insert Integration Components**. This causes the Hyper-V host to mount the ISO for the current Hyper-V additions for the system on to the CD-ROM, D:, so now I can import these into the **Out-of-Box Drivers** area and update my WinPE media.

Importing drivers is as simple as putting the drivers into a directory and right-clicking on **Out-of-Box Drivers** and selecting **Import Drivers**. Point the wizard at the root folder where the driver is located and it'll crawl the directory's tree and import all the drivers it can, as shown in the following image:

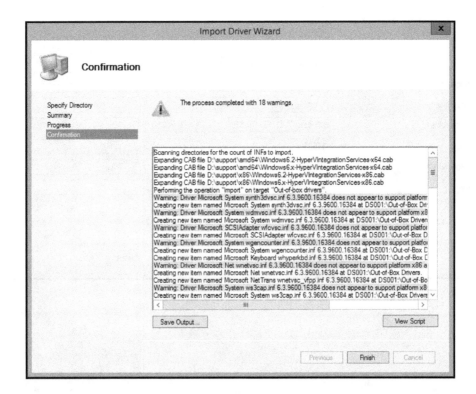

Then your share will reflect drivers in it, as shown in the following image:

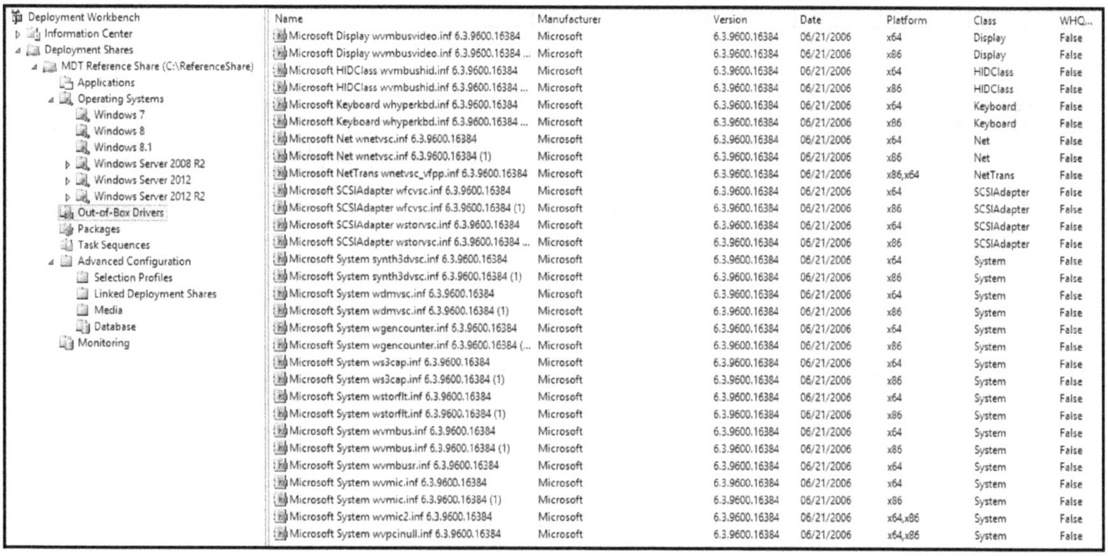

Name	Manufacturer	Version	Date	Platform	Class	WHQ...
Microsoft Display wvmbusvideo.inf 6.3.9600.16384	Microsoft	6.3.9600.16384	06/21/2006	x64	Display	False
Microsoft Display wvmbusvideo.inf 6.3.9600.16384 ...	Microsoft	6.3.9600.16384	06/21/2006	x86	Display	False
Microsoft HIDClass wvmbushid.inf 6.3.9600.16384	Microsoft	6.3.9600.16384	06/21/2006	x64	HIDClass	False
Microsoft HIDClass wvmbushid.inf 6.3.9600.16384 ...	Microsoft	6.3.9600.16384	06/21/2006	x86	HIDClass	False
Microsoft Keyboard whyperkbd.inf 6.3.9600.16384 ...	Microsoft	6.3.9600.16384	06/21/2006	x64	Keyboard	False
Microsoft Keyboard whyperkbd.inf 6.3.9600.16384 ...	Microsoft	6.3.9600.16384	06/21/2006	x86	Keyboard	False
Microsoft Net wnetvsc.inf 6.3.9600.16384	Microsoft	6.3.9600.16384	06/21/2006	x64	Net	False
Microsoft Net wnetvsc.inf 6.3.9600.16384 (1)	Microsoft	6.3.9600.16384	06/21/2006	x86	Net	False
Microsoft NetTrans wnetvsc_vfpp.inf 6.3.9600.16384	Microsoft	6.3.9600.16384	06/21/2006	x86,x64	NetTrans	False
Microsoft SCSIAdapter wfcvsc.inf 6.3.9600.16384	Microsoft	6.3.9600.16384	06/21/2006	x64	SCSIAdapter	False
Microsoft SCSIAdapter wfcvsc.inf 6.3.9600.16384 (1)	Microsoft	6.3.9600.16384	06/21/2006	x86	SCSIAdapter	False
Microsoft SCSIAdapter wstorvsc.inf 6.3.9600.16384	Microsoft	6.3.9600.16384	06/21/2006	x64	SCSIAdapter	False
Microsoft SCSIAdapter wstorvsc.inf 6.3.9600.16384 ...	Microsoft	6.3.9600.16384	06/21/2006	x86	SCSIAdapter	False
Microsoft System synth3dvsc.inf 6.3.9600.16384	Microsoft	6.3.9600.16384	06/21/2006	x64	System	False
Microsoft System synth3dvsc.inf 6.3.9600.16384 (1)	Microsoft	6.3.9600.16384	06/21/2006	x86	System	False
Microsoft System wdmvsc.inf 6.3.9600.16384	Microsoft	6.3.9600.16384	06/21/2006	x64	System	False
Microsoft System wdmvsc.inf 6.3.9600.16384 (1)	Microsoft	6.3.9600.16384	06/21/2006	x86	System	False
Microsoft System wgencounter.inf 6.3.9600.16384	Microsoft	6.3.9600.16384	06/21/2006	x64	System	False
Microsoft System wgencounter.inf 6.3.9600.16384 (...	Microsoft	6.3.9600.16384	06/21/2006	x86	System	False
Microsoft System ws3cap.inf 6.3.9600.16384	Microsoft	6.3.9600.16384	06/21/2006	x64	System	False
Microsoft System ws3cap.inf 6.3.9600.16384 (1)	Microsoft	6.3.9600.16384	06/21/2006	x86	System	False
Microsoft System wstorflt.inf 6.3.9600.16384	Microsoft	6.3.9600.16384	06/21/2006	x64	System	False
Microsoft System wstorflt.inf 6.3.9600.16384 (1)	Microsoft	6.3.9600.16384	06/21/2006	x86	System	False
Microsoft System wvmbus.inf 6.3.9600.16384	Microsoft	6.3.9600.16384	06/21/2006	x64	System	False
Microsoft System wvmbus.inf 6.3.9600.16384 (1)	Microsoft	6.3.9600.16384	06/21/2006	x86	System	False
Microsoft System wvmbusr.inf 6.3.9600.16384	Microsoft	6.3.9600.16384	06/21/2006	x64	System	False
Microsoft System wvmic.inf 6.3.9600.16384	Microsoft	6.3.9600.16384	06/21/2006	x64	System	False
Microsoft System wvmic.inf 6.3.9600.16384 (1)	Microsoft	6.3.9600.16384	06/21/2006	x86	System	False
Microsoft System wvmic2.inf 6.3.9600.16384	Microsoft	6.3.9600.16384	06/21/2006	x64,x86	System	False
Microsoft System wvpcinull.inf 6.3.9600.16384	Microsoft	6.3.9600.16384	06/21/2006	x64,x86	System	False

Tree view (left pane):
- Deployment Workbench
  - Information Center
  - Deployment Shares
    - MDT Reference Share (C:\ReferenceShare)
      - Applications
      - Operating Systems
        - Windows 7
        - Windows 8
        - Windows 8.1
        - Windows Server 2008 R2
        - Windows Server 2012
        - Windows Server 2012 R2
      - Out-of-Box Drivers
      - Packages
      - Task Sequences
      - Advanced Configuration
        - Selection Profiles
        - Linked Deployment Shares
        - Media
        - Database
  - Monitoring

These drivers will auto apply to WinPE base images when you update the deployment share, and they will also be injected (by default) into Windows installations as required by Plug and Play, as part of the task sequence. We will cover this in greater depth in `Chapter 6, Drivers`.

Importing patches

Now that we have imported Hyper-V drivers, let's move on to importing patches. In the following example, I am going to include the `2775511` hotfix in my base Windows 7 image (and 2008 R2 when I get around to importing the Server SKUs as well). The `2775511` hotfix is an enterprise hotfix rollup, which is available for Windows 7 SP1 and Windows Server 2008 R2 SP1.

Downloading a hotfix

First we must acquire the file. This is done by downloading it from Windows Catalog rather than registering and pulling down a hotfix link over e-mail:

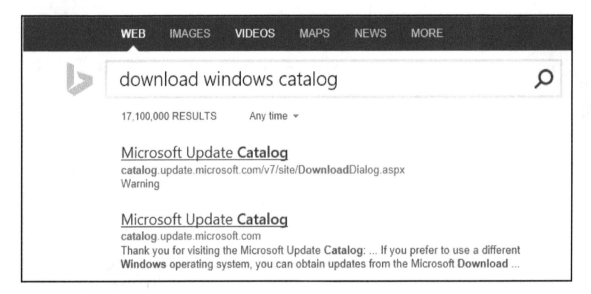

In the catalog engine, put the hotfix ID (2775511) into the search bar and click on **Search**.

Then, you will get the results that hopefully look like the following image:

Add (in this example) all but the **Itanium** option, click on **view basket**, and then select **Download**. Choose a location to download them in a folder on your local system.

Then they will download it in a folder per hotfix in the specified directory:

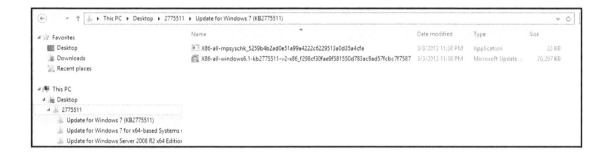

Setting up a packaged import

Point the MDT wizard to the location where you downloaded the hotfix for a package import:

Use the wizard to import the packages:

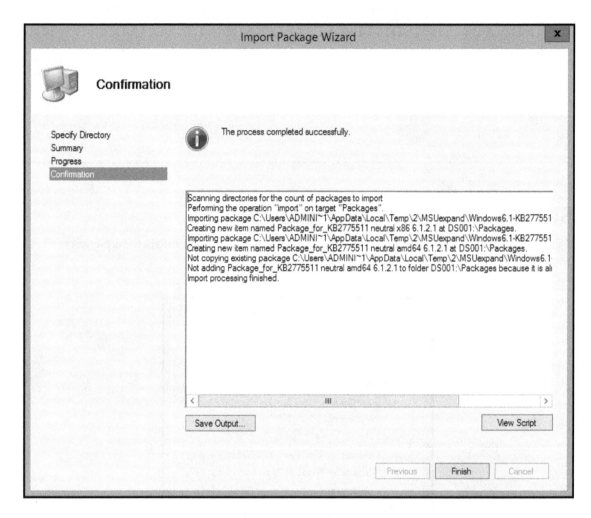

This process is quite easy. For Windows 7, we'll want to add some additional hotfixes, and do the same for 2008 R2. Windows 8, 2012, and higher versions have introduced a servicing stack change that makes it less likely for us to need to pull down one-off hotfixes, but the capability is still here.

Updating the deployment share to include the hotfix

Now that we have added a hotfix, it is time to update the deployment share so that the hotfix can be included in WinPE if needed.

Right-click on **MDT Reference Share** under **Deployment Shares** and select **Update Deployment Share**. You should be able to see a screen similar to the following:

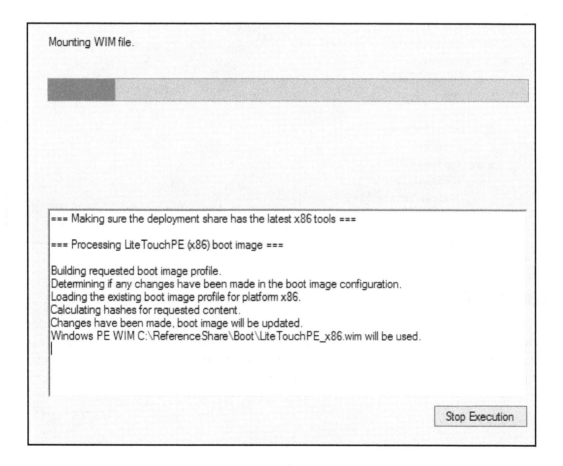

Adding applications to our reference image

Now that we've added patches and drivers, let's add a few applications to our reference image, taking us from a thin image to a hybrid image.

First, we will make a directory structure, as seen in the following image:

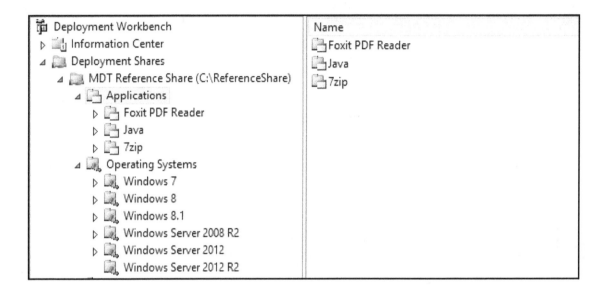

Automating image updates

Now, we can just put `setup.exe` for each of these into the folders and say that we're done. However, you don't want to walk through the installer for each application manually every time we capture a reference image. You want this process to be automated so that when new patches are released, we can just fire off a task sequence and let it update the image automatically.

Finding .msi files with the ITNinja repository

To tweak the setup to be automatic for all your different applications, I would recommend checking `http://www.itninja.com/`. ITNinja is a repository of automatic installation experiences from your peers, which are documented for all time.

So, for Foxit Reader, I went through some gyrations and form filling on Foxit's site, as documented at the ITNinja site, and was rewarded with a `.msi`, which ITNinja says, can be silently installed using the following command:

```
msiexec /i EnterpriseFoxitReader605.0618_enu.msi /qn
```

Your version may change as the product is updated, but this is the general idea.

Placing the .msi file

Place the `.msi` file that we downloaded in its *own* individual directory, as shown in the following screenshot. This directory needs to be unique to the `.msi` file as we'll be navigating to it later:

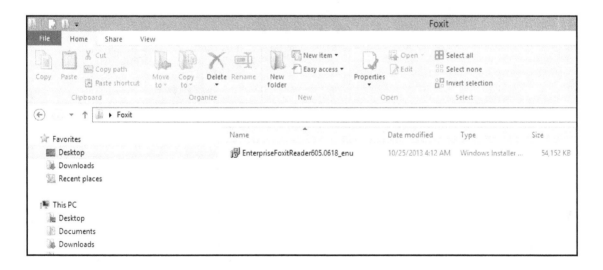

Setting up a new application

To set up our new application in MDT, just like for drivers or patches, we will right-click on the application folder, and select **New Application**. This generates the **New Application Wizard** window, as shown in the following image:

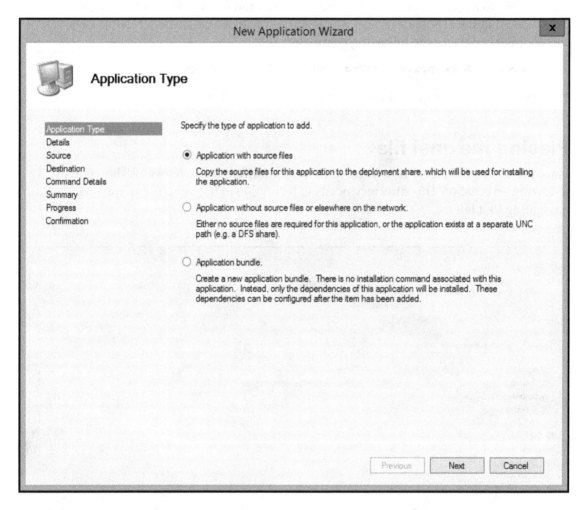

In this particular case, we'll select the first option, as we have the source files (.msi). If one had a lot of packaged applications on a network **Distributed File System (DFS)** or filer scenario, the second option is perfectly viable as well.

Specifying application details

Once we've selected the option that best suits our application, click on **Next**. In the following window, we will fill in the form to specify our application's details:

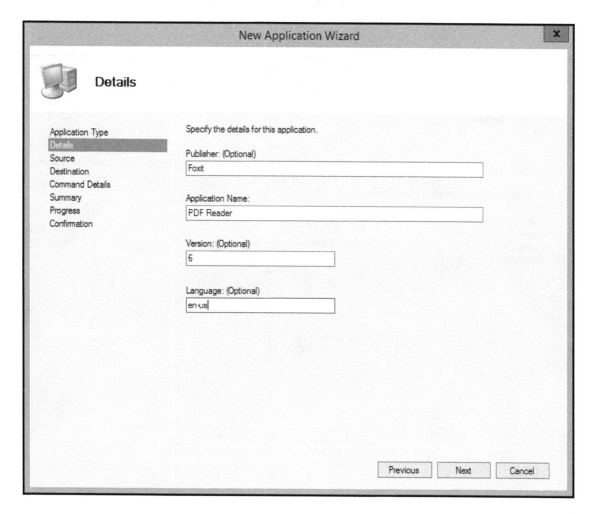

Once you're done, click on **Next**.

Finding the .msi source directory

On the **Source** page, we simply browse to the unique directory that we created previously for our `.msi` file. Since I have no real need for the `.msi` file after this action, I will check the box to **Move the files to the deployment share instead of copying them**, as shown in the following screenshot:

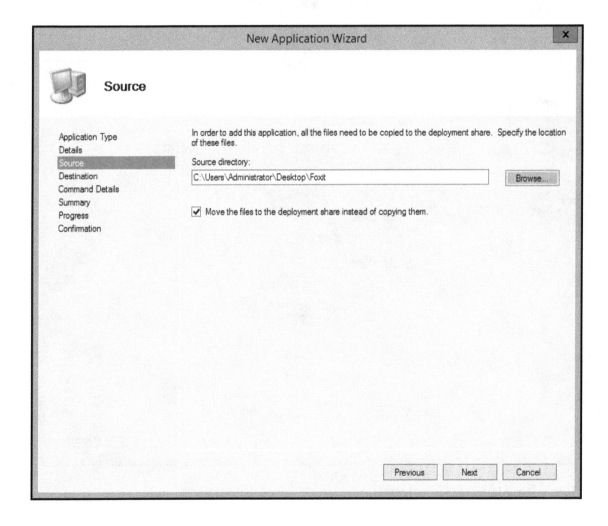

TIP

In an enterprise environment, it may be better to leave this unchecked so that you have a library of the `.msi` files that you have used in the past.

Specifying the destination directory

In the following screen, the directory to be created to move the `.msi` files to is autogenerated based on the information we previously provided:

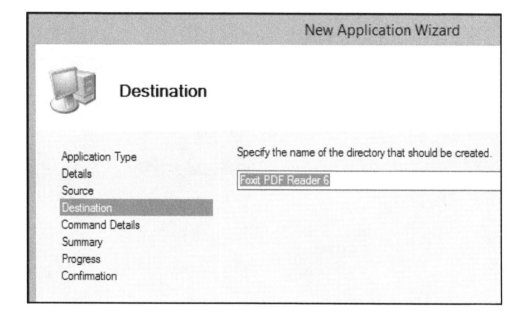

Entering command details

The **Command Details** screen is where the magic happens. We enter the commands to automatically install the application here. For example, Foxit silent install will be configured as `msiexec /i EnterpriseFoxitReader605.0618_enu.msi /qn`:

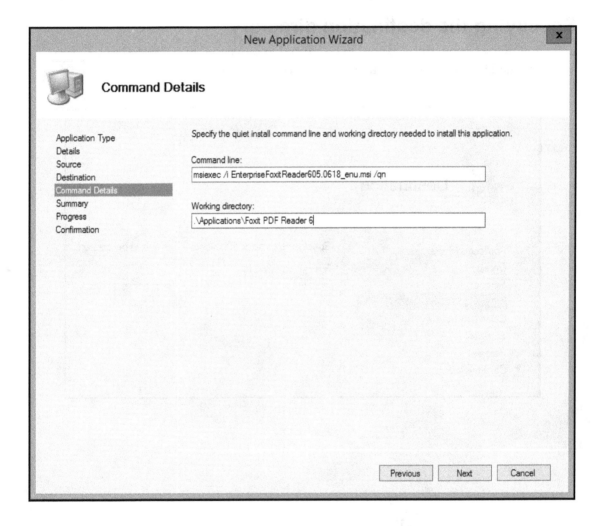

Click on **Next**, confirm whether your settings are correct, and away we go. The application will be created, and then we can use it in a task sequence to essentially embed the application to Windows at deployment time.

I will repeat the process we went through just now for the other two applications (Java and 7-Zip), and now it's time to proceed with creating a task sequence to capture this reference image.

> **Windows 10**
> All the concepts shown in this chapter are still valid for Windows 10 image creation. In addition the following information is relevant to Windows 10 specifically:
>
> - Windows 10 enables sideloading for enterprises in a managable fashion. Therefore you can unlock a device for sideloading using an enterprise policy, or through the settings of the machine. License keys are not required for Windows 10 application sideloading and domain join is not required for sideloading to work properly anymore.
> - Windows 10 as guest VM is only supported on Hyper-V on Server 2012 R2 or newer or Hyper-V on Windows 10. You will need minimum MDT 2013 Update 1. I recommend using newest available MDT (at time of printing this was MDT 2013 Update 2). Please use Windows 10 ADK version 1507 or newer.

Summary

So far, we have created an MDT reference image, downloaded hotfixes, copied Hyper-V drivers, and configured applications for automated installation. In the next chapter, we will be creating our task sequence for a reference image job that we can then use in a repeatable, automated fashion.

3
Creating Reference Images

In the previous chapter, we constructed a reference share on our deployment host. This chapter utilizes this share to craft a task sequence that will be used to create a golden image for later deployment.

In this chapter, we will cover the following topics:

- Task sequence concepts
- Image customizations that can be carried on to the default user profile
- The image factory that will keep reference images up to date with the latest Windows Updates via a Windows Server Update Services configuration
- Sysprep and its run support
- Reference task sequence boot media

Creating a reference image in the management console

In this chapter, we'll spend most of our time modifying the task sequence for **reference image creation**. To create one in the management console, select **Task Sequences**, as shown in the following image, and then select **New Task Sequence**:

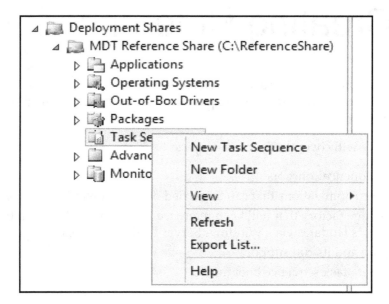

Specifying the general settings

Generally speaking, I recommend **Task sequence ID** to be specified as numerical values. This suites well when we force task sequences based on things such as model number, for instance. **Task sequence name** is better suited for a longer description of what the task sequences' purpose is. Comments, of course, can contain entries such as version control, author, and other operational details, as shown in the following screenshot:

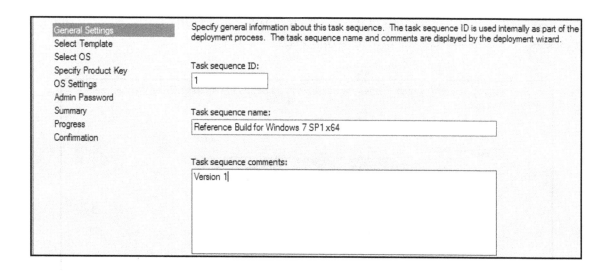

Selecting the template and the OS

On the following screen, **Standard Client Task Sequence** works very well for our intentions here. In fact, the built-in task sequences have a lot of logic built into them, which is hard to reproduce. I recommend always using these as building blocks, instead of building your own from scratch:

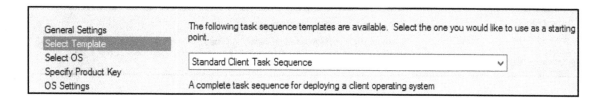

In the following window, we will select our base OS used for the task sequence. On our **General Settings** screen, I indicated this would be a Windows 7 SP1 x64 Reference build, so let's select Windows 7 from the provided options:

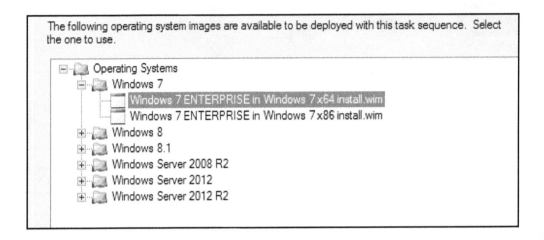

Specifying a product key and OS settings

As we are not building a system per se, but rather constructing a reference image for future use, we do not need to specify a product key at this time:

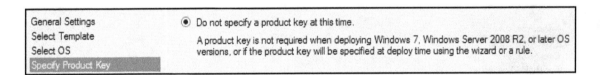

Then, on the next page of the wizard, simply fill in the provided blanks. These are not permanent selections, they can be modified later, so do not worry about them at this point:

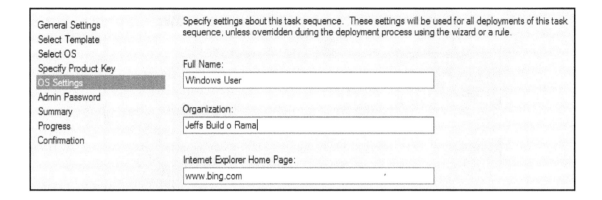

Passwords and security

On the next screen, we specify an administrator account password for the reference image. Make this a fairly simply password, as the password is obfuscated, not encrypted in any strong way; mine will be P@ssword1, for example:

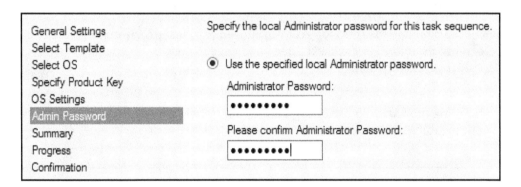

Incidentally, if you chose the other radio button option here, instead of having the reference image automatically build for you, you'll be prompted for the Administrator Password each run. This isn't really desirable in a reference scenario, as we want this to ultimately and ideally be a repeatable and reliable process that can be done hands-off.

Summarising our entries

Finally, we get a summary screen of our entries as shown in the following image:

```
TaskSequenceID:        1
TaskSequenceName:      Reference Build for Windows 7 SP1 x64
TaskSequenceComments:  Version 1
Template:              Client.xml
OperatingSystem:       Windows 7 ENTERPRISE in Windows 7 x64 install.wim
FullName:              Windows User
OrgName:               Jeffs Build o Rama
HomePage:              www.bing.com
AdminPassword:         ********
```

Finalising the task sequence

We will click the **Next** button where we see our task sequence is created in a confirmation page. If we chose to do so, we could view the script used to create the task sequence for later use in automation, or save the output as well so that we can audit for a change management tool or for documentation on what was done for change control or the like.

 To review the script or save output, simply click on the appropriate button at the end of our wizard screen and save the output; by default, it will open in Notepad.

After completing the wizard by selecting **Finish**, there should be a task sequence populated, as shown in the following image:

Name	ID	Version	TaskSequenceTemplate	enable	guid
Reference Build for Windows 7 SP1 x64	1	1.0	Client.xml	True	{9838bfe8-0e29-42fc-87dc-05188247e399}

Right-click and select **Properties** on the task sequence, the following screen shows up and let's walk through the basic concepts:

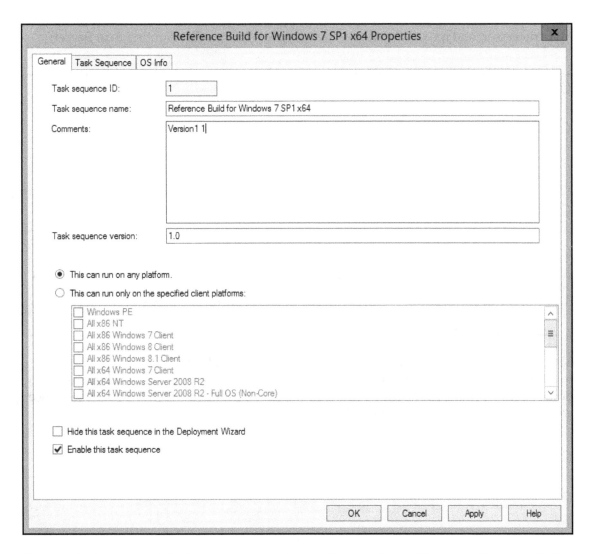

In most deployments, it isn't necessary to select a client platform. However, if you needed to, the flexibility is there to enable the task sequence to only be runnable on certain OSes. If the sequence is a work in progress, it may make sense to hide the sequence in the deployment wizard, or disable it entirely.

However, a common *gotcha* in virtualized reference builds is to have a virtual machine for the reference task sequence that does not have enough memory for Windows PE. You can see from the task sequence that in the **Validation** folder, the **Validate** step looks for a minimum of 768 MB of RAM available to run the task sequence. We also require an 800 MHz processor, and the OS that we are installing is Windows**Client** rather than **Server**:

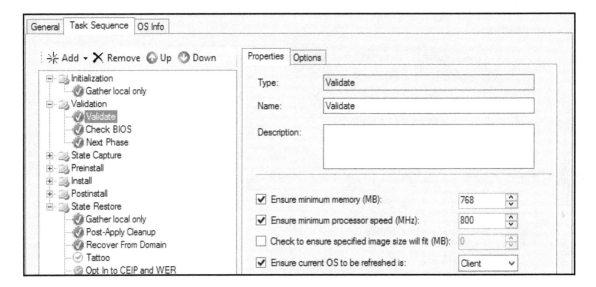

So one must make sure that the virtual machine (or physical host, if you have to go that route) has more than these requirements. You *could* reduce the requirements; however, doing so would likely cause Windows PE to not load, crashing the rest of the task sequence and wasting your time in troubleshooting.

Observing the task sequence

As we observe on the **Task Sequence** tab, the engine breaks the sequence up into seven steps. A brief introduction of them would be as follows:

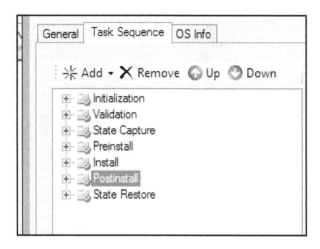

- **Initialization**: In this step, initial variable information is gathered for later consumption.
- **Validation**: In this step, some of the variables are compared against modifiable rules to validate the task sequence can continue.
- **State Capture**: In this step, the state of the machine can be captured. All the task sequences can be run from either inside an OS, or from a WinPE ISO. **User State Migration Tool** (**USMT**)-driven state capture is done here.
- **Preinstall**: This step is broken into multiple areas, based on the stage or type of sequence being run: **New Computer only**, **Offline User State Capture**, and **Refresh only**. This is where the driver injection happens, which can be controlled via selection profiles, which we will cover later.
- **Install**: In this step, the sequence will install the OS specified, laying down the WIM.
- **Postinstall**: In this step, drivers are injected into the Windows installation. Windows Recovery is added to the disk, and finally a reboot takes place.
- **State Restore**: The last step, if any USMT work was done to capture user data, it is restored here. In addition, join domain, installation of applications, enabling BitLocker, and Local GPO packages are applied.

Making configuration changes

Many options are the options with regards to what configuration changes you can make. It all depends on what your needs for your organization are. The following task sequence configuration will suit most reference image capture scenarios:

1. Enable the **Windows Update (Pre-Application Installation)** and **Windows Update (Post-Application Installation)** steps in **State Restore**. To do this, select each item to enable and click on the **Options** tab and uncheck the **Disable this step** checkbox:

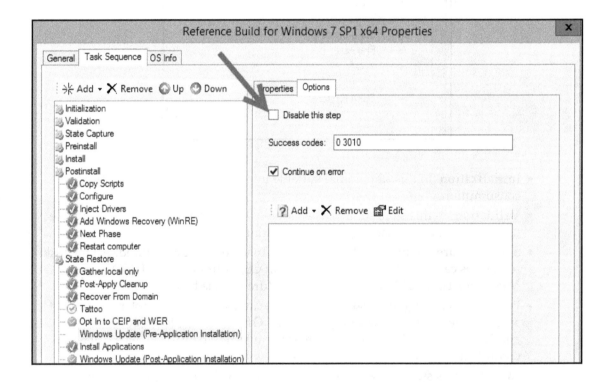

2. Disable the **Enable BitLocker** step by the same method:

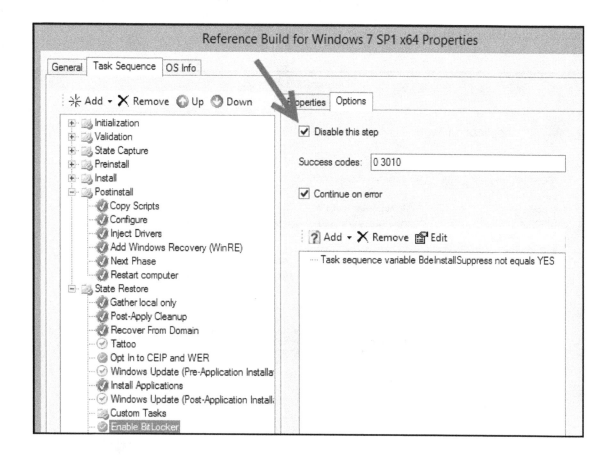

Creating an application bundle

After making these housekeeping item changes, we need to consider what applications we want to place in our default image. What applications do we want in the image for all users, both from a cost and licensing perspective, as well as a workload perspective?

In our examples in the previous chapter, we created the applications for Foxit Reader, Java, and 7-Zip. We could individually make these mandatory applications of the image, but let's do something that is a little easier to manage: make the task sequence install an application bundle containing all three:

So, here we are creating an application bundle with more fluid details, as shown in the following image:

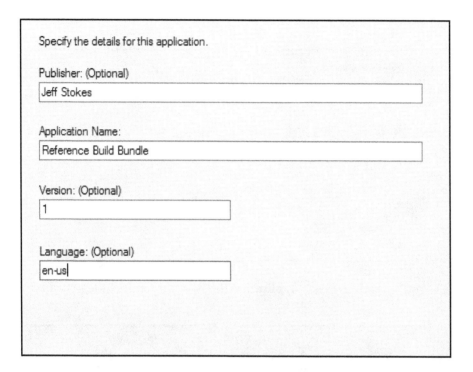

You can click on **Next** and **Finish** to complete the creation of the bundle.

Making an application bundle object

Making an application bundle object is quite easy and straightforward. The details are in the post creation properties, in the **Dependencies** tab:

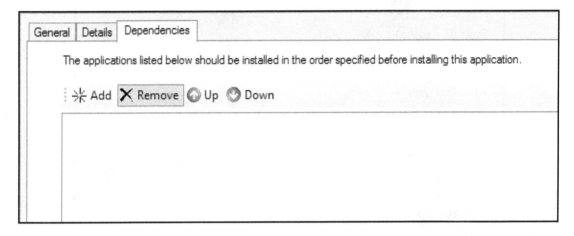

Now, it is as simple as adding each application that we want to include in our bundle:

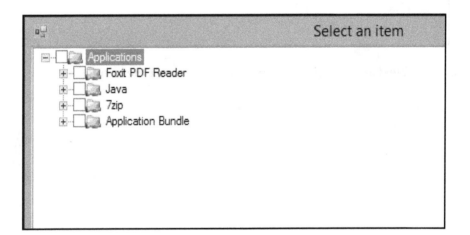

 The order, in this particular case, doesn't really matter. However, it is important to recall that in some cases, such as when installing an application with a Java or .NET dependency, we will install these first.

So, we have selected, for this build, the x64 versions of the applications that have them, and of course, we have *not* selected **Application Bundle**, as that would be recursive:

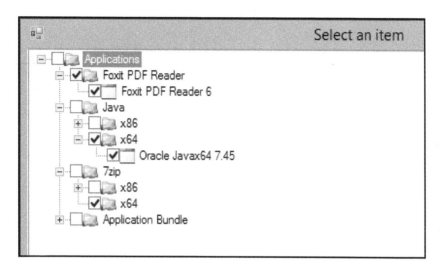

It is then as simple as applying the changes to the application bundle, as shown in the following image:

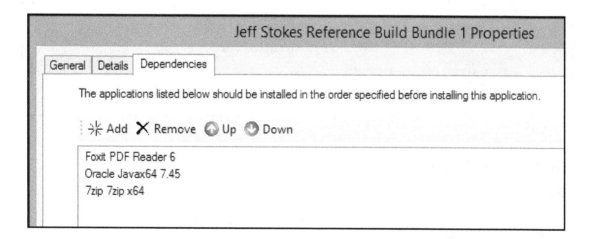

Installing the bundle

After creating our bundle for `Task Sequence 1`, we will go back to the properties of the task sequence and go to the **Install Applications** item, where we can force our bundle to be installed:

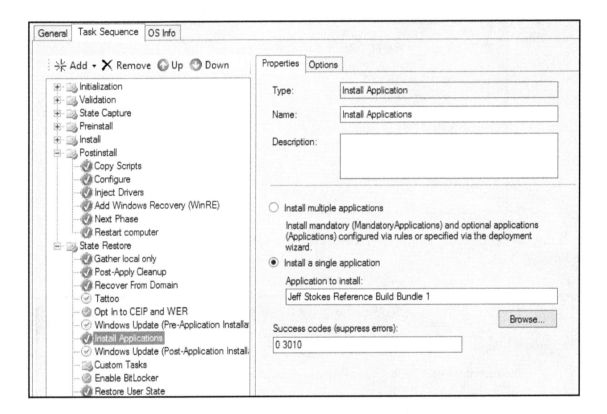

Modifying the bundle

Modifying the bundle is as simple as browsing and selecting the application bundle.

If we did not select the bundle or another application individually, the default behavior is to install multiple applications, and in the task sequence, present a checkbox list for the technician or end user to select and install manually.

For a reference image though, this doesn't make sense. We want our task sequence to be repeatable, as close to a zero-touch event as possible.

Managing updates

So now we have it, a completed task sequence to build a reference image. Additionally, in a large managed environment, we would generally build a standalone **Windows Server Update Services** (**WSUS**) server to manage our updates and approve, or not, the various updates available from the Windows Update Catalog site. This is simply done by adding a property to our `Rules` section, as shown in the following image:

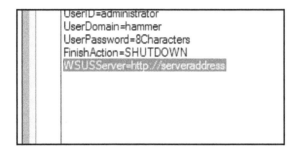

It is unsupported by Microsoft to use a WSUS instance that is SCCM-controlled. For updates that are available from the Catalog, but not available in Windows Updates (so WSUS will not display them), you can either import them directly into WSUS, or add them as a package in MDT.

Sysprep run supportability

Sysprep is primarily a tool used to prepare a Windows installation for cloning. It has been around for some time now, so we won't go into it too much here. Suffice it to say that the tool is alive and well in Windows 7 and 8, and it is one of the tools called by MDT scripts to enable Audit mode, customize images, and build reference images.

Sysprep is famous for having a three-times limit for its run supportability on a single image before it is no longer in a supported state. This is often misunderstood, so let's get a little clarity here.

From `http://technet.microsoft.com/en-us/library/cc766514(v=WS.10).aspx`:

> *"There is no limit to the number of times Sysprep can run on a computer. However, the clock for Windows Product Activation begins its countdown the first time Windows starts. You can use the sysprep /generalize command to reset Windows Product Activation a maximum of three times. After the third time you run the sysprep /generalize command, the clock can no longer be reset."*

The number of `/generalize` passes can be determined by performing `slmgr /dlv` (display license status verbosely) in a command prompt on running the Windows installation. It does require administrative rights.

The following table details the changes in Sysprep limitations, based on the OS:

Windows Version	Documented Sysprep Limitations
Windows XP	Reference and destination computers must have compatible HAL types. The size of the hard disk on the destination computer must be at least the same size as the hard disk on the reference computer. SkipRearm limit of three.
Windows 7	SkipRearm limit of three.
Windows 8	In most Windows 8 deployment scenarios, you no longer have to use the SkipRearm answer file setting to reset the Windows Product Activation clock when you run the `sysprep` command multiple times on a computer. In Windows 8, the SkipRearm setting is used to specify the Windows licensing state. If you specify a retail product key or volume license product key, Windows is automatically activated. You can run the `sysprep` command up to eight additional times on a single Windows image. After running Sysprep eight times on a Windows 8 image, you must recreate your Windows image (from `http://technet.microsoft.com/en-us/library/hh825195.aspx`).

Boot media for the reference task sequence

Boot media is created when the reference share is right-clicked and you select **Update Deployment Share**.

This action runs a PowerShell script to update the WinPE share. This action is known as **UpdateDP**:

```
Import-Module "C:\Program Files\Microsoft Deployment
  Toolkit\bin\MicrosoftDeploymentToolkit.psd1"
New-PSDrive -Name "DS001" -PSProvider MDTProvider -Root
  "C:\ReferenceShare"
update-MDTDeploymentShare -path "DS001:" -Verbose
```

This script updates the boot directory with a WIM and ISO media for easy use in a VM-boot scenario or the creation of USB stick media.

Windows 10

All the concepts shown in this chapter are still valid for Windows 10, but pay attention to the following points:

- If you plan to create a Windows 10 image used for inplace upgrade, only pure OS, features on demand, and patches are allowed. Do not add any applications to an inplace upgrade Image.
- For a normal *wipe and reload* Windows 10 image, you can add applications as shown previously.
- WSUS 4.0 should be patched with KB3095113.
- Changes to the SKU via the Provisioning Package or another mechanism cause an automatic reboot to occur afterward. This reboot is currently not controllable or interruptible. This will result in a **dirty environment** message in MDT due to this reboot *outside* of MDT. Speaking of Windows 10 v1511 / MDT 2013 U2, don't use this feature currently.

Summary

In this chapter, we've covered Sysprep, creating the reference image, and how to do all this in a supported method. The key takeaway from all this is that, with MDT 2013, you can, every month if you chose, build a new golden image in a repeatable supported fashion. We can get away from manual steps, entry points of human error, and questionable methods.

In the next chapter, we'll cover default user profile customization in depth, which will certainly be part of the reference build process for you, going forward.

4
Default User Profile Customization

In the previous chapter, we discussed the technique of collecting a reference build for Windows in a virtual machine on Hyper-V or physical box with boot media on a USB stick. In this chapter, we'll cover how to customize this base image as part of our process. Not from an application build perspective, but to make the image branded, remove or add features, remove the **out-of-box experience** (**OOBE**), and so forth. Now some general things one might want done to their image would be removing the games, setting the Internet Explorer default settings, customizing the background screen, and other branding components, removing the ability to access things in the UI by default, and so on, as well as customizing the image for a kiosk, tablet, cash register, ATM, exec's laptop, VDI image, and so on.

In this chapter, we'll go through the following topics:

- How to customize the Windows image
- Windows System Image Manager and `Unattend.xml`
- The differences between Windows 7 and 8 in UI customizations

Customizing the image

You may customize the image before running your reference task sequence. Customizations are done in many ways; some are script-based, some group policies, some are manual efforts, some are done in a tool known as **Windows System Image Manager** (**WSIM**), and others can be done with PowerShell scripts.

Checking out the customization documentation

The general caveats and principles of image customization are documented for Windows at this KB at http://support.microsoft.com/kb/973289. The essential gist of this is that to customize the user profile of a future user of Windows 7 or 2008 R2, you must customize the default local user profile. When this is done, the settings in the default profile will become the settings of new user profiles on the system. Note that this is the only officially supported method of customizing the default user profile in Windows 7.

For Windows 8.x, things change somewhat. The steps are documented at http://technet.microsoft.com/en-us/library/hh825135.aspx and involve, generally speaking, the same steps as for Windows 7. However, a new functionality is provided to customize the Start menu, documented at http://technet.microsoft.com/en-us/library/jj134269.aspx.

Accessing Windows System Information Manager

An easy way to use this customization, as mentioned previously, is **WSIM**. It's quite easy to access; simply right-click on your task sequence and select the **OS Info** tab, and click on **Edit Unattend.xml**:

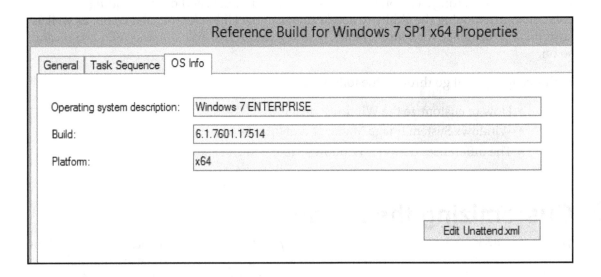

Then you'll be rewarded with a modified view of the typical MMC console layout for
`Unattend.xml` editing, as shown in the following:

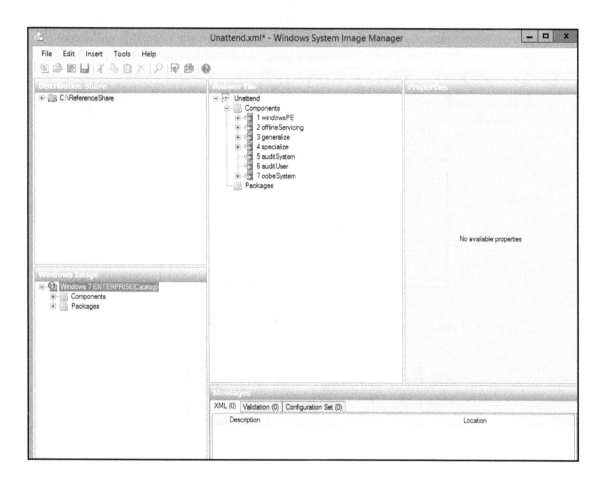

Adding games to our Enterprise image

This interface is a bit intimidating at first, and somewhat unclear about where things should be edited, as they will sometimes appear to be applicable in multiple locations of the XML. For those who have manually edited the Unattend.xml files in the past, this will make little sense perhaps. It may be best to learn by doing, so let's add games to our Windows 7 Enterprise image by performing the following exercise:

1. Ensure the focus is on the **Windows Image** area of the MMC, as shown in the following image:

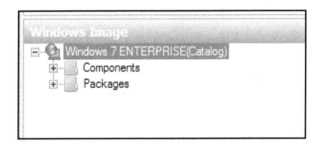

2. Click on **Find…** in the **Edit** menu:

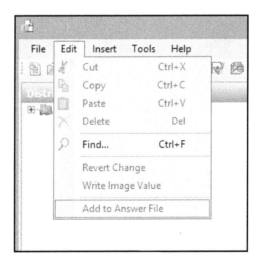

3. Now, simply type `games` here and observe that there are three responses to the query:

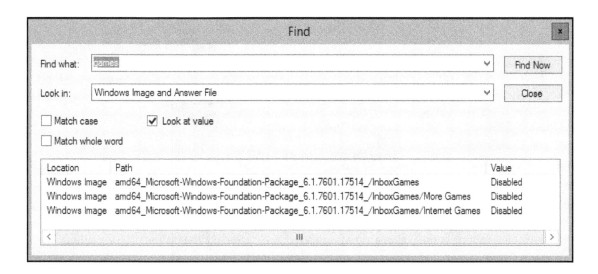

4. In our case, we'll want them all, so select the top one, **InboxGames**. Double-click on it, and then note in the bottom-left pane, we will see it highlighted. Right-click on it and then left-click on **Add to Answer File**:

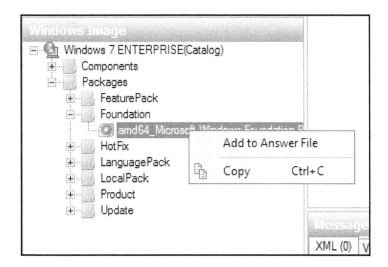

5. Note that the frame of reference in WSIM has changed. In the **Answer File** pane, there is **Packages** listed at the bottom, broken out to **Foundation** and then `amd64_Micrsooft-Windows-Foundation-Package_#Windows Version`; on the far right, we have the break out of all the options for this entry listed. Nested in here is our **InboxGames**, and the property is **Disabled** by default. Each entry is a drop box on the far right, as shown in the following screenshot:

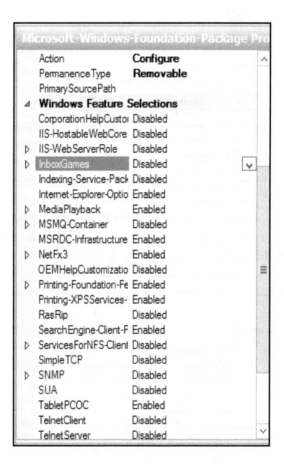

Simply click the **Disabled** text and change to **Enabled**:

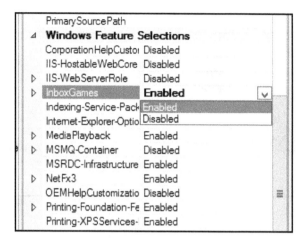

6. Now that we've specified that we want to enable **InboxGames** from our image, click on the **Tools** menu and select **Validate Answer File**:

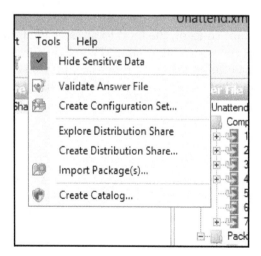

7. Now, in the **Messages** area at the bottom of the screen, you should see that your validation answer file is good and has no warnings or errors:

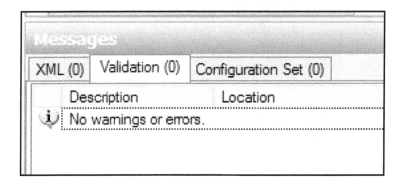

8. Finally, simply save the Unattend.xml file.

Now, from this point forward, this task sequence for Windows 7 Enterprise in this deployment share will have **InboxGames** enabled.

It's an important concept, the Unattend.xml file follows the task sequence, not the operating system. Therefore, we can import Windows 7 Enterprise x64 edition once and make a multitude of different configurations that all use this WIM and modify it differently, based on the need.

Analyzing our changes

What has actually happened here is that the Unattend.xml file for our Windows 7 image in MDT has been modified. The image itself, the WIM file, is fine. It hasn't been modified; however, Unattend.xml, used in this task sequence, has been modified.

For example, Unattend.xml in the Control Directory\1 directory now has a snippet that looks a bit similar to the following code:

```
<?xml version="1.0" encoding="utf-8"?>
<unattend xmlns="urn:schemas-microsoft-com:unattend">
  <servicing>
    <package action="configure">
```

```
<assemblyIdentity name="Microsoft-Windows-Foundation-Package"
  version="6.1.7601.17514" processorArchitecture="amd64"
  publicKeyToken="31bf3856ad364e35" language="" />
<selection name="InboxGames" state="true" />
<selection name="Solitaire" state="true" />
```

Leveraging the Audit mode

What if we wanted to do things outside of the options we find in `Unattend.xml`?

For this, you may want to leverage the audit mode. This is a little known mode of Windows boot, where the Windows installation is booted into the default administrator account (which, on Windows 8, is always disabled by default).

The current definition of audit mode on TechNet (`http://technet.micr osoft.com/en-us/library/cc722413(v=WS.10).aspx`), when writing this text, is as follows:

"Audit Mode. Audit mode is used by OEMs and corporations to add customizations to their Windows images. Audit mode does not require settings in Windows Welcome to be applied. By bypassing Windows Welcome, you can get to the desktop quicker and perform your customizations. You can add additional device drivers, install applications, and test the validity of the installation. OEMs and corps should use audit mode to complete their manual customizations before shipping the computer to an end user."

In audit mode, settings in an unattended answer file in the `auditSystem` and `auditUser` configuration passes are processed. For more information about these configuration passes, see `auditSystem` and `auditUser`.

If you are running in audit mode, to configure the installation to boot to Windows Welcome, run the `sysprep/oobe` command. For more information, see Sysprep Technical Reference. OEMs are required to run `sysprep/oobe` before shipping a computer to an end user.

In the audit mode, all the changes to the **base administrator account** can become the default settings for other users, provided the `CopyProfile=true` switch is flipped in `Unattend.xml` (as we observed previously).

Now, MDT will enter the audit mode for us. However, if we want to customize the image further than just what WSIM provides, we can pause the Task Sequence and modify this logon for all sorts of customizations that WSIM does not expose to us.

There are a few methods of pausing the task sequence. My personal favorite is to modify the MDT Task Sequence Editor as documented at `http://blogs.technet.com/b/deplo ymentguys/archive/2010/08/26/customising-the-mdt-task-sequence-editor.a spx`.

This method adds the following lines to the `actions.xml` XML file, located in the workbench machine:

```xml
<action divider="true" />
<action>
  <Category>Deployment Guys</Category>
  <Name>Pause Task Sequence</Name>
  <Type>SMS_TaskSequence_RunCustomSuspendCommandLineAction</Type>
  <Assembly>Microsoft.BDD.Actions</Assembly>
  <Class>Microsoft.BDD.Actions.ActionRunCommandLine</Class>
  <Property type="string" name="CommandLine"
    default="cscript.exe %SCRIPTROOT%\LTISuspend.wsf" />
  <Property type="string" name="WorkingDirectory" />
  <Property type="string" name="SuccessCodes" default="0 3010" />
  <Property type="string" name="PackageID" />
  <Property type="string" name="RunAsUser" default="false" />
  <Property type="string" name="SMSTSRunCommandLineUserName" />
  <Property type="string" name="SMSTSRunCommandLineUserPassword" />
  <Property type="boolean" name="LoadProfile" default="false" />
  <Property type="string" name="SupportedEnvironment"
    default="WinPEandFullOS" />
</action>
<action>
  <Category>Deployment Guys</Category>
  <Name>Force Update of Group Policy</Name>
  <Type>SMS_TaskSequence_RunCustomGPUpdateCommandLineAction</Type>
  <Assembly>Microsoft.BDD.Actions</Assembly>
  <Class>Microsoft.BDD.Actions.ActionRunCommandLine</Class>
  <Property type="string" name="CommandLine"
    default="gpupdate.exe /force" />
  <Property type="string" name="WorkingDirectory" />
  <Property type="string" name="SuccessCodes" default="0 3010" />
  <Property type="string" name="PackageID" />
  <Property type="string" name="RunAsUser" default="false" />
  <Property type="string" name="SMSTSRunCommandLineUserName" />
  <Property type="string" name="SMSTSRunCommandLineUserPassword" />
  <Property type="boolean" name="LoadProfile" default="false" />
  <Property type="string" name="SupportedEnvironment"
    default="WinPEandFullOS" />
</action>
```

Now, my wizard in the MDT console appears as shown in the following image:

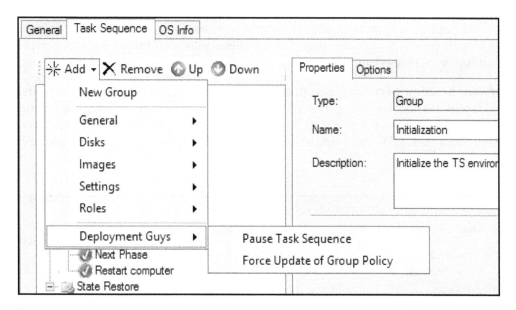

So what I would do here is place the **Pause Task Sequence** step in my **Custom Tasks** folder, as follows:

This will put a friendly link on the desktop to double-click when you choose to resume the task sequence. Thanks **Deployment Guys**!

Local Policy Object Customizations and SCM

In 2008, Aaron Margosis published the **Local Group Policy Object** (**LGPO**) toolset to manage and deploy local group policy objects. With these tools, it became easy to manage settings in local policy. You could insert these policies into your image with the scripts and tools that Aaron published and it worked fairly well.

Fast forward to today, **Security Compliance Manager** (**SCM**) (what LGPO became in essence) is now the tool for doing this. With SCM, you can manage policies, create and compare them, and then back them up. They are then (from a deployment perspective) GPO Packs, and then MDT can import them as part of the task sequence, as shown in the following image:

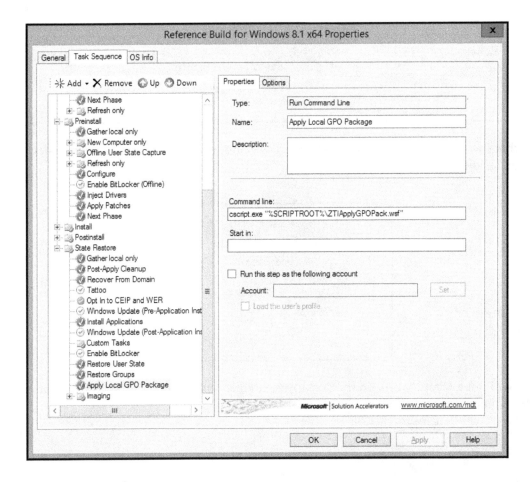

Using this suite of tools, we can then bake into the image customizations that we want to be the default for Windows. Many security-conscious organizations will implement this as a practice so that the machines that are built immediately have a default set of GPO settings applied. These can then be modified remotely via SCM and Active Directory Group Policy processing.

One must, however, consider the policy processing order when making these image modifications. According to `http://technet.microsoft.com/en-us/library/cc7856 65(v=WS.10).aspx`, the ordering of policy processing and precedence is as follows:

"Local Group Policy object—Each computer has exactly one Group Policy object that is stored locally. This processes for both computer and user Group Policy processing."
"Site—Any GPOs that have been linked to the site that the computer belongs to are processed next. Processing is in the order that is specified by the administrator, on the Linked Group Policy Objects tab for the site in Group Policy Management Console (GPMC). The GPO with the lowest link order is processed last, and therefore has the highest precedence."
"Domain-Processing of multiple domain—linked GPOs is in the order specified by the administrator, on the Linked Group Policy Objects tab for the domain in GPMC. The GPO with the lowest link order is processed last, and therefore has the highest precedence."
"Organizational units—GPOs that are linked to the organizational unit that is highest in the Active Directory hierarchy are processed first, then GPOs that are linked to its child organizational unit, and so on. Finally, the GPOs that are linked to the organizational unit that contains the user or computer are processed."

Therefore, changes we make in our LGPO will not be overridden by future updates of Active Directory policies, without modifying the local policy again, that is.

Another reason to utilize a tool such as SCM for configuration templates is that the work put into the templates by Microsoft Consulting Services can be leveraged as a baseline standard for your organization as well. Literally hundreds of man-hours of experience and case work have resulted in these templates for use in a security and management perspective.

Shell customizations

In Windows XP, in the old days, one meticulously set up the desktop and Start menu layout, and then copied the profile over the default profile by hand. This was never a supported method for user customization, and over the years, some problems occurred due to its use as a standard practice.

With the Windows Vista model of user profile customization, this has changed somewhat. Questions on Windows 7, 8, 8.1, and beyond, generally boil down to topics such as how to pin an internal application to the Start menu, how to pin it to the taskbar, and how to customize the Start screen in Windows 8.

Windows 7 Start menu and taskbar

Supported methods of Windows 7customization are well documented in several blogs and support articles by Microsoft. In this text, we'll cover these modifications and the pros and cons of the mentioned methods.

Note that the licensing of Windows 7 in some cases precludes image customization. The TechNet article at `http://technet.microsoft.com /en-us/library/ff730914.aspx`, in particular, discusses Windows 7 Professional and the customization of this image based on your particular licensing scenario. It is not supported in any case to take an OEM image that you get on a factory-built PC and capture and customize it. This image has already been syspreped, and therefore, could cause unpredictability in image creation and deployment, as well as violate the OEM license.

First, Scott McArthur reviewed ways of customizing the Start menu and taskbar in Windows 7 by way of `Unattend.xml`. This is a pretty straightforward method of image customization and is fully supported. The article was posted to AskCore on March 16th 2010, and is located at `http://blogs.technet.com/b/askcore/archive/2010/03/16/how-to-customize-the-windows-7-start-menu-and-taskbar-using-unattend-xml.as px`.

In this blog, Scott goes over two items in `Unattend.xml`, `Microsoft-Windows-Shell-Setup\StartPanelLinks` and `Microsoft-Windows-Shell-Setup\TaskBarLinks`. These settings should be placed in the `oobeSystem` part of the `Unattend.xml` file. The `StartPanelLinks` area is fairly straightforward; it's modifying the part of the Start menu shown in the following red box (the spot above is system-reserved):

To modify these, simply define them as links, as shown in the following example:

```
<StartPanelLinks>
<Link0>%ALLUSERSPROFILE%\Microsoft\Windows\Start
   Menu\Programs\accessories\Notepad.lnk</Link0>
<Link1>%ALLUSERSPROFILE%\Microsoft\Windows\Start
   Menu\Programs\accessories\Windows Explorer.lnk</Link1>
</StartPanelLinks>
```

This example will modify the menu to display `Link0` as `Notepad` and `Link1` as `Windows Explorer`.

To modify the `TaskbarLinks` area, the logic is the same:

```
<TaskbarLinks>
<Link0>%ALLUSERSPROFILE%\Microsoft\Windows\Start
   Menu\Programs\accessories\Notepad.lnk</Link0>
<Link1>%ALLUSERSPROFILE%\Microsoft\Windows\Start
   Menu\Programs\accessories\Windows Explorer.lnk</Link1>
</TaskbarLinks>
```

There are some caveats to this setup that one must consider:

- We need `CopyProfile=true` to be enabled in our `Unattend.xml`. This should be expected for the default profile configuration at this point.
- You cannot remove the icons in the Start menu above the red box that I detailed. If you do, they are simply recreated when a new user logs in. Microsoft does not support removing these icons in any manner.

Windows 7 background, logon screen, and user tiles

Modifying the Windows 7 logon screen is a fairly straightforward process. One simply modifies a `regkey` value, drops in a graphic, and it's done.

The `regkey` is located at `HKLM\Software\Microsoft\Windows\CurrentVersion\Authentication\LogonUI\Background`, and the value of `OEMBackground` is set to 1.

Simply place your custom image in `%windir%\system32\oobe\info\backgrounds`. The desired logon wallpaper should have the `backgroundDefault.jpg` filename.

Images must be less than 256 KB in size. With regards to resolution of the image, set the resolution as you desire. If the monitor is set to an alternate resolution, the graphic will stretched to fit.

The Windows 7 wallpaper is pretty easy too, you can set it in the image prior to `sysprep/capture` through the normal UI; and as long as `CopyProfile=true`, it will keep it as the default setting. Another method might be to set the `HKEY_CURRENT_USER\Control Panel\Desktop` registry key value of wallpaper to the `C:\Windows\Web\Wallpaper\wallpaper.jpg` path, or even use the GPO documented at `http://gpsearch.azurewebsites.net/#141` (Desktop Wallpaper User Policy).

To modify user tile to the company branding, the images are located in the following path:

- `%ProgramData%\Microsoft\User Account Pictures\Guest.bmp`
- `%ProgramData%\Microsoft\User Account Pictures\User.bmp`

However, I think that utilizing the picture of the user for the user tile is even more interesting. On a domain-joined Windows 7 machine, the user tiles are stored for the users in the `C:\ProgramData\Microsoft\User Account Pictures` path. There is an API to pull the tiles from Active Directory. So get to work!

Just kidding. Jacob Steenhagen was kind enough to create a `setUserTile.exe` utility that does the work for you. You can check it out at `http://jacob.steenhagen.us/blog/201 2/02/loading-a-windows-7-user-tile-using-the-picture-in-active-director y/`.

You can use this tool (source documented in the blog post) to set this automatically from your Active Directory User Tile attribute that you have already populated.

Windows 8 customizations

Windows 8 brought us a new Start screen experience that changes the game somewhat with regards to image customization.

With regards to customizing the Start screen, Ben Hunter wrote (`http://blogs.technet.com/b/deploymentguys/archive/2012/10/26/start-screen-customization-with-mdt.aspx`):

> *"There are three approaches that you can use:*
> *1. Use the Unattend.xml file to define which applications will appear in each "slot" on the Start Screen as detailed here.*
> *2. Manually customize the Start Screen, then use CopyProfile to apply the customizations to the default user profile.*
> *3. Manually customize the Start Screen and capture the layout file created, then copy this file to the default user during image deployment."*

We've already discussed `CopyProfile=true` to some extent in this text; the other two options are interesting, where new customization capabilities are present.

So, let's discuss using the `Unattend.xml` file to define apps and the slotting model in the `Unattend.xml` file. This will require the `AppID` key of the applications needed to be pinned by the way, and TechNet covers the how-to at `http://technet.microsoft.com/en-us/library/jj134269.aspx#BKMK_StartTiles`, but in essence, `Get-AppxPackage` will reveal this. Once you have your AppxPackage IDs, you can add the `StartTiles` setting to the `Unattend.xml` file with WSIM or Notepad. You will construct the layout using the Wide Tile##, Square Tile## and DesktopOrSquare Tile##.

In WSIM, these appear as follows:

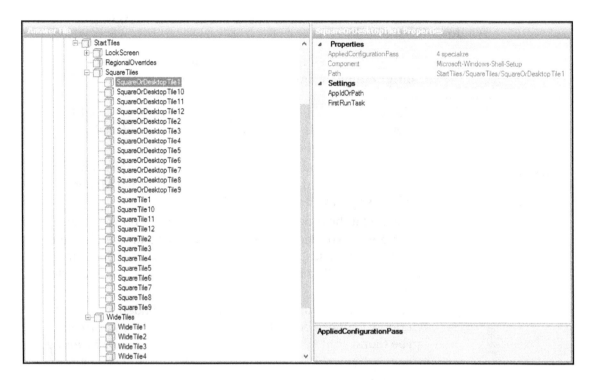

AppsFolderLayout.bin is actually discussed in the same TechNet article at http://tech net.microsoft.com/en-us/library/jj134269.aspx#BKMK_AppFolder. To do this, create a user profile, set up the Start screen, and then copy this design back into your master image using **xcopy**. This works similar to the CopyProfile=true method, except you overwrite AppsFolderLayout.bin from the customized profile to the default user profile while in the audit mode. Then, all future profiles will load this customized layout.

Windows 10

All the concepts shown in this chapter are still valid for Windows 10 image creation. In addition the following information is relevant to Windows 10 specifically:

- Windows 10 comes with a new **Windows Imaging and Configuration Designer** (**Windows ICD**). This Windows ICD is used for configuring features and policies by provisioning packages. This tool is designed specifically for Windows 10 customization and is discussed in Appendix, *Additional Enterprise Configuration Items*, of this book.
- MDT still needs modification of Unattend.xml. Unattend.xml can only be modified with **Windows System Image Manager** (**WSIM**), so you will still need WSIM.
- Currently (at the time of writing) CopyProfile on Windows 10 can create unexpected results. Therefore the recommendation is that you do not use CopyProfile with Windows 10 in your task sequences. This is subject to change with future updates to Windows 10.
- Start menu layout customization has been extended for Windows 10. It can be partially locked down. More information can be found at https://blogs.technet.microsoft.com/d eploymentguys/2016/03/07/windows-10-start-layout-customization/.

Summary

In this chapter, we reviewed image customization and default profile modifications and how to implement changes to these in a supported manner. We also reviewed WSIM and the Unattend.xml file structure, and discussed some of the changes that Windows 8 brings to Start Menu customizations as well.

In the next chapter, the CustomSettings.ini and task sequence engine will be covered in detail and depth.

5

CustomSettings.ini and Task Sequence

In the previous chapter, we discussed some tips and tricks to customize the default user profile via policy, script, halting the MDT process mid-capture and modifying it manually, and so on.

In this chapter, we will review the essence of deployment, the task sequence that is called to perform the automated deployment in MDT. We will discuss the following topics:

- We will discuss the `CustomSettings.ini` file as it relates to the `Unattend.xml` file, what it does, how it works, and how to use it for your environment
- We'll also get into the subject of the task sequence, the scripting environment, logging, and how to use existing, as well as custom variables

The structure of the CustomSettings.ini file

As we look at the structure of the **Rules** tab of a share, we are also looking at the `CustomSettings.ini` file. The structure of the file is fairly basic; there are two sections, the `[Settings]` area and the `[Default]` area:

```
[Settings]
Priority=Default
Properties=MyCustomProperty

[Default]
OSInstall=Y
SkipAppsOnUpgrade=YES
SkipCapture=NO
```

```
SkipAdminPassword=YES
SkipProductKey=YES
_SMSTSOrgName=MDT Reference Task Sequence
SkipBitLocker=YES
SkipDomainMembership=YES
JoinWorkgroup=Workgroup
SkipFinalSummary=YES
SkipLocaleSelection=YES
SkipSummary=YES
SkipTimeZone=YES
SkipUserData=YES
TimeZoneName=Eastern Standard Time
```

Now what we see is under `[Settings]`; there are two entries, `Priority` and `Properties`. `Priority` defines the grouping order that is to be followed when there is a settings conflict. `Properties` is a place to define custom properties, which we will discuss later in this chapter.

So, on `Priority`, note that we only have one section, and its labelled `[Default]`. An example of how we might do this differently than default would be, perhaps, if we wanted to dynamically name workstations or laptops, based on chassis types.

However, let's walk through this as if we just stumbled upon this problem to show the workflow. First, we'd want to designate the machine name as something unique. Every machine has a unique serial number (we hope), so let's use that as follows:

```
[Default]
OSDComputerName=%serialnumber%
```

Well fair enough, we have it set now, so the machine names are unique, but we don't know if it's a laptop or desktop, do we?

For this, some would say we need the MDT Database SQL backend, but that's not really true:

```
[Settings]
Priority=IsLaptop, Default
Properties=MyCustomProperty

[IsLaptop]
Subsection=Laptop-%IsLaptop%
[Laptop-True]
OSDComputerName=L%serialnumber%
```

```
[Laptop-False]
OSDComputerName=D%serialnumber%

[Default]
OSInstall=Y
```

The preceding code will specify, based on the `variables.dat` readout of the chassis type, the computer name at the time of setup. Therefore, the `%serialnumber%` variable is queried and placed in `OSDComputerName` as either an `L` or `D` followed by the variable (a mixture of alphanumeric characters assumedly).

Some organizations will place laptops and desktops into different organizational units in Active Directory as well, and we can accommodate this here quite easily as well:

```
[Settings]
Priority=IsLaptop, Default
Properties=MyCustomProperty

[IsLaptop]
Subsection=Laptop-%IsLaptop%
[Laptop-True]
OSDComputerName=L%serialnumber%
MachineObjectOU=OU= Laptops,OU= User Computers,DC=domain,DC=com

[Laptop-False]
OSDComputerName=D%serialnumber%
MachineObjectOU=OU= Desktops,OU= User Computers,DC=domain,DC=com

[Default]
OSInstall=Y
```

What if the serial number exceeds 15 characters (and the **Network Basic Input/Output System (NetBIOS)** name)? No problem! Remember this is a scripting environment. We can modify the preceding snippet to account for the excessive characters by changing `OSDComputerName` to `L#Right("%serialnumber%",8)#`:

```
[Settings]
Priority=IsLaptop, Default
Properties=MyCustomProperty

[IsLaptop]
Subsection=Laptop-%IsLaptop%
[Laptop-True]
OSDComputerName=L#Right("%serialnumber%",8)#
MachineObjectOU=OU= Laptops,OU= User Computers,DC=domain,DC=com
```

```
[Laptop-False]
OSDComputerName=D#Right("%serialnumber%",8)#
MachineObjectOU=OU= Desktops,OU= User Computers,DC=domain,DC=com

[Default]
OSInstall=Y
```

Now our `OSDComputerName` is a combination of `L` (or `D`) and then the right-most eight characters of the serial number. Now, the name is within the 15-character requirement of NetBIOS.

This same construct of logic can be used in the GUI as well! I will use the following example for this: what if we want to install a set of applications, but we will only install it if it is a VM, or only if it's a particular model number of hardware? For this example, let's assume that we are deploying to HP Servers and VMware VMs and we want to install VMware Tools, only if it is a VM, and the ProliantSupportPack software from HP, only if the task sequence is running on physical machines. Easy! The steps to do so are as follows:

1. Import the applications for each, and then create an application step for each under **Custom Tasks**:

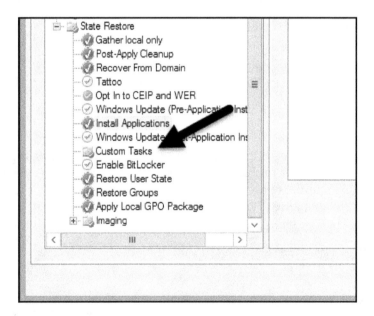

It will appear as shown in the following screenshot:

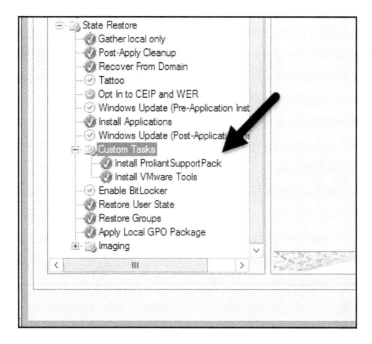

2. Then, in the **Properties** of each step, in the **Options** tab, add an **If Statement Properties** condition, as shown in the following screenshot:

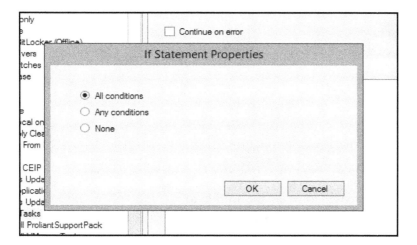

3. Then simply set the condition for physical machine step as follows (**Install ProliantSupportPack** in our example):

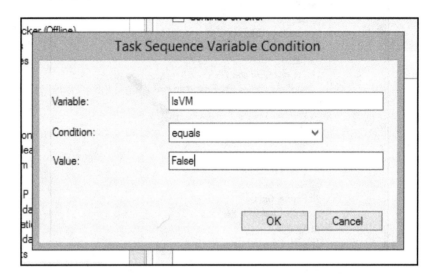

For VMs (in this case, **Install VMware Tools**) set the condition as follows:

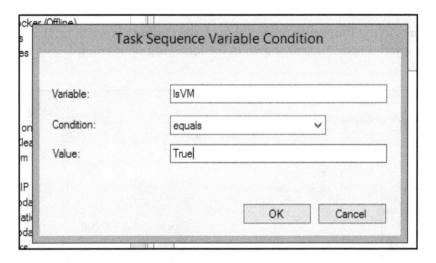

Using this method, we will force an application to run, but only in the conditions for which it is appropriate.

The Unattend.xml structure

Now that we have walked through the `CustomSettings.ini` structure, it is important to see exactly why this is relevant for an unattended installation of Windows. The key takeaway is that the variables, which MDT has created and defined, overlap in many cases with `Unattend.xml`. For example, we previously worked on a subsection in the `CustomSettings.ini` example that hinged on the `OSDComputerName` variable. In our `Unattend.xml` file, this is simply `<ComputerName>`.

We can review our `Unattend.xml` structure by going to our **Task Sequences** tab in our MDT console, right-clicking on a specific task sequence, selecting **Properties**, and then clicking on the **OS Info** tab, as shown in the following screenshot:

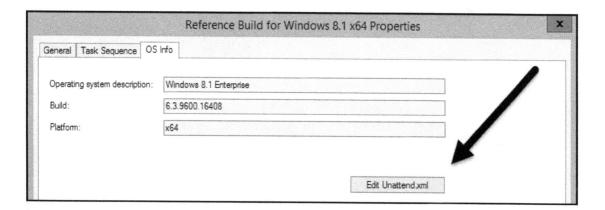

There is a **Edit Unattend.xml** button. This launches **Windows System Image Manager (WSIM)**, so we won't see the raw file contents. To see this, we can easily browse to our reference share using the `C:\ReferenceShare\Control\1` path and the `Unattend.xml` file. Open the file, and by default, Internet Explorer will render it for you, as shown in the following screenshot:

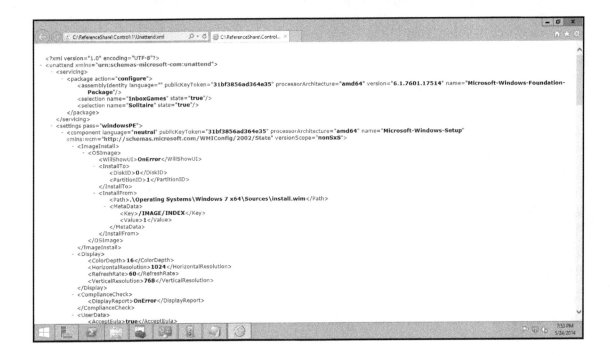

However, to open this file for ease of modification, I prefer to use the keystrokes *Shift +* right-click and navigate to **Open with** | **Notepad**. It will then look like the following code snippet and is fully editable:

```xml
<?xml version="1.0" encoding="utf-8"?>
<unattend xmlns="urn:schemas-microsoft-com:unattend">
  <servicing>
    <package action="configure">
      <assemblyIdentity name="Microsoft-Windows-Foundation-Package"
        version="6.1.7601.17514" processorArchitecture="amd64"
        publicKeyToken="31bf3856ad364e35" language="" />
      <selection name="InboxGames" state="true" />
      <selection name="Solitaire" state="true" />
    </package>
  </servicing>
  <settings pass="windowsPE">
    <component name="Microsoft-Windows-Setup"
      processorArchitecture="amd64" publicKeyToken="31bf3856ad364e35"
      language="neutral" versionScope="nonSxS"
      xmlns:wcm="http://schemas.microsoft.com/WMIConfig/2002/State">
      <ImageInstall>
        <OSImage>
          <WillShowUI>OnError</WillShowUI>
          <InstallTo>
            <DiskID>0</DiskID>
            <PartitionID>1</PartitionID>
          </InstallTo>
          <InstallFrom>
            <Path>.\Operating Systems\Windows 7
              x64\Sources\install.wim</Path>
            <MetaData>
              <Key>/IMAGE/INDEX</Key>
              <Value>1</Value>
            </MetaData>
          </InstallFrom>
        </OSImage>
      </ImageInstall>
```

It is not recommended to edit the `Unattend.xml` file manually, unless you really know what you are doing. The file is picky about the order, and some things that you think you might not need and want to delete are actually core setup process dependencies. So tinker at your own peril!

In the `Unattend.xml` file, we can see how MDT *bootstraps* itself as part of the logon process, as shown in the following code snippet:

```
<FirstLogonCommands>
  <SynchronousCommand wcm:action="add">
    <CommandLine>wscript.exe
      %SystemDrive%\LTIBootstrap.vbs</CommandLine>
    <Description>Lite Touch new OS</Description>
    <Order>1</Order>
  </SynchronousCommand>
```

In the preceding code snippet, note that the first command run at logon is to launch `LTIBootstrap.vbs`, which then resumes and controls the MDT task sequence engine for the setup process.

The variables.dat structure

So, where do we get the list of the variables that exist? The Print-Ready Documentation for MDT 2013 is a perfect library, particularly the `Toolkit Reference.docx` file. To see the values that are being discovered for your hardware, one can easily open the `variables.dat` file. The structure is XML-based (one can simply rename the file to `.xml`), open it in Internet Explorer, and get a better view than Notepad.

However, when the `variables.dat` file is rendered in a browser, it appears as follows:

```
<MediaVarList Version="4.00.5345.0000">
  <var name="LOGPATH">
    <![CDATA[ X:\MININT\SMSOSD\OSDLOGS ]]>
    ...
    <![CDATA[ Bootstrap.ini ]]>
  </var>
  <var name="OSCURRENTVERSION">
    <![CDATA[ 6.3.9600 ]]>
  </var>
  <var name="OSCURRENTBUILD">
    <![CDATA[ 9600 ]]>
  </var>
  <var name="OSVERSION">
    <![CDATA[ WinPE ]]>
  </var>
  <var name="ISSERVEROS">
    <![CDATA[ False ]]>
  </var>
  <var name="ISSERVERCOREOS">
    <![CDATA[ False ]]>
```

```
</var>
...
<var name="HOSTNAME">
  <![CDATA[ MININT-I7GS8HP ]]>
</var>
<var name="ASSETTAG">
  <![CDATA[ 7774-6450-3382-1242-9318-1886-08 ]]>
</var>
<var name="SERIALNUMBER">
  <![CDATA[ 7774-6450-3382-1242-9318-1886-08 ]]>
</var>
<var name="MAKE">
  <![CDATA[ Microsoft Corporation ]]>
</var>
<var name="MODEL">
  <![CDATA[ Virtual Machine ]]>
</var>
<var name="PRODUCT">
  <![CDATA[ Virtual Machine ]]>
</var>
<var name="UUID">
  <![CDATA[ 41498066-DE4A-4C40-918F-F7C8F8BD32D6 ]]>
</var>
<var name="MEMORY">
  <![CDATA[ 2047 ]]>
</var>
<var name="ARCHITECTURE">
  <![CDATA[ X64 ]]>
</var>
<var name="PROCESSORSPEED">
  <![CDATA[ 3400 ]]>
</var>
<var name="CAPABLEARCHITECTURE">
  <![CDATA[ AMD64 X64 X86 ]]>
</var>
<var name="ISLAPTOP">
  <![CDATA[ False ]]>
</var>
<var name="ISDESKTOP">
  <![CDATA[ True ]]>
</var>
```

So, here we have our variables that we called previously, ISDESKTOP and ISLAPTOP.

CustomSettings.ini and the Unattend.xml file

Now that we've reviewed the `CustomSettings.ini` structure, some commonalities between the `Unattend.xml` file and `CustomSettings.ini` may be evident. For example, the `OSDComputerName` value of `CustomSettings.ini` is what will dynamically supersede our task sequence's `<ComputerName>` value of `Unattend.xml` when the task sequence runs.

This is the key value in using MDT for deployment. With a structured `Unattend.xml` file and deployment, you get a hands-off deployment. However, it's machine-specific, typically, hardware-specific. It's also a challenge to manage this and change `Unattend.xml`, even with WSIM. So, this solution of utilizing `Unattend.xml` manually (even per model, for example, for driver considerations) doesn't scale and should not be used in the Enterprise environment, or small and medium businesses.

Dynamic modification

With MDT, we are essentially scaling `Unattend.xml` and dynamically modifying the values as we see fit, for each task sequence run. This is the value of utilizing this system for deployments. If you need to take it even further, you can dynamically modify `CustomSettings.ini` in the manner that we saw earlier in this chapter. However, this modification method of using the scripting environment, native to the MDT, doesn't scale very well.

The next option would be to utilize a concept known as **UserExit scripts** to modify the `CustomSettings.ini` dynamically. Essentially, UserExit scripts are a way to exit the MDT scripting environment and perform some function call and come back and populate variables based on the function call. An example of this might be `https://blogs.techne t.microsoft.com/deploymentguys/tag/user-exit-script/`, which details the setting of the `TaskSequenceID` variable in `CustomSettings.ini` based on the available RAM installed.

Lastly, there is another concept to dynamically modify `CustomSettings.ini`, and that is the MDT SQL DB option. In this setup, a Microsoft SQL Database (installed on the MDT Server or an instance of another existing Microsoft SQL Server in the environment) services the deployment share and `CustomSettings.ini`. In this configuration, you can dynamically populate groups of applications based on role, manage complex selection profile arrangements, or even pre-populate the database with MAC addresses and automatically pick `TaskSequenceID` based on the MAC address of the machine.

Task sequence structure

If we examine the structure of our task sequence, we can see it is broken into a set of folders and underlying actions for each folder (and in some cases, a tree of folders under the top-level folder), as shown in the following screenshot:

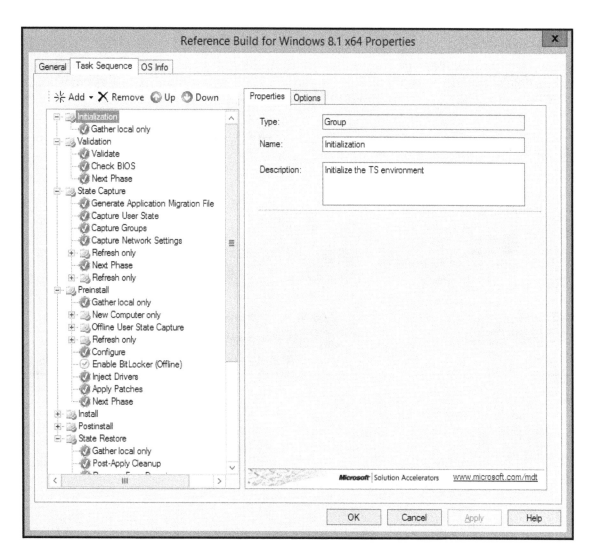

The root-level steps and their functions are explained in the following sections.

Initialization

In this step, the task sequence is initialized and a **Gather local only** step is run. This gathers the data utilizing the script, `ZTIGather.wsf`, and in this step, the original `variables.dat` file is populated.

Validation

In this step, the task sequence checks the local environment to verify that it is suitable to run the rest of the task sequence. In this step, for instance, we will verify that the system has a minimum of 768 MB to run Windows PE, and the processor speed is at least 800 Mhz:

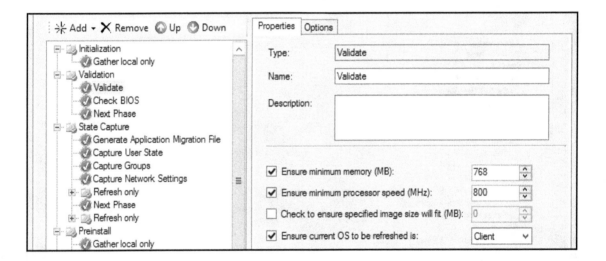

Microsoft Virtual PC had an issue where it would report 0 Mhz for processor speed, so when you ran a task sequence in Windows 7 Virtual PC, you had to uncheck this step or the task sequence would fail.

The next part of this step is an interesting component, **Check BIOS**. This is placed solely for the purpose of validating BIOS. So if you have a model of computer that requires a particular version of BIOS to allow the operating system to install properly, you can modify the file in \Scripts\ZTIBIOSCheck.xml, which ZTIBIOSCheck.wsf calls, and this guidance is provided in the XML file itself:

> If you have a computer BIOS version that needs to be identified during the BDD installation process, you can run the following VBScript program (ZTINextPhase.wsf) to extract out the necessary fields on the computer system.

Then, we will simply run the step, **Next Phase**, which calls ZTINextPhase.wsf, writes to the variables.dat file (for future reference) and logs (for troubleshooting), and then continues to the next step.

State capture

In this step, the task sequence may create the application migration file, capture user state by calling the **User State Migration Tool (USMT)**, appropriate XML configuration files, capture network settings, and so on. I use the word *may* as it will only run these steps if they are called by the task sequence that is currently executing. This is also the area where the **Refresh** steps of a task sequence also may be run, particularly the **Disable BDE Protectors** (to disable BitLocker drive encryption, or suspend it temporarily) and **Apply Windows PE** steps.

Preinstall

Firstly, the **Preinstall** task sequence step runs another **Gather local only** step. Then, it gets interesting. If the task sequence is running in a situation that meets the **NEWCOMPUTER** definition (as defined by the **Options** tab of the **Task Sequence** folder), then it runs the steps under this folder, as shown in the following screenshot:

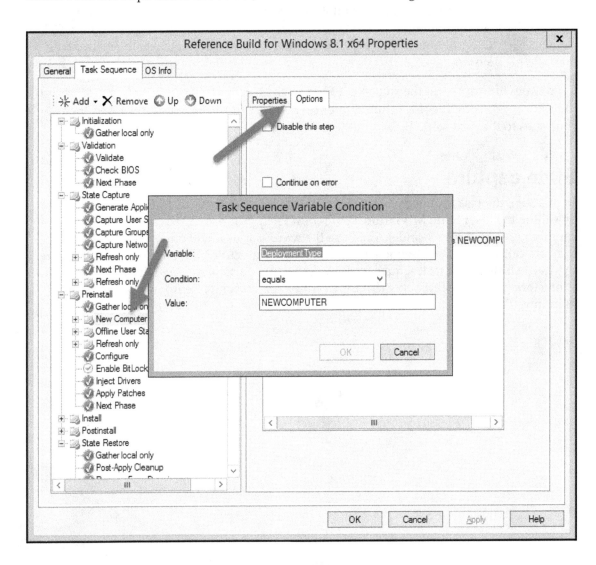

If you observe, under this folder, if it runs, the task sequence will format and partition the hard drive and then copy scripts to be run locally and set up a logging area. If it doesn't run, it will skip to **Offline User State Capture**, or **Refresh only**, again based on the scenario.

After the variables are played out in the task sequence, an **Inject Drivers** occurs. This is an interesting step, where according to the selection profile specified, drivers are injected for the operating system. The `ztidrivers.wsf` script is called, which is described in detail in the word document, `Toolkit Reference.docx`, from the MDT 2013 Documentation. Basically, what happens is a query is made for **Plug and Play** (**PnP**) IDs located on the hardware on which the script is running, and then a query is made against the XML file that is the master inventory of the deployment share's `Out-of-Box Drivers` directory (where you would import the third-party drivers) and any matches are copied over and made available for installation.

Now, one key concept here is, as I mentioned, according to the selection profile specified. So this step, by default, would pick *every* driver as a possibility for the installation of Windows. In some instances, it is okay to leave this as a default, let the PnP magic happen in the scripts, and auto-pick your drivers.

What if you have two Lenovo laptops, both of which resolve a piece of hardware that they have installed to the same PnP ID, but there are actually two drivers for this PnP ID in your `Out-of-Box Drivers` folder? What happens? Which driver is installed on which model? It's somewhat random. Therefore, in this scenario, for example, the mass storage device (your SATA controller, for instance, that connects the system board to the SSD/HD of the device) might have the correct driver and allows the system to boot fine, or if the wrong driver were to be loaded, the system would blue screen, probably quite quickly, with **STOP 0x0000007B (INACCESIBLE_BOOT_DEVICE)**, something such as documented at `http://support.microsoft.com/kb/324103`, for instance.

For this and other considerations, refer to `Chapter 6`, *Drivers*. The key to note here is that you can specify alternate selection profiles to address this potential hiccup in your deployment.

After the **Inject Drivers** step is complete, **Apply Patches** runs. This is similar to the **Inject Drivers** step, but instead it utilizes DISM to apply Windows Updates, Language Packs, and so forth to the WIM offline. It retrieves these from the `Packages` directory of the deployment share. Later on, we'll discuss a step to download updates from Windows Updates, or a **Windows Server Update Services** (**WSUS**) Server, for online action. However, for now, we offline-install patches in this step.

Install

In the install phase of task sequence, the actual operating system is applied. What is actually happening is a script is running, which calls DISM/Apply-Image to apply the WIM that you select onto the storage you select. This is modifiable by the way!

Note that in the following screenshot, the WIM has a **Browse...** button to select an alternate WIM, for instance, if you wanted to switch from Windows 8.1 with Update 1 to Windows 8.1 with Update 2 if and when it comes out. You can also select the logical drive to be applied to the OS being installed:

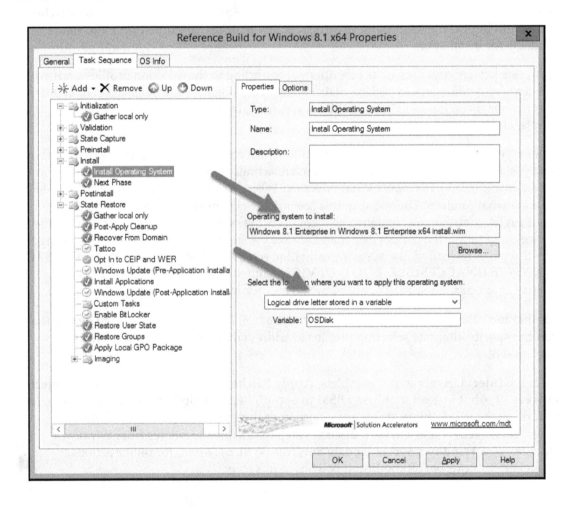

Postinstall

In the **Postinstall** task sequence phase, scripts are copied to the drive that we previously formatted and performed the DISM /Apply-Image to, and then driver injection occurs and a **Windows Recovery Environment (WinRE)** is applied to the volume. Then, the machine is rebooted. It is pretty simple and straightforward.

State restore

In the **State Restore** phase, a domain join action—**Recover From Domain**—can run to join the machine to the domain automatically. The registry is tattooed, options to opt in to CEIP and WER are presented, and then Windows Updates can run (though it is disabled by default). This will hit the Internet Windows Updates servers, unless one specifies a value in CustomSettings.ini for WSUS server Then, the step will point directly to the specified WSUS server, which ordinarily should be a quicker and less bandwidth-hungry operation.

> This WSUS server *cannot* be an SCCM server or WSUS server touched by SCCM. It is not supported and odd update experiences will occur.

Logging

In MDT 2010, an option to log the task sequence runs was introduced as a variable. This SLShareDynamicLogging variable requires you to point to a UNC path where deployments would be written to in real time. Therefore, as Michael Niehaus pointed out in his blog back in 2009, you could run Trace32.exe against the BDD.LOG file in the share for each deployment and see it happening in real time versus waiting for the deployment to fully complete and then harvesting BDD.LOG from the deployed or failed deployment machine.

In MDT 2012, a feature known as MDT Monitoring was introduced. You can find the settings for it by right-clicking on the deployment share and selecting **Properties**. The last tab is **Monitoring** and should look similar to the following screenshot, by default:

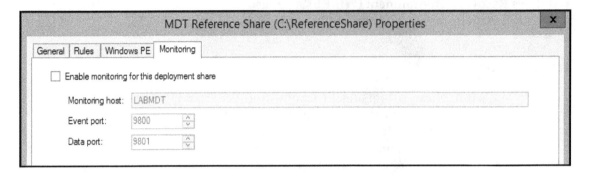

To enable monitoring, simply tick the box and click on **Apply**. Note that checking the box here adds a line to our CustomSettings.ini and rules entry, EventService=http://LABMDT:9800. Also the default share used is a directory on the C:\events local MDT host. This is a configurable option using the MDT task sequence variable, EventShare, where EventShare=\\host\events. Also, a service must be running for this to work, it is installed automatically and enabled when you click **Apply**.

One can also utilize PowerShell to access the data in the monitoring service using the cmdlet Get-MDTMonitorData; an example is as simple as (Get-MDTMonitorData -Path DS001:).Count

Windows 10
Windows 10 does not significantly modify the instructions of this chapter. Task sequence customization continues as any other operating system at the time of writing this.

Summary

In this chapter, we've discussed the task sequence and how variables are utilized by the stock scripts; we also discussed how to create our own variables for different hardware configurations.

We've also looked at the structure of the `CustomSettings.ini` and `variables.dat` files and `Unattend.xml` file. More importantly, we've discussed the interconnectedness of `CustomSettings.ini` and how it is used to *variable-ize* `Unattend.xml` dynamically. On top of this, the task sequence itself can make `Unattend.xml` values into variables as well for our deployment purposes.

We've also walked through the deployment task sequence structure and covered the gotchas, frequently used areas, and best practices.

Lastly, we've gone over monitoring, from its roots to its current incarnation of PowerShell-enabled cmdlets.

In the next chapter, we'll cover driver concepts, when drivers are applications and when they are drivers, how to handle both scenarios, and mandatory driver profiles.

6
Drivers

In the previous chapter, we discussed the `CustomSettings.ini` file as it relates to `Unattend.xml`, what it does, how it works, and how to use it for your environment. We discussed that not only can we define global rules that apply to all task sequences, but we can also take advantage of variables to perform condition-based actions based on things such as hardware type, model, default gateway, or any variables that MDT defines during the gather phase, or even your own custom variables that you have created. These concepts are very important in our next topic of driver management.

In this chapter, we will discuss how to utilize MDT to make the complex world of device drivers into a much more manageable experience. We will focus on how drivers get installed via MDT, how to specifically control which drivers get installed, and general best practices around proper driver management.

We will cover the following topics in this chapter:

- Understanding offline servicing
- The MDT method of driver detection and injection
- Populating the Out-of-Box Drivers node of MDT
- Utilizing model variable to control what drivers are installed
- Drivers as applications
- Win PE drivers

Understanding offline servicing

Those of us who created images for deployment of Windows XP were often met with an enormous challenge of dealing with drivers for many different models of hardware. We were already forced to create separate images for different HAL families. Additionally, in order to deal with different hardware models within the same HAL family, the standard practice way was usually to have a `C:\Drivers` folder, which contained a copy of every possible driver that could be required by this image for all the different hardware models it would be installed to. There was an `OemPnPDriversPath` entry in the registry that individually listed each of the driver paths (subfolders under the `C:\Drivers` directory) for the Windows **Plug and Play** (**PnP**) process to locate and install the driver. As you can imagine, this was not a very efficient way to manage drivers. One reason is that every driver for every machine was staged in the image, causing the image size to grow; another reason being that we were relying on PnP to figure out the right driver to install, which gives us less control of what driver actually gets installed, based on a driver ranking process.

Fast forward to Windows Vista and the current versions of Windows, and we can now utilize the magic of offline servicing to inject drivers into our WIM as it gets deployed. With this in mind, consider the concept of having your customized Windows image created through your reference image build process, but it contains no drivers. Now, when we go to deploy this image, we could utilize a process to detect all of the hardware in the target machine and then grab only the correct drivers that we need for this particular machine. Then, we can utilize DISM to inject them into our WIM before the WIM actually gets installed, thereby making the drivers available to be installed as Windows is installed on this machine. MDT is doing just that.

The MDT method of driver detection and injection

When we boot a target machine via our LiteTouch media, one of the initial task sequence steps will enumerate (via `PnPEnum.exe`) all of the PnP IDs for every device in the machine. Then, as part of the Inject Drivers task sequence step, we will search all of our Out-of-Box Driver INF files to find the matching driver, then MDT will utilize DISM to inject these drivers offline into the applied WIM.

Note that, by default, we will be searching our entire Out-of-Box drivers repository and letting PnP figure things out.

We will later discuss how to force MDT to only choose from the drivers that we specify, thereby gaining strict control over which drivers actually get installed.

The preceding scenario indicates that this whole process hinges on the fact that we are searching through driver INF files to find the matching PnP IDs in order to correctly detect and install the correct driver. This brings up a concern; what if the driver does not contain an INF file, but rather it simply has to be installed via an EXE program? In this scenario, we cannot utilize the driver injection process; instead, we would treat this driver as an **application** in MDT, meaning that we would add a new application using the EXE program, and its accompanied files if present, as the source files, specifying the command-line syntax to launch the driver install program and install silently, and then adding this application as a task sequence step. I will later demonstrate how to utilize conditional statements in your task sequence to only install this driver program on the model that it applies to, thereby keeping our task sequence flexible in order to be able to install correctly on any hardware.

Populating the Out-of-Box Drivers node of MDT

The first step will be to visit the OEM Manufacturer's website and download all device drivers for each model machine that we will be deploying to. Note that many OEMs now offer a deployment-specific download or CAB file that has all of the drivers for a particular model compressed into one single CAB file. This benefits you as you will not have to go through the hassle of downloading and extracting each individual driver for each device separately (NIC, video, audio, and so on). Once you have downloaded the necessary drivers, to store them in a folder for each specific model, you will need to extract the drivers within your folder before importing them into MDT.

Next, we want to create a folder structure under the **Out-of-Box Drivers** node in MDT to organize our drivers. This will not only allow easy manageability of drivers as new drivers are released by the OEM; but if we name the folders to match the model names exactly, we can later also introduce logic to limit our PnP search to the exact folder that contains the correct drivers for our particular hardware model. As we will have different drivers for x86 and x64, as well as for different operating systems, a general best practice would be to create the first hierarchy of your folder structure. Perform the following steps:

1. In order to create the folder structure, simply click on **Out-of-Box Drivers** and choose **New Folder**, as shown in the following screenshot:

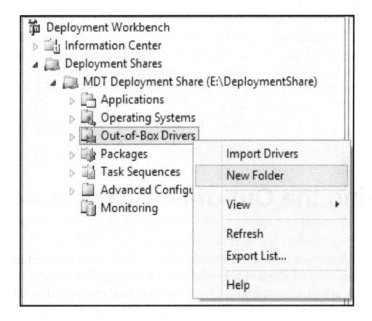

2. Next, we will want to create a folder for each model that we will be deploying to:

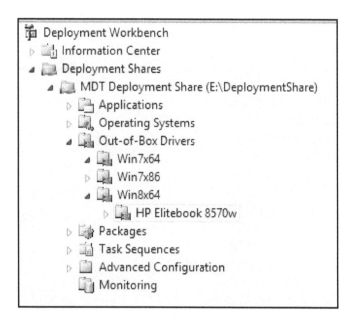

3. In order to ensure that you are using the correct model name, you can use the following WMI query to see what the hardware returns as the model name:

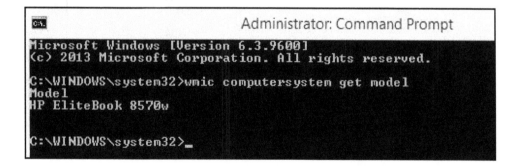

4. Once you have your folder structure created, you are ready to inject the drivers. Right-click on the model folder and choose **Import Drivers**. Point the driver source directory to the folder where you have downloaded and extracted the OEM drivers:

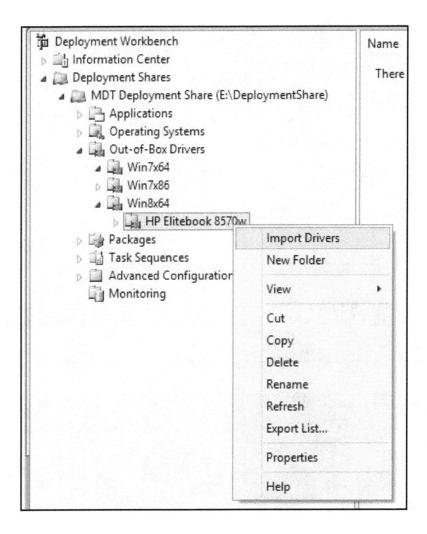

There is a checkbox stating **Import drivers even if they are duplicates of an existing driver**. This is because MDT is utilizing the **Single Instance Storage** (**SIS**) technology to store the drivers in the actual deployment share. If you are importing multiple copies of a driver to different folders, MDT only stores one copy of the file in the actual filesystem by default, and the folder structure you see within the MDT Workbench will be pointing duplicates to the same file in order to not waste any space.

As new drivers are released from the OEM, you can simply replace the drivers by going to the particular folder for this model, removing the old drivers, and importing the new drivers. Then, next time you install your WIM to this model, you will be using the new drivers, and you don't have to make any modifications or updates to your WIM.

Utilizing model variable to control what drivers are installed

As mentioned earlier, while using a default MDT task sequence, the Inject Drivers task sequence step will search your entire Out-of-Box drivers repository to find a matching driver. If you only have a few hardware models, and all models are from the same manufacturer, then this could very well suit your needs without problem; but let's consider the following scenario.

Let's say you have a Dell model that has a rebranded Broadcom Network Adapter. You also have an HP model that has a rebranded Broadcom Network Adapter of the same chipset. Now, Broadcom, Dell, and HP each have a driver. Based on what we discussed earlier about how PnP finds a matching driver, it would be possible for any of these three drivers to be a match, if both devices reported the same PnP ID, then Windows' driver ranking process would determine which driver is installed based on signed versus unsigned, version number, inbox versus Out-of-Box, and so on. So, we could get in a situation where perhaps the HP driver was installed on the Dell. For us to have more control over which driver gets installed, while also keeping the task sequence flexible to work on any model, we can take advantage of variables and conditional statements.

During the MDT Gather phase, MDT has already determined the exact model name of the machine we are installing to and has stored this value in a `%model%` variable. MDT also utilizes another built-in `DriverGroup00x` variable in order to set the path of where to look for the drivers. So, we can place a step in the task sequence to set `DriverGroup001` to point to a dynamic path that gets filled in with the exact model name by use of the `%model%` variable, as shown in the following screenshot example:

1. In the task sequence that you are using to deploy your image, under the **Preinstall** section, we will modify the **Inject Drivers** step to use the selection profile of **Nothing**, as shown in the following screenshot:

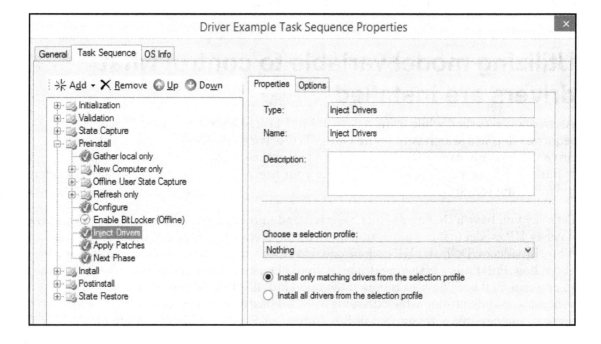

2. Next, we will add a step above the **Inject Drivers** step to set our
   `DriverGroup001` variable to point to the path of the model we are installing to,
   which will have the `%model%` variable filled in with the correct information, as
   follows:

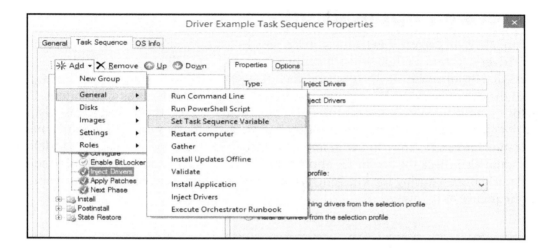

3. Configure the **Properties** page as outlined in the following screenshot:

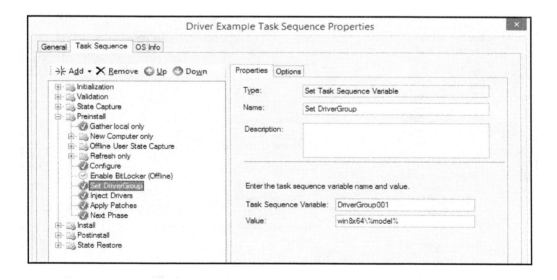

Now, you can be sure that when PnP is searching for and installing drivers, the drivers are only coming from the correct folder for this model and you have full control over the process instead of hoping things just work out on their own.

Drivers as applications

Unfortunately, all drivers don't adhere to the usual `.inf`/`.sys` format, and in this case, the MDT driver injection method will not apply to these drivers. What I'm referring to is drivers that install via a `.exe` format and cannot be extracted to the usual `.inf`/`.sys` format that we are used to. In this case, we need to treat these drivers as applications. Let's say, for example, I have a trackpad driver for a particular laptop that I need to install and the driver installation program must be installed via a `.exe` program. I can import a new application into MDT. The command line must be configured to perform a silent install and you should also check the box in the application's **Properties** to hide the application so that it will not show up during the LiteTouch Deployment wizard. We will add the driver to our **Task Sequence** as follows:

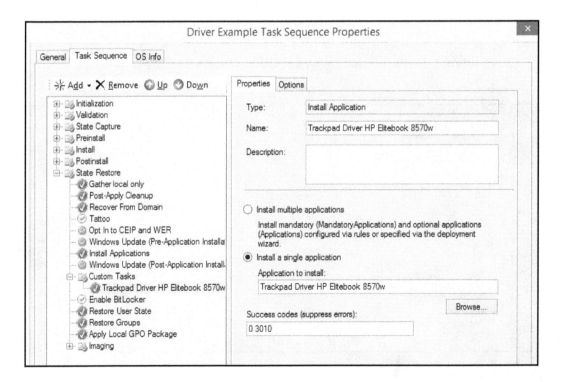

Now, to ensure that this application/driver only gets installed on the machines that we need to install it on, we can take advantage of conditional statements to make this happen. This way, the task sequence will still apply to any hardware, but will only execute this step on the hardware the driver is targeted to. We can accomplish this as outlined in the following screenshot:

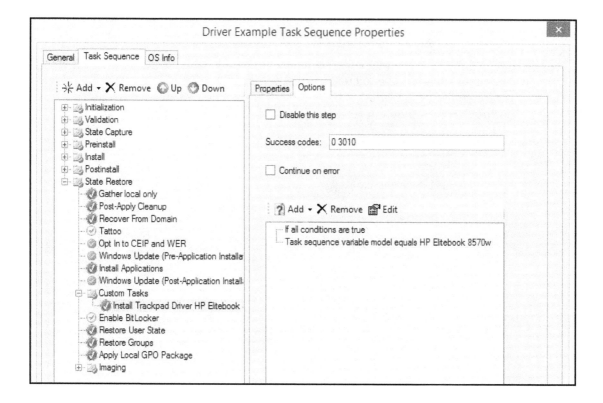

Win PE drivers

By default, MDT will inject all network adapter and mass storage drivers into the LiteTouchPE_x86/LiteTouchPE_x64 ISO/WIM file(s). If you want to specifically control which drivers are injected, you can create separate folders under your Out-of-Box Drivers node for WinPE_x86 and WinPE_x64 drivers, then create selection profiles for each of these folders. Navigate to the **Properties** of your deployment share | **Windows PE** tab | **Drivers and Patches** tab, and select the **Selection profile** for each architecture. The steps to inject specific drivers are as follows:

1. The first step would be to create a selection profile to point to the specific folder where you have imported your Win PE drivers. You can accomplish this as outlined in the following screenshot:

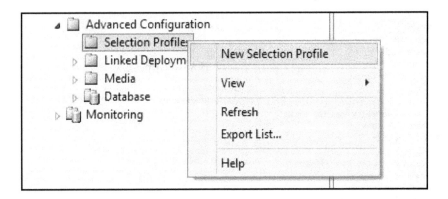

2. In the next step, name the selection profile. In this example, we are naming it WinPEx64, as shown in the following screenshot:

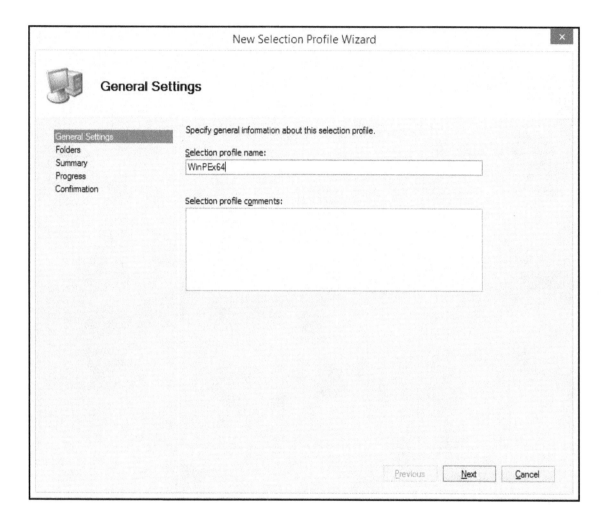

3. We will then only select the folder that we want to include in the selection profile, as shown in the following screenshot:

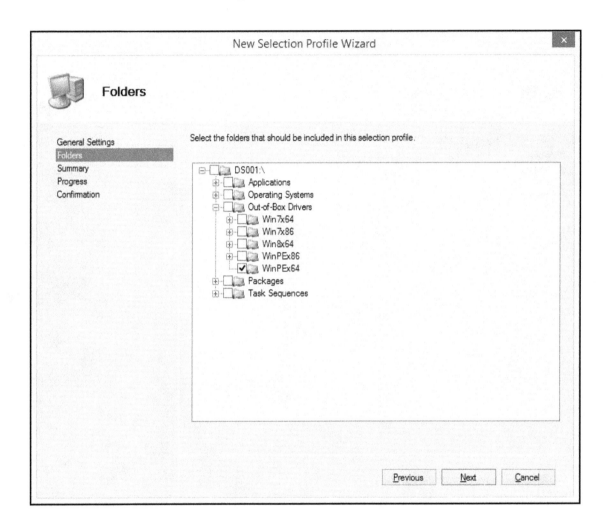

4. Once we have created our selection profile, we will then go to the **Properties** of our deployment share and then to the **Windows PE** tab, choose the **Platform (x64)** from the drop-down list, and then go to the **Drivers and Patches** tab. From the **Selection profile** drop-down list, choose the selection profile that you created for WinPEx64, as shown in the following screenshot:

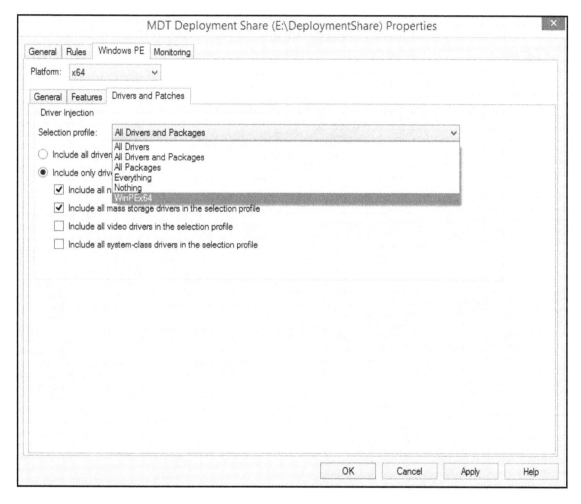

Now, when you update your deployment share to generate new LiteTouch media, it will only inject drivers into Windows PE from the folder that you specified in your selection profile. This will give you more control over which drivers actually get injected into your LiteTouch media.

Windows 10

All the concepts shown in this chapter are still valid for Windows 10, but please pay attention to the following points:

- While the plan is definitely to enforce the new driver signing model (signed by Microsoft directly), current builds (1507 and 1511) allow the legacy driver signing model by default.
- This was to work around upgrade challenges that will be removed in the Redstone timeframe.
- Moving forward, drivers will continue to be migrated and loaded successfully (even if not signed *properly*), but all new device drivers installed will require the new model.
- When considering a Windows 10 deployment the same driver considerations apply as any other Windows installation. In some specific device installations such as Surface Pro 4 devices or Surface Book, driver packages need to be installed to perform device firmware updates. Therefore Microsoft and OEM provided drivers are perhaps more important to keep up to date in Windows 10 than in other operating systems.

Summary

In this chapter, we covered driver concepts, when drivers are applications and when they are drivers, how to handle both scenarios, and we also discussed mandatory driver profiles. In the next chapter, we'll look at the deployment share configuration, deployment best practices, and guidelines to secure the deployment share.

7
Image Deployment

In the previous chapter, we discussed driver management in MDT. We discussed how to perform offline servicing in order to inject drivers into our image post-capture. We also discussed how plug and play works with MDT and driver profiles using variables in MDT to force drivers into an installation based on properties such as model number.

In this chapter, we will go over how to deploy our image, both for capturing a reference image, as well as doing deployments in test and production environments. Various caveats and situations will be covered and several real-world scenarios will be examined as well.

We will cover the following topics in this chapter:

- Reference image deployment and image types
- Virtual machine creation
- Deployment steps
- Deployment share
- Deployment scenarios and network considerations

Reference image deployment

In previous chapters, we've discussed drivers, `CustomSettings.ini` configuration, task sequence, and many other items. All these concepts are utilized here as we build our reference image deployment task sequence and virtual machine. In our examples in this chapter, we're going to be utilizing Hyper-V as a virtualization host for simplicity and cost; other solutions can be used, but they add a complication layer in terms of drivers that need to be inserted into both the **Windows Preinstallation Environment** (**Win PE**) and actual driver store for the image itself. However, Hyper-V can pose the same concern with driver-versioning needs.

What this means is the native Hyper-V drivers that are shipped with Windows 7, for instance, will not work in a Hyper-V virtual machine hosted in Windows Server 2012 R2, for example. Back-level drivers will still need to be provided so that the Win PE and installation task sequence can see the network, and thus communicate with the deployment share.

When we design our reference image, it behooves us to review the business needs and consider the scenarios of thick, thin, and hybrid images. There are many scenarios and business cases where Windows is used, and a blanket statement that one image type is better than another is a slippery slope. Let's review the options and discuss when it would be proper to implement the specific type of image.

Thick image

The thick image is one that contains all the applications needed by the overall business. Depending on the bandwidth constraints connecting the sites for image replication, this may be a viable and correct option.

For example, I had a customer implement the thick image due to limited connectivity between their deployment sites. Replicating more than a single image took a very long time to finish. Therefore, the solution was to have a master thick image. They then had multiple task sequences that used the WIM and uninstalled select applications based on the appropriate scenario (laptop, desktop, and so on).

Thin image

The thin image contains a patched WIM of Windows and scant else. It is a barebones kit, where applications are installed (or streamed via an application provisioning/virtualization layer) at deployment, or even at the initial run of the application. These deployments tend towards the campus deployment scenario, where high bandwidth and low latency are present. Some VDI implementations go this route, particularly with the application streaming components in place.

Another use case for this would be flexibility. You only need to rebuild a single image if you need to apply additional updates, and so on. This makes maintenance of your deployment images much easier and still gives the flexibility of multiple task sequences for different business needs.

Hybrid image

Perhaps the most common of deployment methodologies, the base thin image is crafted with a task sequence that (in addition to patching) adds universal applications that any user at the business is licensed for and might feasibly use. An example would be a build with Windows Updates, Office 2013, and Updates applied, but not the HR application nor the accounting one. This type of image usually makes the most sense from licensing, bandwidth, servicing, and deployment perspective.

Now the reader should keep in mind that any of these images can be the subject of many task sequences that change `CustomSettings.ini`, `Unattend.xml`, and so on, and customize the deployment in whatever manner needed. Therefore, in considering the type of image to craft, consider this a skeletal design onto which you will later craft many different and diverse task sequences against (potentially, some shops get by with one or two images).

Virtual machine creation

The screenshots and text are taken from Windows 8.1 Update 1, which is quite similar to Windows Server 2012 R2 as well. Most concepts will apply to down-level Hyper-V hosts as well though.

1. The first action item is to create a virtual machine. Generally speaking, a virtual machine with one core and 2 GB of RAM is adequate for our purpose. We'll walk through the wizard and create our virtual machine as follows:

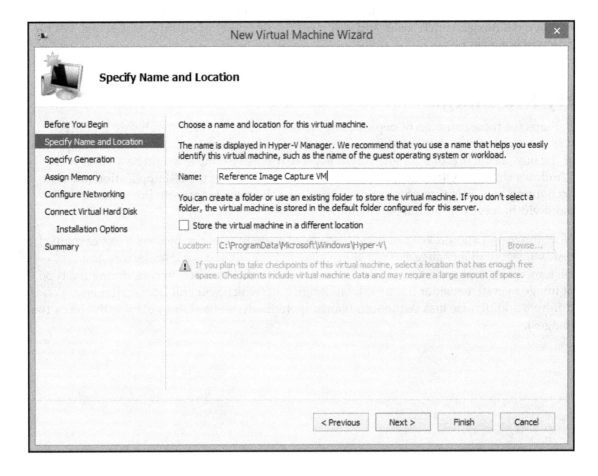

Virtual Machine name

2. In the next step, we'll want to select **Generation 1**. This is to support both x86 and x64 versions of Windows, and also Windows 7 and Server 2008 R2, as well as newer OSes:

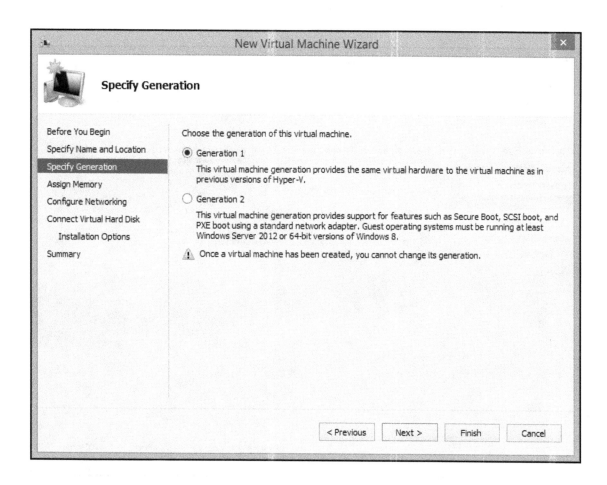

Generation 1 selection

3. In our next selection, we'll specify **2,048** MB for **Startup memory**, and not check the box for **Use Dynamic Memory for this virtual machine**. We don't want the hypervisor to try to reduce the RAM footprint of our system while it's installing software, Windows Updates, and so on:

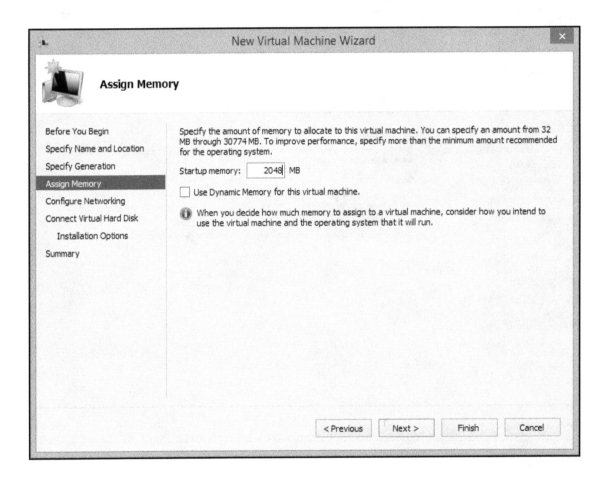

No Dynamic Memory here!

4. Then on the next screen, we need the virtual machine to be connected to a network that has access to several items. The deployment server, preferably a DHCP server, DNS, and either an external path to Windows Updates or an internal WSUS server. We will simply place the virtual machine in this network in Hyper-V.

5. We'll cover static IP address considerations later in this chapter:

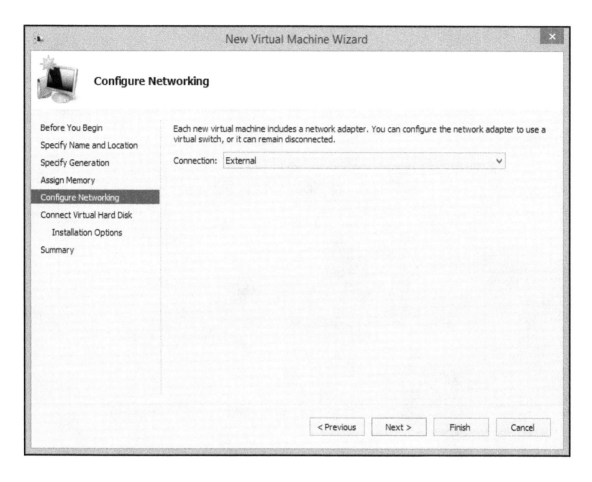

External network

6. On the next screen, we need to allocate a virtual disk. If we don't already have a virtual disk defined, we can simply ask Hyper-V to make one for us now. The drive location should be speedy and have space for a Windows installation and applications:

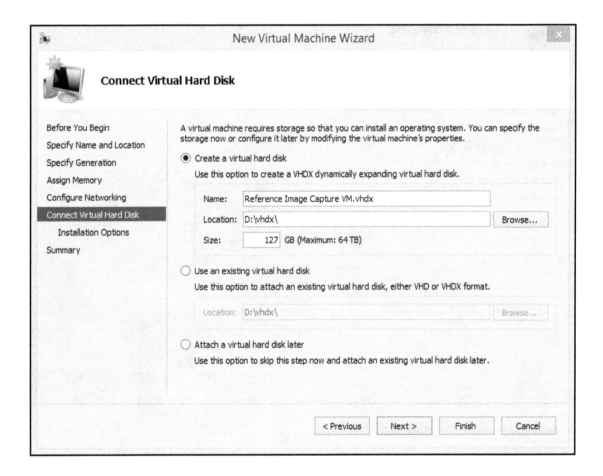

VHDX location

7. On the next screen we are asked whether we want to install an OS now? Well, sort of. What we want to do here is specify the ISO of the MDT reference share. This ISO will be configured in the `Bootstrap.ini` and `CustomSettings.ini` to know to talk to our reference share, run task sequences, and so forth. This ISO is located in `C:\ReferenceShare\Boot` on our MDT server. Copying it from the reference share to the Hyper-V host so that it appears in a local disk is recommended:

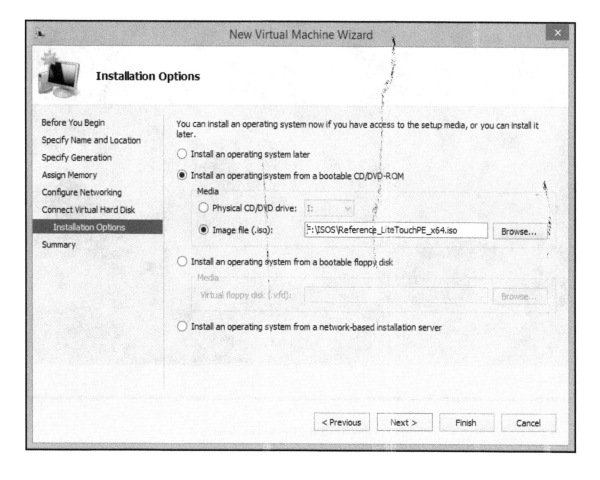

The ISO must be on a local volume for the Hyper-V host

8. Then, it is a simple matter of clicking **Finish** and starting the virtual machine. The machine will go through a boot process.

Deployment

The virtual machine will go through the boot process, as shown in the following screenshot:

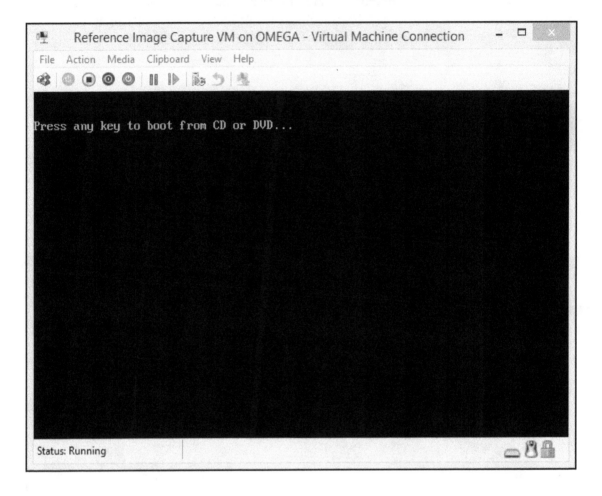

Here, BIOS in the virtual machine has posted and it is booting up

We must then specify the task sequence that we wish to run:

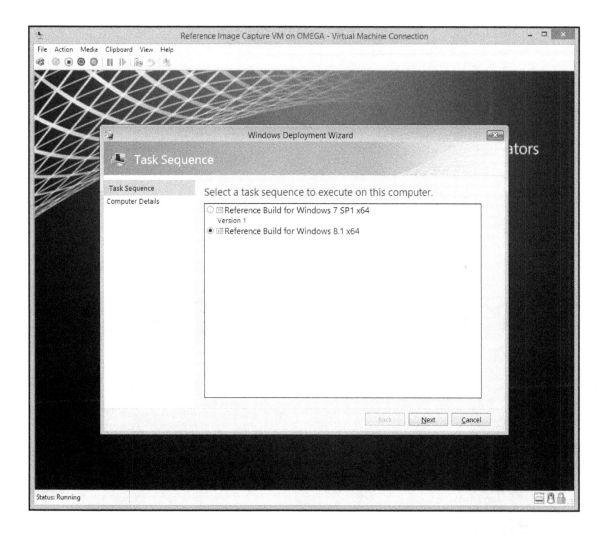

Note that now our task sequence engine skipped some screens. Our `CustomSettings.ini` has specified the following:

```
SkipCapture=NO
SkipAdminPassword=YES
SkipProductKey=YES
SkipBitLocker=YES
SkipDomainMembership=YES
JoinWorkgroup=Workgroup
SkipFinalSummary=YES
SkipLocaleSelection=YES
SkipSummary=YES
SkipTimeZone=YES
SkipUserData=YES
```

As we specified `SkipCapture=NO` in the preceding code, the **Capture Image** screen wizard is displayed as follows:

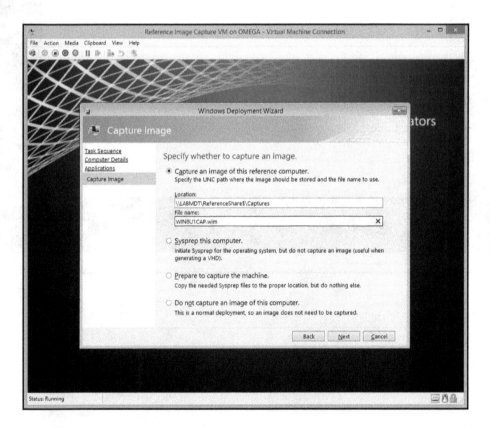

The task sequence will then execute through the OS install, apply Windows updates and application installations, and then Sysprep and capture the image:

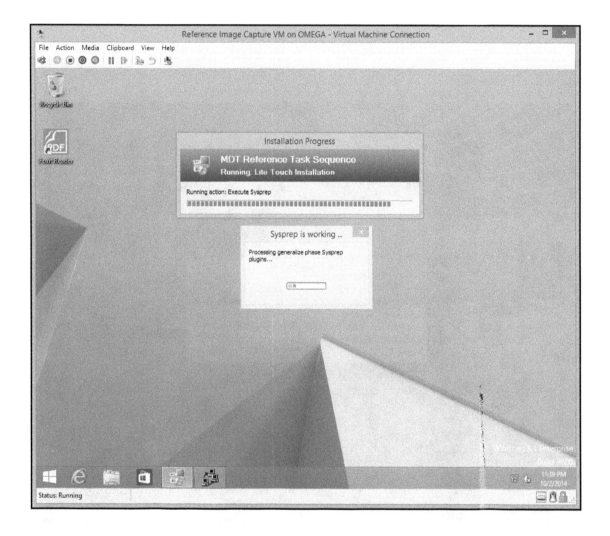

After the Sysprep is complete, the WIM is captured. This cannot be done with the running system, so MDT needs to start a Win PE by applying Win PE to the virtual machines' disk, changing the boot entry to Win PE, then rebooting to Win PE, and running a DISM `/captureimage` command:

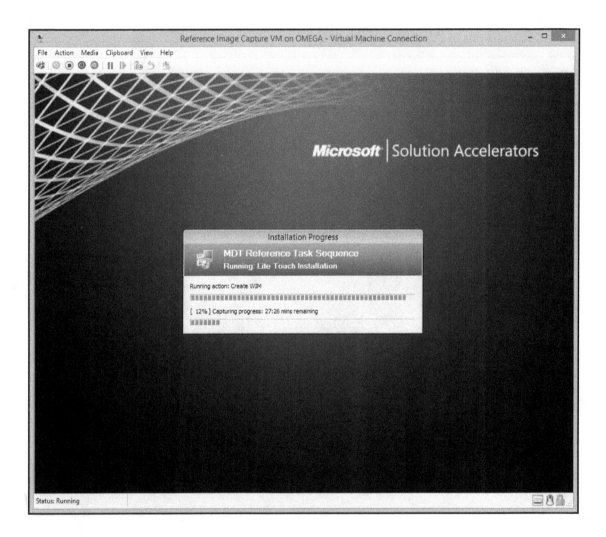

The end product after running both our task sequences should be that our `Captures` directory on the MDT reference share looks something similar to the following image:

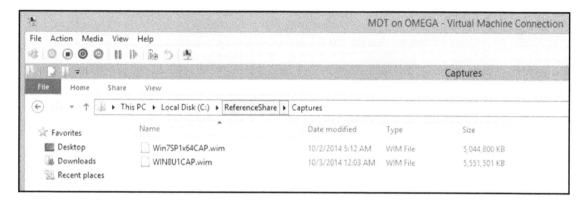

Here we can see that we have two WIM files, both approximately 5 GB in size.

Now the process is to import these WIM files as OSes into our deployment share. We haven't created a deployment share yet, but the steps are essentially the same as creating the reference share.

Deployment share

The deployment share is quite similar to our reference share. Most of the content of the `CustomSettings.ini` and `Bootstrap.ini` will be the same. The OSes of the deployment share are simply the WIM files, which we just captured, the product of our reference share task sequences. The applications will be complex drivers for specific hardware devices or applications applied post-OS deployment. However, our base images are somewhat set in stone at this point. The WIM files from our reference share form the base operating system of our deployment task sequences.

Again, creation of the deployment share follows the reference share, with some naming differences:

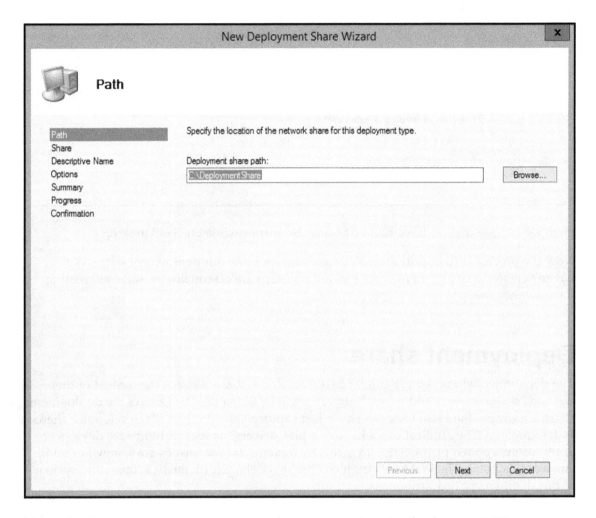

Name the directory `DeploymentShare` to keep our naming standards correct. We absolutely want to keep the reference share and deployment share work separate. This gives us the flexibility of experimenting in the reference share space, building baseline images, tweaking task sequences, and so on, without impacting deployment share, where deployments will actually occur, replication with partners will take place, and so forth.

We will continue through the wizard until we get to the **Options** area, where depending on need, we'd likely want it set as shown in the following image:

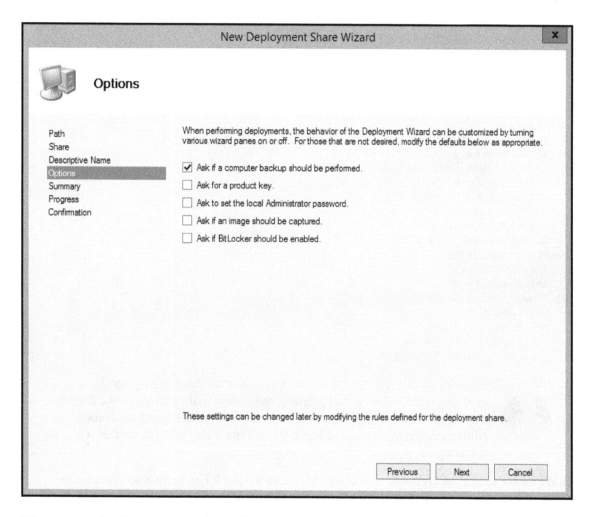

We may need to backup a machine if we run the `litetouch.vbs` script on an existing Windows installation and perform a replace scenario. We don't want to capture an image though, so we uncheck this. We've already done our capture work in reference share.

Some changes that we might want to make in `CustomSettings.ini` are as follows:

```
SMSTSOrgName=MDT Deployment Task Sequence
SkipDomainMembership=YES
JoinDomain=Contoso
DomainAdmin=Administrator
```

So, it will look something similar to the following:

```
OSInstall=Y
SkipAppsOnUpgrade=YES
SkipCapture=YES
SkipAdminPassword=YES
SkipProductKey=YES
_SMSTSOrgName=MDT Deployment Task Sequence
SkipBitLocker=YES
SkipDomainMembership=YES
JoinWorkgroup=Workgroup
SkipFinalSummary=YES
SkipLocaleSelection=YES
SkipSummary=YES
SkipTimeZone=YES
SkipUserData=YES
TimeZoneName=Eastern Standard Time
UserID=administrator
UserDomain=contoso
UserPassword=Password
FinishAction=RESTART
```

`FinishAction=RESTART` or `SHUTDOWN` is important in managed environments. If this is not present, the action will be to leave the freshly deployed machine that is joined to the domain and logged on as local administrator, which could leave the system vulnerable to end user shenanigans.

Don't forget to import Hyper-V driver additions, so WIN PE has them and update the deployment share as well. For Hyper-V on Server 2008 R2 or 2012 R2, log on to a virtual machine and insert integration service setup disk. If you do not have a virtual machine up and running, you can mount `%windir%\system32\vmguest.iso`.

Here, we will import the custom WIM file as an OS:

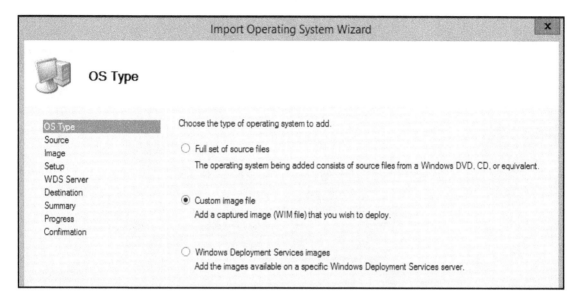

Also specify the file noted in the reference share. Note the checkbox, you can move the file to speed the process. However, I prefer to keep the WIM files in the reference share to keep a library of work:

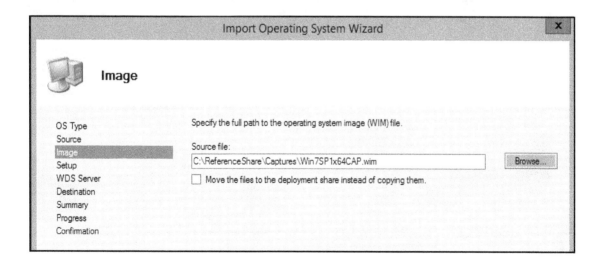

After we specify the WIM, on the next screen, we will specify the setup files needed from the OS media. It is important to pick the one appropriate to bitness and version matching the WIM file. Point to the official ISO for the OS you built/captured the WIM from:

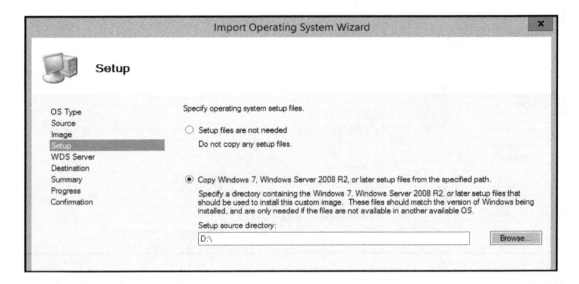

Then we give it a friendly name:

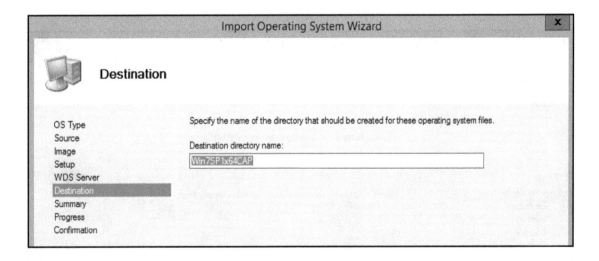

Deployment scenarios and network considerations

During the capture process, the task sequence follows the steps, determining the variables, making decisions whether to continue on error, and so on, all according to the task sequence created in the share. We've gone over the task sequence engine, settings, and variables, but we have not yet discussed the scenarios on the share itself, deployment strategies, replication for enterprise environments, and so on. We'll cover some of these scenarios now.

Firstly, deployment in most enterprises is considered a dangerous event. I've seen several misconfigured environments that started running SMS or MDT-based task sequences on production systems. User data is lost, days of productivity are lost, and IT careers are altered in a negative way. One such incident that is helpful to dissect occurred at a healthcare provider in the United States.

SMS advertised a deployment task sequence over an agent that told the agent to format the existing hardware and install Windows 7. This includes all laptops, desktops, and servers in the environment.

Deployment networks

For this reason alone, I typically advise customers to create a virtual network (VLAN) for deployments. The MDT deployment share resides on this VLAN, and hosts that are to be migrated are moved onto the VLAN temporarily for servicing. As laying down a fresh image on a host happens rarely (one would hope), this should mitigate the accidental task sequence push to all clients.

So, deploy in a VLAN. This brings us to the concept of how to configure this network.

Configuration of the deployment network

Use Multi-Cast on the deployment VLAN. Multi-Cast transmission will allow Win PE boot media to start listening to the broadcast anywhere in the image stream, as it is transmitted to all endpoints on the VLAN. Therefore, Win PE can start listening as soon as it is network-ready, and when the whole deployment transmissions is complete, it can begin running the task sequence.

DHCP should be configured on the network, even in an environment that does not use DHCP. The pain associated with manual static IP address assignments in a mass-deployment scenario is possible with a lot of work, or a DHCP server.

The network should be as fast as possible, given that it's going to be deploying and (potentially) migrating user data via **User State Migration Tool** (**USMT**). A sizing estimation for data migration should also be done. The size of the user profile area on your hosts * number of hosts being migrated at once = the general amount of storage you might need (multiply the result by two or three so that you have extra. You can never have enough storage).

More details about USMT and it's configuration will be discussed in `Chapter 8`, *USMT – The User State Migration Tool.*

Geographical considerations

When we are deploying across geographical sites, we would want to use linked deployment shares (available in the advanced area of the MDT share). The key here is to manage your share centrally from the master deployment share, then use linked deployment shares to essentially act as a floodgate to your downstream deployment points (ideally hosted in DFS).

You may not (at the time of writing) utilize an active directory associated DFS share for replication. Therefore, a deployment standalone DFS infrastructure is recommended. This sounds like a lot of work; but in reality, it is quite simple to stand up.

So again, Master deployment share is linked to another share (which acts as a kind of floodgate). This link will reside as a folder structure in a standalone DFS configuration. You can then use block-level differential copying native in DFS to save bandwidth and time in replicating changes between geographical sites.

Windows 10

All the concepts shown in this chapter are valid for Windows 10, but pay attention to the following points:

- Windows 10 as a guest virtual machine is only supported on Hyper-V on Server 2012 R2 or newer or on Hyper-V on Windows 10.
- I recommend using a Generation 2 virtual machine to create the Windows 10 images.
- If you plan to create a Windows 10 image used for inplace upgrade, only pure OS features on demand and patches are allowed. Do not add any application to an inplace upgrade Image.
- For a normal *wipe and reload* Windows 10 image, you can add applications as shown previously.

Summary

In this chapter, we discussed the basics of deploying the image. We discussed how to set up a capture share, how to set up a deployment share, and their basic configuration. The concepts in this chapter are, in some instances, all you need for a deployment engagement.

However, many times, user data needs to be migrated, which is sometime problematic; especially, when you have used redirection of user data folders and user profile contents.

In the next chapter, we'll discuss precisely how to migrate user data, supported by Microsoft methodology using USMT. We will guide you for XML configuration and show how to troubleshoot USMT.

8
USMT – The User State Migration Tool

In the previous chapter we discussed deploying the image. The concepts in that chapter are in some instances all you need for a deployment engagement. However, many times user data is at rest on the endpoints, particularly when migrating from Windows XP where the redirection of user data folders and user profile contents was not a good story.

In this chapter, we'll discuss precisely how to migrate user data, supported by Microsoft methodology:

- We'll look over the existing functionality of the toolset provided in the ADK
- We'll look at the practice of customizing the toolset for some user data configuration samples
- We'll also look at how to troubleshoot USMT specifically and talk about some supportability caveats with MDT and USMT

History

The **User State Migration Tool (USMT)** was designed as a command-line tool to move settings and data from one computer to another or to save and restore settings in case of break-fix. (break-fix is the repair of an IT system when computer equipment fails, the network stops functioning or software programs are not working by reinstalling the OS.) Some other GUI tools (for example, Windows Easy Transfer) rely on the technical base.

The first version of USMT migrated Windows 95/98 and Windows NT 4.0 computers to Windows 2000 using customized INF Files. This version was never available publicly for download. The first public version USMT 2.x added support for Windows 2000 source computers and Windows XP destinations.

The USMT 3.x version brought considerable changes, including the use of XML files for migration customization, file security migration, encrypted data storage and Windows Vista manifest support.

USMT 4.0 was included in **Windows Automated Installation Kit** (**WAIK**) and adds significant capabilities and complexity by introducing new data collection helper functions, UsmtUtils tool, offline and hard-link migrations and support for Window 7 as source and target, and removes Windows XP as target.

USMT 5.0 has the same capabilities as 4.0 but adds support for Windows 8 as source and target and removes Windows Vista as target. Additionally some tools for compressed store validation and recovery are added.

Beginning with USMT 5.0, the internal versioning of `scanstate.exe` and `loadstate.exe` changed to version numbers identical to the OS. So you will see 6.2.xxxx or 6.3.xxxx or 10.0.xxxx versions depending which OS/ADK you are using.

Here is a compatibility chart explaining the source (left column) and target (top row) OS supported by each USMT version:

	Windows XP	Windows Vista	Windows 7	Windows 8
Windows XP	USMT 3	USMT 4	USMT 4, 5	USMT 5
Windows Vista	Not supported	USMT 4	USMT 4, 5	USMT 5
Windows 7	Not supported	Not supported	USMT 4, 5	USMT 5
Windows 8	Not supported	Not supported	Not supported	USMT 5

Compatibility chart for USMT 3.x, 4.0, and 5.0

Supported scenarios and minimum requirements

USMT does not have any explicit or its *own* CPU, RAM, graphics or HDD requirements. It relies furthermore on the system requirements of the operating system it is executed on. If you do not use hard-link migration or external disk or network path, the hard drives must have sufficient space to contain the migration store, whether compressed or not. Additionally, it will need some temporary space. If unsure, you can estimate the needed space by using `scanstate.exe /p`.

 USMT supports migration to the same OS or a newer OS, but it does not support migration to an older OS. It supports migrating from 32-bit to 32-bit, 32-bit to 64-bit and 64-bit to 64-bit. It does not support migrating from 64-bit to 32-bit. ARM is completely unsupported and so you cannot migrate from any ARM edition nor to any ARM edition.

The following table lists the operating systems supported in USMT 5.0:

Operating System	ScanState (Source PC)	LoadState (Destination PC)
Windows XP Professional	YES	NO
Windows XP Professional x64 Edition	YES	NO
Windows Vista (32-bit)	YES	YES
Windows Vista (64-bit)	YES	YES
Windows 7 (32-bit)	YES	YES
Windows 7 (64-bit)	YES	YES
Windows 8 (32-bit)	YES	YES
Windows 8 (64-bit)	YES	YES
Windows RT (WOA)	NO	NO

USTM also does not support any Windows Server editions, Starter editions or Basic editions.

USMT does support migration between **Multilingual User Interfaces** (**MUIs**), but it does not support migration between OS languages.

The user running `ScanState` and `LoadState` must be a member of the local administrators group and run it in elevated mode. If you modified the default privileges, make sure the user still
has `SeBackupPrivilege`, `SeDebugPrivilege`, `SeRestorePrivilege`, `SeSecurityPriv` `ilege`, and `SeTakeOwnership` granted.

What USMT will migrate and won't migrate

There is a complete list of settings, restrictions, applications, and file types in the *What does USMT migrate?* section of the USMT User's Guide. I will highlight the most important capabilities and limitations.

USMT will migrate the following things:

- Profile data for all local users as well as the *all users* profile including My Documents, My Pictures, Shared Documents, and Shared Favorites
- EFS files and certificates (need to add `/efs:copyraw` option)
- All file types defined in `MigUser.xml` (can be edited)
- Application settings for certain apps defined in `MigApps.xml` (*) (can be edited)
- **Access control lists** (**ACL**) with files and folders
- Operating system data such as mouse and keyboard, taskbar, and also group membership and more
- Computer settings
- Local user to local user or local user to domain user
- Domain user to a (new) domain user

USMT will *NOT* migrate the following things:

- Applications themselves, though it will migrate application settings. (You need to install the applications on the destination computer prior to restoring settings with `LoadState`.)
- Applications to a newer version; the source and destination must be the same version. (Except Microsoft Office, where it is supported to migrate to a newer version.)
- Application settings not modified by the user.
- Operating system settings such as local and network printers, permissions for shared folders, hardware settings, some firewall settings from XP, files, and settings between different language OS.

USMT 5.0 migrates the following Microsoft and third party applications settings and data files. Those must be installed on the source and destination computer prior to running `ScanState` and `LoadState`:

Product	Version
Adobe Acrobat Reader	9
AOL Instant Messenger	6.8
Adobe Creative Suite	2
Adobe Photoshop CS	8, 9
Adobe ImageReady CS	Any
Apple iTunes	6, 7, 8
Apple QuickTime Player	5, 6, 7
Apple Safari	3.1.2
Google Chrome	Any
Google Picasa	3
Google Talk	Any
IBM Lotus 1-2-3	9
IBM Lotus Notes	6, 7, 8
IBM Lotus Organizer	5
IBM Lotus WordPro	9.9
Intuit Quicken Deluxe	2009
Money Plus Business	2008
Money Plus Home	2008
Mozilla Firefox	3
Microsoft Office	2003, 2007, 2010, 2013
Microsoft Office Access	2003, 2007, 2010, 2013
Microsoft Office Excel	2003, 2007, 2010, 2013
Microsoft Office FrontPage	2003, 2007, 2010, 2013
Microsoft Office OneNote	2003, 2007, 2010, 2013

Microsoft Office Outlook	2003, 2007, 2010, 2013
Microsoft Office PowerPoint	2003, 2007, 2010, 2013
Microsoft Office Publisher	2003, 2007, 2010, 2013
Microsoft Office Word	2003, 2007, 2010, 2013
Opera Software Opera	9.5
Microsoft Outlook Express	Only mailbox file
Microsoft Project	2003, 2007, 2010, 2013
Microsoft Office Visio	2003, 2007, 2010, 2013
RealPlayer Basic	11
Sage Peachtree	2009
Skype	3.8
Windows Live Mail	12, 14
Windows Live Messenger	8.5, 14
Windows Live MovieMaker	14
Windows Live Photo Gallery	12, 14
Windows Live Writer	12, 14
Windows Mail	Only shipped with Windows Vista
Microsoft Works	9
Yahoo Messenger	9
Microsoft Zune	3, 4

Where to download

Older versions up to USMT 3.x can be downloaded separately on Microsoft Download Center. Beginning with 4.0, USMT was integrated into the **Windows Automated Installation Kit** (**WAIK**) for Windows 7. USMT 5 and later versions are included in the **Windows Assessment and Deployment Kit** (**Windows ADK**) for Windows 8/8.1/8.1 Update.

The latest USMT (10.x) can be found in the newest released ADK, which is currently Windows ADK for Windows 10, v1511, available at `https://msdn.microsoft.com/en-u s/windows/hardware/dn913721.aspx`. When executing the `adksetup.exe` web installer, you have to select **User State Migration Tool (USMT)**

How USMT works

At first glance, USMT with its various executables looks complex and confusing. We will explain the basics of USMT, the role of included XML files, and give insight to the `ScanState` and `LoadState` process with its steps and rule processing. With this knowledge, using USMT will be less confusing.

USMT basics

USMT 5.0 and newer consists of the following components:

- `scanstate.exe`
- `loadstate.exe`
- `usmtutils.exe`
- The `MigDocs.xml`, `MigApps.xml`, and `MigUser.xml` migration files

- The downlevel and replacement manifests for Windows XP, Windows Vista, and Windows 7
- Various libraries and supporting files

The interactions between these components are shown in the following figure:

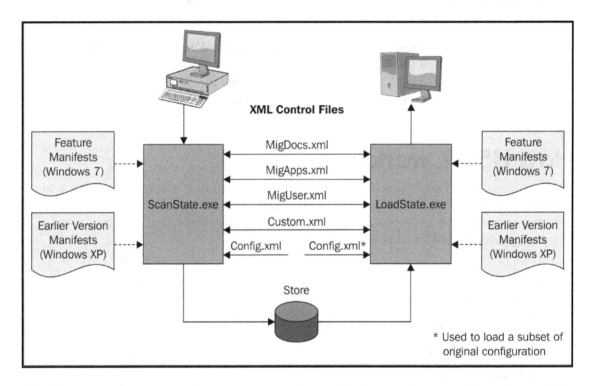

USMT uses a two-part migration process consisting of gather and restore. The gather, which can be done in online and offline mode, uses the command-line scanstate.exe to collect user and computer settings and data based on XML files included with USMT, included in the operating system, and provided by the customer.

The restore uses the command-line `loadstate.exe` to reinstate those files to a computer using the same or different XML files.

The `usmtutils.exe` is not required for the migration process but is recommended for validating compressed stores. It can also recover data from a store that cannot be restored by `loadstate.exe` normally.

USMT migrates application settings and user data based on rules defined in XML files:

- `MigApps.xml`: Rules to migrate application settings
- `MigDocs.xml`: Rules that use the `MigXmlHelper.GenerateDocPatterns` helper function, which automatically finds user documents on a computer without the need to author extensive custom migration XML files
- `MigUser.xml`: Rules to migrate user profiles and user data

To perform a data-only migration, use only the `MigDocs.xml` and a `Config.xml` with all migrate entries set to `no`.

Use the default migration `.xml` files as models. It is recommended that you create a separate XML file instead of adding your XML code to one of the existing migration `.xml` files.

 Microsoft does not recommend using `MigUser.xml`. It is included for backwards compatibility, but it misses many files and does not migrate file ACLs outside the user profiles.

The ScanState process

The ScanState tool needs to be executed on the source computer. ScanState can be executed from within a running OS or from a **Windows Preinstallation Environment (Windows PE)**. When running from within a running OS, it is recommended to perform a reboot before executing to reduce the number of blocked/locked files.

`scanstate.exe` gathers everything in a user's profile and then does a file extension-based search of most of the system for other user data. If data does not match either of these criteria, the data does not migrate.

When you execute ScanState, the following steps are processed:

1. ScanState first parses and validates the command line parameters and starts writing to a ScanState log file (by default `ScanState.log`).

2. All XML files specified in the command line are read and information about all migration components that need to be migrated is being collected. A migration component is a logical group of files, registry keys, and values. Typically, all settings (files, registry keys, values) representing an application are grouped into a single migration component. Additionally, since Vista and newer OS the built-in manifest files from the source computer (`%SYSTEMROOT%\Windows\WinSxS`) are also read and evaluated. You cannot edit these files directly. If you want to exclude certain operating system settings you need to create and modify a `Config.xml` file.

3. ScanState determines next which user profiles need to be migrated. By default, all user profiles on the source computer are migrated. You can specify user options to include and exclude certain users using the user arguments (`/ue`, `/ui`, `/uel`). The `All Users` (XP)/`Public` (Vista and later) profile is always migrated and cannot be excluded.

4. ScanState starts the *Scanning* phase and checks every user profile. Depending on the component setting (`User`, `System`, or `UserAndSystem`) and the type of the user profile the component is processed or ignored. For each processed component of the correct type, ScanState evaluates the `<detects>` section. If the `<detects>` section evaluates to true, the component is further processed. Otherwise the component is dropped and the next component gets evaluated. For all still valid components the `<rules>` section is evaluated next. Rules are again listed in types (`User`, `System`, and `UserAndSystem`). Depending on the user profile, ScanState processes the rule or continues to next rule of the component. ScanState creates a list of migration units by processing all subsections under each `<rules>` section. Each unit is collected if it is mentioned in an `<include>` subsection and there is not a more specific rule with the `<exclude>` subsection or a general `<unconditionedExclude>` subsection.

5. Next ScanState starts the *Collecting* phase by creating a master list of all valid evaluated migration units combining all lists created for each profile.

6. The last phase of ScanState is the *Saving* phase. All collected migration units from the master list are now written to the store location.

ScanState does not modify the source computer. No files and data are changed except the creation of a store folder, for copying or hard linking the files, and a temporary folder for the administrative user executing ScanState.

The LoadState process

The LoadState process is very similar to the ScanState process. Except for looking into user profiles and searching the system, LoadState collects the migration units from the store location and applies them to the destination computer.

When you execute LoadState, the following steps are processed:

1. LoadState first parses and validates the command line parameters and starts writing to a LoadState log file.
2. All XML files specified in the command line are read and information about all migration components need to be migrated is being collected.

    Additionally, since Vista and newer OSes, the built-in manifest files from the destination computer (`%SYSTEMROOT%\Windows\WinSxS`) are also read and evaluated. You cannot edit these files directly. If you want to exclude certain operating system settings you need to create and modify a `Config.xml` file.

3. LoadState determines all user profiles which should be migrated. By default, all user profiles in the store location are migrated. You can specify user options to include and exclude certain users using the user arguments (`/ue, /ui, /uel`). The `All Users` (XP)/`Public` (Vista and later) profile is always migrated and cannot be excluded.

    - If a local user account is migrated and does not already exist on the destination computer, the migration will fail. In this case, you need to create a user account before or specify the `/lac` argument.
    - With `/md` and `/mu` arguments user accounts can be renamed on the destination computer.

4. Next, LoadState will run the *Scanning* phase. Similar to the *Scanning* phase of ScanState each user profile type is checked, each component is evaluated, each rule and subsection processed. Additionally the LoadState evaluates the destination-specific subsections, for example, `<destinationCleanup>` or `<locationModify>`. Also, the manifest files are processed, if migrating from a downlevel OS.
5. The last phase executed by LoadState is the *Apply* phase. LoadState writes all evaluated migration units to the destination computer. If there is no `<merge>` rule defined for the object, registry keys are overwritten by default and files are renamed by default.

ScanState and LoadState syntax

Writing down a full list of all possible ScanState and LoadState syntax and their possible combinations would exceed the limits of this chapter by far (and would also be very boring content).

For this reason, we will only highlight some particularly noteworthy command syntax you should take a closer look at, marked by ScanState only, LoadState only, and generally valid for both.

Command-Line Argument	Description
`/o` (ScanState only)	Required to overwrite any existing data in the store location or `Config.xml` file. We recommend to delete migration store between executions.
`/hardlink`	Needs to be combined with the `/nocompress` option. It will enable the hard-link migration. `StorePath` needs to be on the same volume. When migrating files on different volumes and using `/hardlink` option the migration store spans also multiple volumes.
`/vsc` (ScanState only)	Enables the volume shadow copy service to help with *locked* and *in use* files. It eliminates most file-locking errors. It cannot be combined with the `/hardlink` option.
`/encrypt [/key|/keyfile]` (ScanState only)	Encrypts the store. By default, encryption is disabled. Use caution with this parameter, because everyone who has access to your ScanState command line can read your encryption key. `/encrypt` and `/nocompress` cannot be used together. Also, `/encrypt` and `/hardlink` cannot be used together.
`/decrypt [/key|/keyfile]` (LoadState only)	Decrypts the store. Use caution with this parameter, because everyone who has access to your LoadState command line can read your encryption key. `/decrypt` and `/nocompress` cannot be used together. Also, `/decrypt` and `/hardlink` cannot be used together.

`/nocompress`	• Disables compression of data and saves all files separately in store location. • Good for troubleshooting to view what ScanState is stored. • `/nocompress` and `/encrypt` cannot be used together. It can be used without `/hardlink` option, but in this case only recommended for testlab.
`/auto:<path to default XML>`	If no path is specified, `.xml` files will be searched in the USMT binaries folder. It has the same effect as using the following arguments: • `/i:MigDocs.xml` • `/i:MigApp.xml` • `/v:5`
`/localonly` (ScanState only)	Excludes all removable drives and network drives regardless of the rules in the `.xml` files specified on command line.
`/v:<Verbosity>`	The default value is 0. For troubleshooting, use the `/v:5` option. Higher levels are only readable by attached debuggers, lower levels are not as useful for troubleshooting.

`/offlineWinDir:<Path>`
`/offlineWinOld:<Path>`
(ScanState only)
	• The `/offlineWinDir` argument is only for PE environment scenarios. This can be helpful when the source OS cannot be started any more or if even `/vsc` results in locked files.
	• The `/offlineWinOld` argument is for already **inplace** migrated/reinstalled scenarios where old data resides in the `Windows.old` folder.

`/c`	• ScanState/LoadState will continue even if non-fatal errors occur. Using `/c` can result in data loss. • Better use the new `<ErrorControl>` section in `Config.xml` for fine granular error control.

`/ui:DomainName\UserName` `/ui:ComputerName\UserName`	• By default, all users are included in the migration. `/ui` only needs to be specified when also using `/ue` and/or `/uel`. `DomainName` and `UserName` can contain asterisk wildcard (*). Usernames with spaces need to be surrounded by quotation marks. Multiple `/ui` arguments can be specified. • `/ui` inclusions take precedence over `/ue` and `/uel` exclusions.

`/uel:<NumberOfDays>`
`/uel:<Date>`
`/uel:0`
	• Excludes users depending on their `LastModified` date of `NTUser.dat`. For example, `/uel:30` excludes all users not logged on within the last 30 days. `/uel:0` migrates only users currently logged on.
	• `/ue` exclusions override `/uel`.
	• `/uel` cannot be used in offline migrations.

`/ue:DomainName\UserName` `/ue:ComputerName\UserName`	• Excludes specified user accounts. `DomainName` and `UserName` can contain asterisk wildcard (*). Usernames with spaces need to be surrounded by quotation marks. Multiple `/ue` arguments can be specified. • `/ui` inclusions take precedence over `/ue` exclusions.

`/md:OldDomain:NewDomain`
`/md:ComputerName:NewDomain`
(LoadState only)
	With this argument, users can be migrated to a `NewDomain`. An `OldDomain` may contain the asterisk wildcard (*). Multiple `/md` arguments can be specified. If conflicting `/md` commands are specified, only the first rule is applied.

`/mu:OldUserName:NewUserName`
`/mu:OldDomain\OldUserName:[NewDomain\]NewUserName`
(LoadState only)
	Specified user gets renamed. Wildcard character is not supported. Multiple `/mu` arguments can be specified.

`/lac[:Password]` (LoadState only)	• If (non-domain) account does not exist, specifying `/lac` will create such an account. Otherwise, LoadState will stop with an error. • The created user account will be disabled. You need to enable it manually or specify `/lae`. • When no password is given, the user will be created with an empty password. If you specify a password, it will be plain-text readable. Also, if multiple users need to be created, all migrated users will have the same password.

`/lae` (LoadState only)	Enables the account which was created by `/lac` argument.

UsmtUtils tool

The UsmtUtils tool is used for deleting a hard-link store, validating a compressed file store and extracting data from a compressed file store. Additionally, it can determine cryptographic capabilities of source and destination computer for use with the `/encrypt` command.

Delete hard-link migration store

Hard-link migration stores cannot be deleted by Windows Explorer or the command prompt. To delete these stores you need to use UsmtUtils with the `/rd` option.

If the migration store spans multiple volumes, it will be deleted from all volumes. Sometimes the `/rd` option needs a reboot to delete all files. To override the accept prompt you can specify the `/y` argument additionally.

Some examples include the following:

- `usmtutils /rd C:\HardLinkStore`
- `usmtutils /rd D:\HardLinkStore /y`

Verify compressed migration store

You can use the `usmtutils.exe /verify` argument when you want to validate whether a compressed migration store is *OK* or contains corrupted files. The `/verify` argument implements different types of reports specified by `/verify[:<reportType>]`:

- `Summary`: Returns only the number of files corrupted and the number of files that are intact. This summary type is the default report type if no type is specified.
- `all`: Returns a list of all files in the compressed migration store and the status of the file (tab delimited). It also reports the status of the Catalog of the store. If the Catalog is corrupted, LoadState cannot open the migration store.

- `failureonly`: Returns a list of only the corrupted files in the compressed migration store.
- `Catalog`: Returns only the status of the catalog.

If the migration store is encrypted, you need to specify the `/decrypt` option as you would with LoadState.

Some examples include the following:

- `usmtutils /verify C:\MigrationStore\Store.mig`
- `usmtutils /verify:all C:\MigrationStore\Store.mig /decrypt:AES_256 /key:"secret encryption key"`
- `usmtutils /verify:failureonly C:\MigrationStore\Store.mig /decrypt /keyfile:C:\encryptionKey.txt`

Recover files from a compressed migration store

You can use the `/extract` argument to recover files from a compressed migration store, for example, if it is corrupted and will not restore normally with LoadState, or if you need to extract some files without doing the full LoadState process.

You need to specify `<path to Store.mig>` and `<destination path for the extracted files>`. Additionally, you can specify an `include` and/or `exclude` pattern which supports the wildcard asterisk (`*`). It is possible to specify multiple patterns by separating them with a comma or semicolon. Include patterns take precedence over exclude patterns.

If the migration store is encrypted, you need to specify the `/decrypt` option like you would with LoadState.

The `/o` option will overwrite existing output files.

Some examples include the following:

- `usmtutils /extract C:\MigrationStore\Store.mig C:\ExtractedFiles /o`
- `usmtutils /extract C:\MigrationStore\Store.mig C:\ExtractedFiles /i:"*.docx,*,xlsx" /e:"~*.*" /decrypt:AES_192 /keyfile:C:\encryptionKey.txt`

Supported cryptographic algorithms on the current system

To get a list of supported cryptographic algorithms (AlgIDs) on the current system, you can use the /ec argument. When using encryption it is important to check that the source and destination computer support the selected/specified AlgID before running the ScanState tool.

Valid values for AlgID include the following: AES_128, AES_192, AES_256, 3DES, or 3DES_112.

If no AlgID for /encrypt or /decrypt is specified, the system will use 3DES by default.

Customization of XML files

USMT does not include graphical editing tools.

By default, a huge list of files is already migrated. For a complete and up to date list see TechNet – **What Does USMT Migrate?**, available at https://technet.microsoft.com/en-us/library/hh825238.aspx. For easy activation/deactivation of single components inside default XML files you can use /genconfig and edit the resulting Config.xml.

If you need to modify or create USMT XML files you should use an XML editor to do it safely. You can also use Visual Studio 2012 (Express) or newer.

To create a clean XML sample, open Visual Studio and select a new Visual C# project with a blank application. To add a blank XML, go to **Solution Explorer**, right click and add a new item, selecting the XML file item type.

Go to the **XML** menu, select **Schemas...**. In the Schemas dialog, add the MigXML.xsd from the USMT folder.

Now you can create your custom XML, excluding or including content.

Some examples are as follows:

Migrate registry keys

The following `.xml` file migrates HKLM registry keys in a system context.

```
<migration urlid="http://www.microsoft.com/migration/1.0/migxmlext/test">
<component type="Application" context="System">
  <displayName>Component to migrate two registry keys and one registry
    value string</displayName>
  <role role="Settings">
    <rules>
      <include>
        <objectSet>
          <pattern type="Registry">HKLM\Software\
            PacktPublishing\Toolbar\* [*]</pattern>
          <pattern type="Registry">HKLM\Software\
            PacktPublishing\Configuration\* [*]</pattern>
          <pattern type="Registry">HKLM\Software\
            PacktPublishing [ShowHelp]</pattern>
        </objectSet>
      </include>
    </rules>
  </role>
</component>
</migration>
```

Migrate a folder from a specific drive

The following are two samples, one with and one without subdirectories.

Including subdirectories

The following `.xml` file migrates all files and subfolders from various locations, including `C:\PacktPublishing` and `C:\UserData`, to the destination computer:

```
<migration urlid="http://www.microsoft.com/migration/1.0/migxmlext/test">
<component type="Documents" context="System">
  <displayName>Component to migrate all Packt Publishing Documents
    including subfolders</displayName>
  <role role="Data">
    <rules>>
      <include>
        <objectSet>
          <pattern type="File">C:\PacktPublishing\* [*]</pattern>
        </objectSet>
      </include>
```

```
      </rules>
    </role>
</component>
<component type="Documents" context="System">
  <displayName>Component to migrate all User Data Documents including
    subfolders</displayName>
  <role role="Data">
    <rules>
      <include>
        <objectSet>
          <pattern type="File">C:\UserData\* [*]</pattern>
        </objectSet>
      </include>
    </rules>
  </role>
</component>
</migration>
```

Excluding subdirectories

The following .xml file migrates all files from C:\PacktPublishing, but it does not migrate any subfolders within C:\PacktPublishing:

```
<migration urlid="http://www.microsoft.com/migration/1.0/migxmlext/test">
<component type="Documents" context="System">
  <displayName>Component to migrate all Packt Publishing Documents without
    subfolders</displayName>
  <role role="Data">
    <rules>
      <include>
        <objectSet>
          <pattern type="File"> C:\PacktPublishing\ [*]</pattern>
        </objectSet>
      </include>
    </rules>
  </role>
</component>
</migration>
```

More samples can be found under TechNet – USMT – **Include Files and Settings**, at https://technet.microsoft.com/en-us/library/hh824833.aspx.

Migration options

All USMT scenarios can be split in the following two common migration scenarios: PC Refresh and PC Replacement.

PC Refresh scenario

The source and destination computer are the same. This scenario is used when upgrading the OS or reinstalling OS for break-fix. The administrator migrates the user and computer state to an intermediate store. This intermediate store can be a remote server/file share, an external drive, or a hard-link migration store on the same drive (if no repartitioning or change of partition type is needed). After installing the new OS on the same computer, the migrated data and settings are brought back and the migration store is deleted.

When using a remote server/file share, using a compressed (and encrypted) migration store is recommended.

When there is no need for repartitioning/formatting the hard disk, a hard-link migration store is recommended due to the speed benefit.

If the source computer OS is broken and cannot be started any more, use a PE environment and the `/offlineWinDir` argument.

When the OS was already reinstalled/upgraded before using USMT and `Windows.old` still exists, you can try the `/hardlink` and `/offlineWinOld` argument.

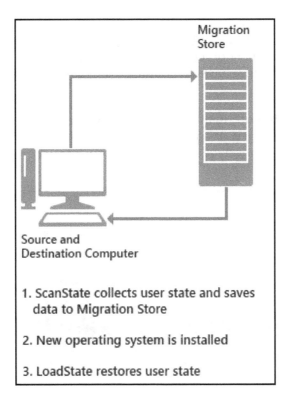

PC Replacement scenario

The source and destination computers are different. This scenario is used when hardware is being replaced (with or without an upgrade of OS).

The administrator migrates the user and computer state to an intermediate store. This intermediate store can be a remote server/file share or an external HDD. A hard-link migration store is not usable. After installing the new OS on the destination computer, the migrated data and settings are brought back and the migration store is deleted. The source computer can be repurposed or discarded.

When using a remote server/file share, using a compressed (and encrypted) migration store is recommended.

If the source computer OS is broken and cannot be started again, use a PE environment and the `/offlineWinDir` argument.

When planning a larger number of replacements, try to group users, as you will need a huge amount of space on a file share depending on the habits of users and usage patterns of the local data.

Network migration can be done manually or automated/managed by using MDT. I recommend using the managed scenario and prepare/test common use XML files (`MigApps.xml`, `MigDocs.xml`, `MigUser.xml`). The process is shown as follows:

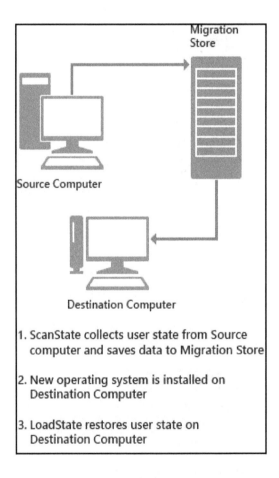

Source Computer

Migration Store

Destination Computer

1. ScanState collects user state from Source computer and saves data to Migration Store

2. New operating system is installed on Destination Computer

3. LoadState restores user state on Destination Computer

Online versus offline migration

When comparing the online migration (running ScanState from the source OS) with offline migration (running ScanState from a PE environment with `/offlineWinDir` or running ScanState on the destination OS with `/offlineWinOld`) I will outline the highs and lows of both methods.

The offline migration is normally not blocked by any *in use* files, but on the other hand it is not possible to migrate all data. The following settings cannot be migrated (partly or at all) as they utilize plugin DLLs that cannot load in that environment:

- COM+ applications
- Handwriting recognition
- Internet Explorer networking
- National language
- Offline files
- Connection manager
- Regional and language options
- Shell configuration
- Shell HTTP handler
- Windows Media Player
- Windows remote management

In a normal scenario, you should stick with the online migration. But in the case of a broken OS, offline migration is a better option than nothing, even if it doesn't migrate everything.

File copy versus hard-link

A hard-link is a simply way for NTFS to point to the same file from multiple locations on the same volume, using only one time space of file. A hard-link has nothing to do with USMT. USMT is just a consumer of a hard-link.

Instead of copying the data, the hard-link only creates additional pointers. The file itself exists only once. This means when USMT is *storing* a hard-link copy of a file it is just telling NTFS to make another pointer of the same file data without touching the data itself.

When comparing USMT copy times versus USMT hard-link times of the same amount of data, there is a constantly increasing gap, as shown in the following figure:

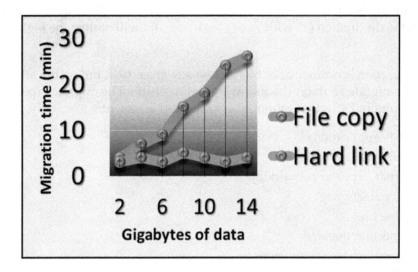

Whenever possible, you should use a hard-link migration store to benefit from the speed increase.

Windows 8 (.1) upgrades also use hard-links, which is one reason why those upgrades are much faster than Windows 7.

Note: Any changes to a hard-linked file through one path or another always reflect on the same physical file on the disk. When you delete one of these representations of the file, the hard-link is deleted. When the last one is deleted, you are also deleting the actual file data.

Using Windows XP with ADK 8.1

With the introduction of Windows ADK for Windows 8.1 and the integrated USMT 6.3, support for Windows XP as the source computer OS was dropped. MDT 2013 and ConfigMgr 2012 R2 require ADK 8.1. If you are in the unlucky situation needing to backup Windows XP and migrate it with ADK 8.1 you can use the following workaround. Run your backup with the older USMT 5.0 and restore with the newer USMT 6.3.

Best practices

A summary from TechNet (available at `https://technet.microsoft.com/en-us/libr ary/hh825108.aspx`) and experiences from the field are outlined as follows:

- **Install applications before running the LoadState tool**: This helps ensure that migrated settings are preserved. For Microsoft Office, this is required for migration to work correctly.

- **Do not use MigUser.xml and MigDocs.xml together**: If you use both `.xml` files, some migrated files may be duplicated if conflicting instructions are given about target locations. You can use the `/genmigxml` command-line option to determine which files will be included in your migration, and to determine if any modifications are necessary.

- **Use MigDocs.xml for a better migration experience**: If your dataset is unknown or if many files are stored outside of the standard user-profile folders, the `MigDocs.xml` file is a better choice than the `MigUser.xml` file, because the `MigDocs.xml` file will gather a broader scope of data. The `MigDocs.xml` file migrates folders of data based on location, and on registered file types by querying the registry for registered application extensions. The `MigUser.xml` file migrates only the files with the specified file extensions and in user profiles.

- **Close all applications before running either the ScanState or LoadState tools**: Although using the `/vsc` switch can allow the migration of many files that are open with another application-except with `/hardlink`—it is a best practice to close all applications in order to ensure all files and settings migrate. Without the `/vsc` or `/c` argument, USMT fails when it cannot migrate a file or setting. When you use the `/c` option, USMT will ignore any files or settings that it cannot migrate and log an error each time, but this also potentially leads to data loss on the destination computer.

- **Log off after you run the LoadState tool**: Some settings, such as fonts, wallpaper, and screensaver settings, will not take effect until the next time the user logs on. For this reason, you should log off after you run the LoadState tool.

- **Use migration to create a managed environment**: USMT can move all of the end user's documents from their various locations into their Documents (`%CSIDL_PERSONAL%`) folder. Since Windows 7 and Windows 8 do not allow standard users to create folders on the root of the `C:` drive, they will start to use the more appropriate managed profile areas, making folder redirection, offline files, and roaming folders easier to manage. The end users will naturally require training to know where their data moved after migration.

- **Use Chkdsk.exe and usmtutils.exe /verify**: We recommend that you run `Chkdsk.exe` before running the ScanState and LoadState tools. `Chkdsk.exe` creates a status report for a hard disk drive and lists and corrects common errors. You should also `usmtutils.exe /verify` after creating a compressed store file and before wiping any source machine data to insure integrity and prevent a disaster later.

- **Migrate in groups**: If you decide to perform the migration while users are using the network, it is best to migrate user accounts in groups. To minimize the impact on network performance, determine the size of the groups based on the size of each user account. Migrating in phases also allows you to make sure each phase is successful before starting the next phase. Using this method, you can make any necessary modifications to your plan between groups.

- **Encrypting file system (EFS)**: Take extreme caution when migrating encrypted files, because the end user does not need to be logged on to capture the user state. By default, USMT fails if an encrypted file is found. Do not use `/efs:skip` or `/efs:decryptcopy` without good cause; this may lead to data loss or compromised data. Always provide `/efs:copyraw` or `/efs:hardlink` if you are unsure that users are encrypting data, as the default behavior is for USMT to fail when it detects an encrypted file and does not have an `/efs` argument specified. Ensure there is at least one Data Recovery Agent assigned and operating in the environment. Do not disable the certificate manifests (`CAPI2_certs-DL.man` or `CAPI2_certs-repl.man`) using `Config.xml`.

- **Protect/encrypt the store**: Use the `/encrypt` option with the ScanState command to protect the compressed store. Use ACLs on the file server storing the data that does not grant unnecessary access. Transmit data through IPSEC or VPN tunnels to prevent access to the store files on the wire, especially if using an uncompressed or unencrypted store. However, use extreme caution with this set of options, because anyone who has access to the ScanState command-line script also has access to the encryption key.

- **Virus scan**: We recommend that you scan both the source and destination computers for viruses before running USMT. In addition, you should scan the destination computer image. To help protect data from viruses, it is strongly recommended running an antivirus utility before migration. Along with this, you might consider disabling any AV software during the backup/restore itself, so it doesn't interfere with USMT.

- **Maintain security of the file server and the deployment server**: It is recommended that you manage the security of the file and deployment servers. It is important to make sure that the file server where you save the store is secure. You must also secure the deployment server, to ensure that the user data that is in the log files is not exposed. It is also recommended that you only transmit data over a secure Internet connection, such as a virtual private network. For more information about network security, see Microsoft Security Compliance Manager.

- **Password migration/knowledge**: To ensure the privacy of the end users, USMT does not migrate passwords, including local user passwords and those for applications such as Live Mail, Internet Explorer, Remote Access Service connections, or mapped network drives. Ensure that end users know their passwords or reset them before migrating if they no longer remember cached passwords.

- **Legally bond your migration team**: The users creating the migration store have access to the store encryption key as well as access to all data in the store itself. They must be trusted at the highest levels by the company as they have total access to all client data, no matter what the local security permissions are on the files, except for EFS-encrypted files. As local administrators on the destination computers, they also have complete access to install malware or remote control software. Microsoft suggests legally bonding administrators against exceeding their access and contacting law enforcement authorities if suspecting employees of theft.

- **Specify the same set of Mig*.xml files in both the ScanState and the LoadState tools**: If you used a particular set of `Mig*.xml` files in the ScanState tool, either called through the `/auto` option, or individually through the `/i` option, then you should use same option to call the exact same `Mig*.xml` files in the LoadState tool.

- **The <CustomFileName> in the migration urlid should match the name of the file**: Although it is not a requirement, it is good practice for `<CustomFileName>` to match the name of the file. For example, the following is from the `MigApps.xml` file:

```
<?xml version="1.0" encoding="UTF-8"?>
<migration
  urlid="http://www.microsoft.com/migration/1.0/migxmlext/migapp">
```

- **Use an XML editor and use the XML Schema (MigXML.xsd) when authoring .xml files to validate syntax**: You can load the `MigXML.xsd` schema in Visual Studio Express 2011 to ensure proper authoring of custom `.xml`. Do not use `Notepad.exe` or other primitive text tools to create or edit XML files for any product, especially USMT. `Notepad++` would be a lightweight alternative to Visual Studio, and provides XML syntax highlighting.

- **Use the default migration XML files as models**: To create a custom `.xml` file, you can use the migration `.xml` files as models to create your own. If you need to migrate user data files, model your custom `.xml` file on `MigUser.xml`. To migrate application settings, model your custom `.xml` file on the `MigApps.xml` file.

- **Consider the impact on performance when using the <context> parameter**: You affect migration performance when you use the `<context>` element with the `<component>` element; for example, as in when you want to encapsulate logical units of file- or path-based `<include>` and `<exclude>` rules.

  - In the `User` context, a rule processes one time for each user on the system
  - In the `System` context, a rule processes one time for the system
  - In the `UserAndSystem` context, a rule processes one time for each user on the system and one time for the system

Note: The number of times a rule is processed does not affect the number of times a file is migrated. The USMT migration engine ensures that each file migrates only once.

- **Do not modify factory XML files**: We recommend that you create a separate `.xml` file instead of adding your `.xml` code to one of the existing migration `.xml` files. For example, if you have code that migrates the settings for an application, you should not just add the code to the `MigApps.xml` file.

- **Do not delete or modify manifest files**: You should not alter the `DLmanifest`, `DlManifest7`, `ReplacementManifest`, `ReplacementManifest7`, or `%SYSTEMROOT%\Windows\WinSxS` files. If you want to exclude certain operating system settings from the migration, you should create and modify a `Config.xml` file. Set the `Config.xml` so as not to migrate the built-in manifest settings you wish, then create a custom XML to provide any subset of those now-missing behaviors.

- **Do not create custom .xml files to alter the operating system settings that are migrated**: These settings are migrated by manifests and you cannot modify those files. If you want to exclude certain operating system settings from the migration, you should create and modify a `Config.xml` file.
- **Perform backups before migrating**: Prior to performing a ScanState, perform a bare-metal backup of a source computer to ensure the ability to restore the machine in an emergency or if the store cannot be recovered. SCCM and MDT offer this as a built-in task option in their workflows.

Troubleshooting USMT

Troubleshooting USMT is very easy, as many error messages are very descriptive. First you should examine the console output for errors.

Next you should use the `/v:5` argument on ScanState, LoadState, and UsmtUtils to get most of the details in the log file. The ScanState and LoadState debug logs—when run with verbosity `/v:5`—contain the information needed to diagnose nearly all USMT failures that get past the console error phase. Key to understanding the logs is examining *normal* working scenarios versus logs which encounter errors. With this method, errors will be much more obvious and easier to understand. Like all debug logs, some entries can appear to report errors, which are actually expected and not problematic. Not comparing the log with a *working* version can result in going down the wrong path.

If you still encounter errors, you can enable a special (optional) diagnostic log to determine which migration units are detected and chosen. To activate this log you need to define a system environment variable with the path where this log should be created:

```
SET MIG_ENABLE_DIAG=C:\MigDiag.xml
```

Use this log file only if there are no other console-related errors or errors with XML files.

The last step to perform is to determine if the behavior is *expected* and the lack of migration is *by design*. This requires understanding the files or settings that are not migrating, then examining the XML and component manifest files to see if any rules actually apply to them and copy their data.

For better investigation, if a missing file/setting was not scanned or was not migrated back, use the `/nocompress` argument to get single files. Then check whether the file/setting does exist in the migration store to see if it was correctly collected by ScanState. If it exists in the migration store, but not on the destination computer, troubleshoot the LoadState process.

In many cases, a customer will assume that something is wrong with USMT when in fact, it is not migrating a setting because it is not told to do so.

Additionally, *Michael Niehaus* collected a great summary of all possible return codes and their troubleshooting, mitigation, and workarounds.

The USMT can report various errors. While these do vary somewhat for each version of USMT, they are mostly consistent between versions.

The following are the return codes reported by USMT 5.0:

Return code value	Return code	Error message	Troubleshooting, mitigation, workarounds
0	USMT_SUCCESS	Successful run	Not applicable
1	USMT_DISPLAY_HELP	Command line help requested	Not applicable
2	USMT_STATUS_CANCELED	Gather was aborted because of an EFS file	Not applicable
		User chose to cancel (such as pressing *Ctrl + C*)	Not applicable
3	USMT_WOULD_HAVE_FAILED	At least one error was skipped as a result of /c	Review the ScanState, LoadState, or UsmtUtils log for details about command-line errors.
11	USMT_INVALID_PARAMETERS	/all conflicts with /ui, /ue, or /uel	Review the ScanState log or LoadState log for details about command-line errors.
		/auto expects an optional parameter for the script folder	Review the ScanState log or LoadState log for details about command-line errors.
		/encrypt can't be used with /nocompress	Review the ScanState log or LoadState log for details about command-line errors.
		/encrypt requires /key or /keyfile	Review the ScanState log or LoadState log for details about command-line errors.
		/genconfig can't be used with most other options	Review the ScanState log or LoadState log for details about command-line errors.
		/genmigxml can't be used with most other options	Review the ScanState log or LoadState log for details about command-line errors.
		/hardlink requires /nocompress	Review the ScanState log or LoadState log for details about command-line errors.
		/key and /keyfile both specified	Review the ScanState log or LoadState log for details about command-line errors.
		/key or /keyfile used without enabling encryption	Review the ScanState log or LoadState log for details about command-line errors.
		/lae is only used with /lac	Review the ScanState log or LoadState log for details about command-line errors.
		/listfiles cannot be used with /p	Review the ScanState log or LoadState log for details about command-line errors.
		/offline requires a valid path to an XML file describing offline paths	Review the ScanState log or LoadState log for details about command-line errors.

		`/offlinewindir` requires a valid path to offline windows folder	Review the ScanState log or LoadState log for details about command-line errors.
		`/offlinewinold` requires a valid path to offline windows folder	Review the ScanState log or LoadState log for details about command-line errors.
		A command was already specified	Verify that the command-line syntax is correct and that there are no duplicate commands.
		An option argument is missing	Review the ScanState log or LoadState log for details about command-line errors.
		An option is specified more than once and is ambiguous	Review the ScanState log or LoadState log for details about command-line errors.
		By default `/auto` selects all users and uses the highest log verbosity level. Switches such as `/all`, `/ui`, `/ue`, `/v` are not allowed.	Review the ScanState log or LoadState log for details about command-line errors.
		Command line arguments are required. Specify `/?` for options.	Review the ScanState log or LoadState log for details about command-line errors.
		Command line option is not valid	Review the ScanState log or LoadState log for details about command-line errors.
		EFS parameter specified is not valid for `/efs`	Review the ScanState log or LoadState log for details about command-line errors.
		File argument is invalid for `/genconfig`	Review the ScanState log or LoadState log for details about command-line errors.
		File argument is invalid for `/genmigxml`	Review the ScanState log or LoadState log for details about command-line errors.
		Invalid space estimate path. Check the parameters and/or file system permissions	Review the ScanState log or LoadState log for details about command-line errors.
		List file path argument is invalid for `/listfiles`	Review the ScanState log or LoadState log for details about command-line errors.
		Retry argument must be an integer	Review the ScanState log or LoadState log for details about command-line errors.
		Settings store argument specified is invalid	Review the ScanState log or LoadState log for details about command-line errors. Make sure that the store path is accessible and that the proper permission levels are set.
		Specified encryption algorithm is not supported	Review the ScanState log or LoadState log for details about command-line errors.
		`/efs:hardlink` requires `/hardlink`	Review the ScanState log or LoadState log for details about command-line errors.
		The `/target` Windows 7 option is only available for Windows XP, Windows Vista, and Windows 7	Review the ScanState log or LoadState log for details about command-line errors.
		The store parameter is required but not specified	Review the ScanState log or LoadState log for details about command-line errors.
		The source-to-target domain mapping is invalid for `/md`	Review the ScanState log or LoadState log for details about command-line errors.

		The source-to-target user account mapping is invalid for `/mu`	Review the ScanState log or LoadState log for details about command-line errors.
		Undefined or incomplete command-line option	Review the ScanState log or LoadState log for details about command-line errors.
		Use `/nocompress`, or provide an XML file path with `/p"pathtoafile"` to get a compressed store size estimate	Review the ScanState log or LoadState log for details about command-line errors.
		User exclusion argument is invalid	Review the ScanState log or LoadState log for details about command-line errors.
		Verbosity level must be specified as a sum of the desired log options: Verbose (`0x01`), Record Objects (`0x04`), Echo to debug port (`0x08`)	Review the ScanState log or LoadState log for details about command-line errors.
		Volume shadow copy feature is not supported with a hard-link store	Review the ScanState log or LoadState log for details about command-line errors.
		Wait delay argument must be an integer	Review the ScanState log or LoadState log for details about command-line errors.
12	USMT_ERROR_OPTION_PARAM_TOO_LARGE	Command-line arguments cannot exceed 256 characters	Review the ScanState log or LoadState log for details about command-line errors.
		Specified settings store path exceeds the maximum allowed length of 256 characters	Review the ScanState log or LoadState log for details about command-line errors.
13	USMT_INIT_LOGFILE_FAILED	Log path argument is invalid for `/l`	When `/l` is specified in the ScanState command line, USMT validates the path. Verify that the drive and other information, for example, file system characters, are correct.
14	USMT_ERROR_USE_LAC	Unable to create a local account because `/lac` was not specified	When creating local accounts, the command-line options `/lac` and `/lae` should be used.
26	USMT_INIT_ERROR	Multiple Windows installations found	`Listfiles.txt` could not be created. Verify that the location you specified for the creation of this file is valid.
		Software malfunction or unknown exception	This is a common error when using `/i` to load the `Config.xml` file in USMT. Check all the loaded `.xml` files for syntax errors.
		Unable to find a valid Windows directory to proceed with requested offline operation; Check if offline input file is present and has valid entries	Verify that the offline input file is present and that it has valid entries. USMT could not find valid offline operating system. Verify your offline directory mapping.
27	USMT_INVALID_STORE_LOCATION	A store path can't be used because an existing store exists; specify `/o` to overwrite	Specify `/o` to overwrite an existing intermediate or migration store.
		A store path is missing or has incomplete data	Make sure that the store path is accessible and that the proper permission levels are set.
		An error occurred during store creation	Make sure that the store path is accessible and that the proper permission levels are set. Specify `/o` to overwrite an existing intermediate or migration store.

		An inappropriate device such as a floppy disk was specified for the store	Make sure that the store path is accessible and that the proper permission levels are set.
		Invalid store path; check the store parameter and/or file system permissions	Invalid store path; check the store parameter and/or file system permissions.
		The file layout and/or file content is not recognized as a valid store	Make sure that the store path is accessible and that the proper permission levels are set. Specify /o to overwrite an existing intermediate or migration store.
		The store path holds a store incompatible with the current USMT version	Make sure that the store path is accessible and that the proper permission levels are set.
		The store save location is read-only or does not support a requested storage option	Make sure that the store path is accessible and that the proper permission levels are set.
28	USMT_UNABLE_GET_SCRIPTFILES	Script file is invalid for /i	Check all specified migration .xml files for errors. This is a common error when using /i to load the Config.xml file.
		Unable to find a script file specified by /i	Verify the location of your script files, and ensure that the command-line options are correct.
29	USMT_FAILED_MIGSTARTUP	A minimum of 250 MB of free space is required for temporary files	Verify that the system meets the minimum temporary disk space requirement of 250 MB. As a workaround, you can set the environment variable USMT_WORKING_DIR=<path> to redirect the temporary files working directory.
		Another process is preventing migration; only one migration tool can run at a time	Check the ScanState log file for migration .xml file errors.
		Failed to start main processing, look in log for system errors or check the installation	Check the ScanState log file for migration .xml file errors.
		Migration failed because of an XML error; look in the log for specific details	Check the ScanState log file for migration .xml file errors.
		Unable to automatically map the drive letters to match the online drive letter layout; use /offline to provide a mapping table	Check the ScanState log file for migration .xml file errors.
31	USMT_UNABLE_FINDMIGUNITS	An error occurred during the discover phase; the log should have more specific information	Check the ScanState log file for migration .xml file errors.
32	USMT_FAILED_SETMIGRATIONTYPE	An error occurred processing the migration system	Check the ScanState log file for migration .xml file errors, or use online help by typing /? on the command line.
33	USMT_UNABLE_READKEY	Error accessing the file specified by the /keyfile parameter	Check the ScanState log file for migration .xml file errors, or use online help by typing /? on the command line.
		The encryption key must have at least one character	Check the ScanState log file for migration .xml file errors, or use online help by typing /? on the command line.

34	USMT_ERROR_INSUFFICIENT_RIGHTS	Directory removal requires elevated privileges	Log on as Administrator, and run with elevated privileges.
		No rights to create user profiles	Log on as Administrator, and run with elevated privileges.
		No rights to read or delete user profiles	Log on as Administrator, and run with elevated privileges.
35	USMT_UNABLE_DELETE_STORE	A reboot is required to remove the store	Reboot to delete any files that could not be deleted when the command was executed.
		A store path can't be used because it contains data that could not be overwritten	A migration store could not be deleted. If you are using a hard-link migration store, you might have a locked file in it. You should manually delete the store, or use `usmtutils /rd` command to delete the store.
		There was an error removing the store	Review the ScanState log or LoadState log for details about command-line errors.
36	USMT_ERROR_UNSUPPORTED_PLATFORM	Compliance check failure; please check the logs for details	Investigate whether there is an active temporary profile on the system.
		Use of `/offline` is not supported during apply	The `/offline` command was not used while running in the Windows PE.
		Use `/offline` to run gather on this platform	The `/offline` command was not used while running in Windows PE.
37	USMT_ERROR_NO_INVALID_KEY	The store holds encrypted data but the correct encryption key was not provided	Verify that you have included the correct encryption `/key` or `/keyfile`.
38	USMT_ERROR_CORRUPTED_NOTENCRYPTED_STORE	An error occurred during store access	Review the ScanState log or LoadState log for details about command-line errors. Make sure that the store path is accessible and that the proper permission levels are set.
39	USMT_UNABLE_TO_READ_CONFIG_FILE	Error reading `Config.xml`	Review the ScanState log or LoadState log for details about command-line errors in the `Config.xml` file.
		File argument is invalid for `/config`	Check the command line you used to load the `Config.xml` file. You can use online help by typing `/?` on the command line.
40	USMT_ERROR_UNABLE_CREATE_PROGRESS_LOG	Error writing to the progress log	The progress log could not be created. Verify that the location is valid and that you have write access.
		Progress log argument is invalid for `/progress`	The progress log could not be created. Verify that the location is valid and that you have write access.
41	USMT_PREFLIGHT_FILE_CREATION_FAILED	Can't overwrite existing file	The progress log could not be created. Verify that the location is valid and that you have write access.
		Invalid space estimate path. Check the parameters and/or file system permissions	Review the ScanState log or LoadState log for details about command-line errors.
42	USMT_ERROR_CORRUPTED_STORE	The store contains one or more corrupted files	Review the UsmtUtils log for details about the corrupted files. For information on how to extract the files that are not corrupted, learn how to **Extract Files from a Compressed USMT Migration Store** at `https://technet.microsoft.com/en-in/library/hh824962.aspx`.
61	USMT_MIGRATION_STOPPED_NONFATAL	Processing stopped due to an I/O error	USMT exited but can continue with the `/c` command-line option, with the optional configurable `<ErrorControl>` section or by using the `/vsc` command-line option.

71	USMT_INIT_OPERATING_ENVIRON MENT_FAILED	A Windows Win32 API error occurred	Data transfer has begun, and there was an error during the creation of migration store or during the apply phase. Review the ScanState log or LoadState log for details.
		An error occurred when attempting to initialize the diagnostic mechanisms such as the log	Data transfer has begun, and there was an error during the creation of migration store or during the apply phase. Review the ScanState log or LoadState log for details.
		Failed to record diagnostic information	Data transfer has begun, and there was an error during the creation of migration store or during the apply phase. Review the ScanState log or LoadState log for details.
		Unable to start. Make sure you are running USMT with elevated privileges	Exit USMT and log in again with elevated privileges.
72	USMT_UNABLE_DOMIGRATION	An error occurred closing the store	Data transfer has begun, and there was an error during migration store creation or during the apply phase. Review the ScanState log or LoadState log for details.
		An error occurred in the apply process	Data transfer has begun, and there was an error during migration store creation or during the apply phase. Review the ScanState log or LoadState log for details.
		An error occurred in the gather process	Data transfer has begun, and there was an error during migration store creation or during the apply phase. Review the ScanState log or LoadState log for details.
		Out of disk space while writing the store	Data transfer has begun, and there was an error during migration store creation or during the apply phase. Review the ScanState log or LoadState log for details.
		Out of temporary disk space on the local system	Data transfer has begun, and there was an error during migration store creation or during the apply phase. Review the ScanState log or LoadState log for details.

GUI wrappers for USMT

USMT does not provide any GUI for its three command-line tools. Additionally, USMT command-line input can be very complex. There are many third-party GUI frontends available on the Internet, and also commercial products incorporating the USMT engine. I will pick some of the GUI frontends you should have a closer look at:

- **USMTGUI** (`http://usmtgui.ehler.dk/`): A very powerful *one window GUI* for USMT. Newer versions of USMTGUI are now *Donation ware*. Depending how much you donate, you will get the basic or the pro version. The new pro version is now also able to handle all advanced USMT features for offline migration.
- **Workstation Migration Assistant** (`http://dcunningham.net/applications/workstation-migration-assistant/`): This nice looking UI was written by Dan Cunningham and is now open source, and the source code is available on GitHub. It is highly customizable so you can adapt it to your needs.

Windows 10

All the concepts shown in this chapter are still valid for Windows 10, but please pay attention to following compatibility matrix:

	Destination OS					
Source OS	Windows XP	Windows Vista	Windows 7	Windows 8	Windows 8.1	Windows 10
Windows XP	USMT 3	USMT 3, 4	USMT 4, 5	USMT 5	Not supported	Not supported
Windows Vista	Not supported	USMT 3, 4	USMT 4, 5	USMT 5	Not supported	USMT 10
Windows 7	Not supported	Not supported	USMT 4, 5, 6.3, 6.3 Update, 10	USMT 5, 6.3, 6.3 Update, 10	USMT 6.3, 6.3 Update, 10	USMT 10
Windows 8	Not supported	Not supported	Not supported	USMT 5, 6.3, 6.3 Update, 10	USMT 6.3, 6.3 Update, 10	USMT 10
Windows 8.1	Not supported	Not supported	Not supported	Not supported	USMT 6.3, 6.3 Update, 10	USMT 10

Windows 10	Not supported	Not supported	Not supported	Not supported	Not supported	USMT 10

Here:

USMT 3-Windows Vista (MSI download)

USMT 4-Windows 7 AIK

USMT 5-Windows 8 ADK

USMT 6.3-Windows 8.1 RTM ADK (6.3.9600.16384)

USMT 6.3 Update-Windows 8.1 Update ADK (6.3.9600.17029)

USMT 10-Windows 10 ADK

Note: Always use the Windows 10 ADK version of USMT that matches the OS release (that is, 1507 ADK version with Win10 1507, 1511 ADK version with Win10 1511, and so on.)

Summary

In this chapter we have learned how to utilize the USMT. We showed which benefits and drawbacks this solution provides. By talking about best practices and looking at third-party GUI extensions and troubleshooting tips you should be able to incorporate USMT well in your environment.

In the next chapter we will have a deeper look into troubleshooting in MDT itself.

9
Troubleshooting Deployment Logs

In the previous chapter, we discussed how to migrate user data. Now it is time to discuss what to do when things go wrong or do not deliver the expected results.

The Windows deployment process contains many moving targets—scripts, tools, utilities, and other stuff are brought together for a complete end-to-end deployment process. In a perfect world, all of these things would work perfectly and there would be no need to troubleshoot.

However, as you may already realize, perfection is hard to achieve and will probably never be achieved. This means that we will need to do some troubleshooting.

In this chapter, we'll discuss which logs we should look at if the deployment fails. We will give a summary of the logs you will be most concerned with when troubleshooting a failed OS deployment via Microsoft Deployment Toolkit 2013. We will show some common error codes and how to solve them.

We will also discuss frequent pitfalls and common mistakes and how to circumvent or avoid them, and we will give tips about how to troubleshoot effectively.

Delving into Windows logs

During the operating system deployment process, several logs are created. Depending on what portion of setup phase we are talking about, the location of the logs will move around to different paths and drive letters.

Starting point for troubleshooting basic operating system deployment errors is usually the main `setupact.log` file. This log keeps track of everything that happens during the deployment process.

Whereas, `setuperr.log` only contains error entries from the main log file. Very often you will need the information lines before and after the error occurred in order to determine the root cause. So, `setuperr.log` should be seen as an *indicator* and cannot be used standalone. If its file size is larger than 0 bytes, take a look at `setupact.log`:

Whenever possible, you should grab the whole `Panther` directory. This is typically found under `C:\Windows\Panther`, including all subdirectories. This directory is often referenced as *the Panther logs*. The `Panther` log directory will contain all logs for specialize, OOBE, and Sysprep phases.

```
2013-10-02 11:34:47, Info              CONX   installprep.exe: Started Logging ...
2013-10-02 11:34:47, Info   [0x090008] PANTHR CBlackboard::Open: C:\$WINDOWS.~BT\Sources\Panther\installinfo succeeded.
2013-10-02 11:34:47, Info              CONX   installprep.exe Launched from G:\Sources
2013-10-02 11:34:47, Info              CONX   Initialized Sources Folder = C:\$WINDOWS.~BT\Sources
2013-10-02 11:34:47, Info              CONX   Initialized Panther Folder = C:\$WINDOWS.~BT\Sources\Panther
2013-10-02 11:34:47, Info              CONX   Initialized Setup DU Folder = C:\$WINDOWS.~BT\DUDownload\Setup
2013-10-02 11:34:47, Info              CONX   Initialized Blackboard C:\$WINDOWS.~BT\Sources\Panther\installinfo
2013-10-02 11:34:47, Info              CONX   Install pkg location G:\Sources\install.wim
2013-10-02 11:34:47, Info              CONX   CSetupFileCopier::CopySetupFiles: start copying setup files
2013-10-02 11:34:47, Info              CONX   CSetupFileCopier::GenerateCopyListFromConfigFile: Number of file names found: 113
2013-10-02 11:34:47, Info              CONX   CSetupFileCopier::GenerateCopyListFromConfigFile: Number of folder names found: 6
2013-10-02 11:34:51, Info              CONX   CSetupFileCopier::CopySetupFiles: successfully complete copying setup files
2013-10-02 11:34:51, Info              CONX   Command line arguments stored to BB --
2013-10-02 11:34:51, Info              CONX   Command line to use to launch install:  /downlevel
2013-10-02 11:34:51, Info   [0x090009] PANTHR CBlackboard::Close: c:\$windows.~bt\sources\panther\installinfo.
2013-10-02 11:34:51, Info              CONX   Launching C:\$WINDOWS.~BT\Sources\install.exe  /downlevel
2013-10-02 11:34:51, Info              CONX   install.exe: Started Logging ...
2013-10-02 11:34:51, Info   [0x090008] PANTHR CBlackboard::Open: C:\$WINDOWS.~BT\Sources\Panther\installinfo succeeded.
2013-10-02 11:34:51, Info              CONX   InitializeWorkingDirectory: Successfully initialized working directory
2013-10-02 11:34:51, Info              CONX                     Running Mode = 1
2013-10-02 11:34:51, Info              CONX                     ~BT Directory = C:\$WINDOWS.~BT
2013-10-02 11:34:51, Info              CONX                     Working Directory = C:\$WINDOWS.~BT\Sources\Panther
2013-10-02 11:34:51, Info              CONX                     Logging Directory = C:\$WINDOWS.~BT\Sources\Panther
2013-10-02 11:34:51, Info              CONX                     Setup DU Directory = C:\$WINDOWS.~BT\DUDownload\Setup
2013-10-02 11:34:51, Info              CONX                     Driver DU Directory = C:\$WINDOWS.~BT\DUDownload\Drivers
2013-10-02 11:34:51, Info              CONX                     Component DU Directory = C:\$WINDOWS.~BT\DUDownload\Components
2013-10-02 11:34:51, Info              CONX   Command line parameters: /downlevel
2013-10-02 11:34:51, Info              CONX   CSetupLangIniLoader::Initialize: LANG.INI Directory = C:\$WINDOWS.~BT\Sources
2013-10-02 11:34:51, Info              CONX   CSetupLangIniLoader::Initialize: Language Pack Root = ..\Langpacks
2013-10-02 11:34:51, Info              CONX   CSetupLangIniLoader::Initialize: 1 languages found.
2013-10-02 11:34:51, Info              CONX   CSetupLangIniLoader::Initialize: Adding language: index: 0
```

Snippet from a setupact.log

The described Windows logs are plain text files starting with date and time and an `Info,` `Warning,` or `Error` indicator. When something is critical, it is additionally marked with `!!!`. Always look for the first encounter of an error, as most other errors are *following errors* caused by the first one. From the position of the first error, look around for surrounding Warnings.

Here is a summary of the most useful logs created on the client during deployment process. Dig into these log files first to get an impression what was going wrong.

The Client Log files are mentioned in the following table:

Log file:	`setupact.log`
Description:	This is the main log file written by the operating system installation process. This log keeps track of everything that happens during the deployment process. This is useful for investigating failed installations. For more details, refer to `http://support.microsoft.com/kb/927521.`
Path(s):	`C:\$WINDOWS.~BT\Sources\Panther` (early migration phase) `X:\$WINDOWS.~BT\Sources\Panther` (in Windows PE phase) `C:\Windows\Panther` (for specialize phase) `C:\Windows\Panther\UnattendGC` (for OOBE phase) `C:\Windows\System32\Sysprep\Panther` (for Sysprep phase)
Log file:	`setuperr.log`
Description:	This is the log file containing only error entries from the main log file. Very often you will need the info lines before and after the error occurred in order to determine the root cause. This is useful as an indicator: if >0 bytes, take a look at `setupact.log.`
Path(s):	`C:\$WINDOWS.~BT\Sources\Panther` (early migration phase) `X:\$WINDOWS.~BT\Sources\Panther` (in Windows PE phase) `C:\Windows\Panther` (for specialize phase) `C:\Windows\Panther\UnattendGC` (for OOBE phase) `C:\Windows\System32\Sysprep\Panther` (for Sysprep phase)
Log file:	`CBS.log`
Description:	This is the log file containing details for servicing operations executed by the servicing stack. This is helpful for analyzing file mismatch and corrupted files.
Path(s):	`C:\Windows\Logs\CBS`

Log file:	`dism.log`
Description:	This is the log file containing all DISM command results that are executed during the installation process. Use this log file for issues with security update installation, language pack installation, driver injection, and so on.
Path(s):	`C:\Windows\Logs\DISM`

Log file:	`setupapi.app.log` **and** `setupapi.dev.log`
Description:	These are the log files containing all PnP device driver installation details during the installation process. This is useful for failed driver installations and determining what drivers were used for which device. If you encounter very long setup time during detection and configuration of devices phase, take a closer look at lines starting with `Error` or `!!!`.
Path(s):	`X:\Windows\Inf` (drivers loaded in Windows PE phase) `C:\Windows\Inf`

Log file:	`netsetup.log`
Description:	This is the log file containing all domain join attempts and the result of each attempt. This file contains all domain join details that were specified (except password). This is useful for troubleshooting domain join issues.
Path(s):	`C:\Windows\Debug`

Log file:	`WindowsUpdate.log`
Description:	This is the log file containing details related to software update installation. This is useful for determining the source that was used (Windows Update, WSUS, or SCCM), which updates where detected and downloaded, and so on.
Path(s):	`C:\Windows`

Log file:	`wpeinit.log`
Description:	This is the log file containing details about the Windows PE initialization process. This is useful for analyzing PE network initialization issues, slow start up times of PE, and failed commands during PE initialization. If Windows PE does not reboot automatically, look for hanging/failed commands during Init.
Path(s):	`X:\Windows\System32` (in Windows PE phase)

If you are using a Windows server-based **Windows Deployment Services** (**WDS**), you should also take a look into the following file created on the server when WDS / PXE is failing.

The Server Log file is explained in the following table:

Log file:	`wdsserver.log`
Description:	This is the log file containing details about all PXE requests and multicast transmissions processed by WDS. This log has to be enabled on the server, as it is disabled by default. Details on how to enable it in the different WDS server versions can be found at `http://support.microsoft.com/kb/936625`.
Path(s):	`C:\Windows\Tracing`

Microsoft deployment toolkit logs and task sequencer logs

Each MDT script creates its own individual log file during execution. These log files normally match the script name (for example, `ZTIGather.log`, `ZTIDiskpart.log`, and so on) or begin with the script name (for example, `ZTIConfigureDHCP_DISM.log`). Additionally, each script writes to the common `BDD.log`. The information written to both log files is the same; so normally, it is okay to just take a look at the aggregated `BDD.log` as it contains everything needed.

The position of `BDD.log` and individual script logs changes several times during the deployment process. During the Windows PE phase, when there is no partition accessible/existing, the log file will be hosted under `X:\MININT\SMSOSD\OSDLOGS`. As soon as partition is accessible/created, logs will be transferred to `C:\MININT\SMSOSD\OSDLOGS`. MDT copies the scripts without deleting the logs in the old location, so make sure to view at the newest/up-to-date copy of the logs.

After completion of LiteTouch, log files are copied to `C:\Windows\Temp\DeploymentLogs`. The `BDD.log` file is also copied to a network location at the end of the deployment if the SLShare variable is defined in `CustomSettings.ini`.

Another important log file, `SMSTS.log`, is used by the task sequencer of MDT. This log file is useful for verifying the evaluation of conditions and investigating the failed task sequence step, especially when no other log was written. For example, if the script name was not correct. `SMSTS.log` is typically stored in `%TEMP%\SMSTSLog` (during Windows PE phase) or in `C:\_SMSTaskSequence\Logs` (or in some rare cases, under `X:\SMSTSLog` `/C:\SMSTSLog`).

Unfortunately, the BDD log format is designed to be read by Trace32 (used with SMS 2003 and SCCM 2007) or CMTrace (used with SCCM 2012 and higher versions). Although you can view the logs with Notepad, we strongly recommend using this tool to read the log whenever possible, as it makes it not only more readable, but also highlights errors and warnings. Lines containing the word `Warning` will be highlighted in yellow and lines containing the word `Error` are highlighted in red. Additionally, Trace32 and CMTrace can easily calculate elapsed time when marking two or more entries.

Here is an example of `BDD.log` opened in Notepad. It's quite unreadable if you are not familiar to the XML style:

```
<![LOG[Waiting for Drive to Exist: 100%]LOG]!><time="11:39:04.000+000" date="04-04-2015" component="ZTIDiskpart" context="" type="1"
thread="" file="ZTIDiskpart">
<![LOG[ZTI ERROR - Unhandled error returned by ZTIDiskpart: Object required (424)]LOG]!><time="11:39:04.000+000" date="04-04-2015"
component="ZTIDiskpart" context="" type="3" thread="" file="ZTIDiskpart">
<![LOG[Property LogPath is now = X:\MININT\SMSOSD\OSDLOGS]LOG]!><time="11:39:04.000+000" date="04-04-2015" component="LiteTouch"
context="" type="1" thread="" file="LiteTouch">
<![LOG[Command completed, return code = -2147467259]LOG]!><time="11:39:04.000+000" date="04-04-2015" component="LiteTouch" context=""
type="1" thread="" file="LiteTouch">
<![LOG[Litetouch deployment failed, Return Code = -2147467259  0x80004005]LOG]!><time="11:39:04.000+000" date="04-04-2015"
component="LiteTouch" context="" type="3" thread="" file="LiteTouch">
<![LOG[For more information, consult the task sequencer log ...\SMSTS.LOG.]LOG]!><time="11:39:04.000+000" date="04-04-2015"
component="LiteTouch" context="" type="1" thread="" file="LiteTouch">
<![LOG[Property RetVal is now = -2147467259]LOG]!><time="11:39:04.000+000" date="04-04-2015" component="LiteTouch" context="" type="1"
thread="" file="LiteTouch">
<![LOG[Unable to copy log to the network as no SLShare value was specified.]LOG]!><time="11:39:04.000+000" date="04-04-2015"
component="LiteTouch" context="" type="1" thread="" file="LiteTouch">
<![LOG[CleanStartItems Complete]LOG]!><time="11:39:05.000+000" date="04-04-2015" component="LiteTouch" context="" type="1" thread=""
file="LiteTouch">
<![LOG[TSCore.dll not found, not unregistering.]LOG]!><time="11:39:05.000+000" date="04-04-2015" component="LiteTouch" context="" type="1"
thread="" file="LiteTouch">
<![LOG[About to run command: wscript.exe "X:\Deploy\Scripts\LTICleanup.wsf"]LOG]!><time="11:39:05.000+000" date="04-04-2015"
component="LiteTouch" context="" type="1" thread="" file="LiteTouch">
<![LOG[Microsoft Deployment Toolkit version: <VERSION>]LOG]!><time="11:39:05.000+000" date="04-04-2015" component="LTICleanup" context=""
type="1" thread="" file="LTICleanup">
<![LOG[Removing AutoAdminLogon registry entries]LOG]!><time="11:39:05.000+000" date="04-04-2015" component="LTICleanup" context=""
type="1" thread="" file="LTICleanup">
<![LOG[VSSMaxSize not specified using 5% of volume.]LOG]!><time="11:39:05.000+000" date="04-04-2015" component="LTICleanup" context=""
type="1" thread="" file="LTICleanup">
<![LOG[Property definition is now = Summary_Definition_ENU.xml]LOG]!><time="11:39:06.000+000" date="04-04-2015" component="Wizard"
context="" type="1" thread="" file="Wizard">
```

BDD.log viewed in Notepad

When opening the same `BDD.log` inside CMTrace, it is instantly formatted and much more readable. With the error/warning highlighting, you easily see if something is going wrong, and CMTrace has the possibility to autoscroll, so you can read logs live:

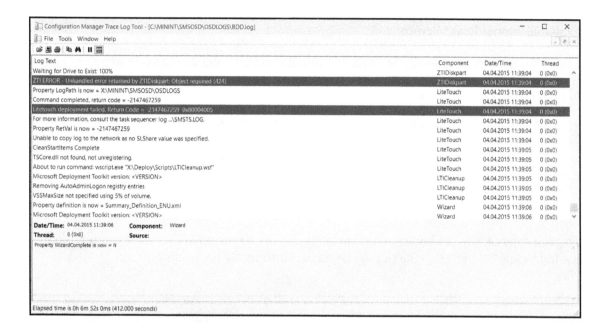

BDD.log viewed in CMTrace

Getting CMTrace

`Trace32.exe` is part of the Microsoft SCCM 2007 Toolkit. However, `Trace32.exe` is an x86 binary, so it cannot be used directly on a x64 Windows PE environment, as it has no WoW emulation. There is also a `Trace64.exe` x64 native binary, but is (officially) only available internally at Microsoft.

However, with the release of Microsoft SCCM 2012 Toolkit, things changed. The toolkit includes the new `CMTrace.exe`, which is an x86/x64 dual binary. The x64 part is a little bit hidden inside the x86 executable.

To get a x64 version, you need to download System Center 2012 R2 Configuration Manager Toolkit (`https://www.microsoft.com/en-us/download/details.aspx?id=50012`) and install the Client Based Tools on a x64 OS. When executing `CMTrace.exe` (located in `C:\Program Files(x86)\ConfigMgr 2012 Toolkit R2\ClientTools\`), the process will create a dynamically named temporary x64 file in `%TEMP%` and execute this `CMTrace_amd64.exe` image.

To get a copy of this x64 binary, view the `CMTrace.exe` process in Process Explorer. Note the following `TRAD85.tmp` file (it may be named differently on your system):

⊟ 🗐 CMTrace.exe	15184	608 K	3.196 K Configuration Manager Trac...	Microsoft Corporation
🗋 TRAD85.tmp	2920	1.324 K	6.328 K CMTrace_amd64.exe	Microsoft Corporation

Look at the properties of the `.tmp` file, as shown in the following image:

Get a copy of this file, rename it to, for example, `CMTrace64.exe` and enjoy. This version is also usable on x64 Windows PE.

Clearing a failed (dirty) MDT deployment

BDD.log and SMSTS.log are the *brain* of MDT. After each reboot, MDT tries to resume with the next step/action in the task sequence. If your task sequence failed, and you start a new try with remaining parts of MININT and _SMSTaskSequence directory, the results will be unpredictable.

In MDT versions prior to MDT 2013 (such as 2012 Update 1), this cleanup needs to be done manually. A lot of tips state using diskpart clean. However, if you want to preserve the other data/files/settings, this is not a good idea. Also, it needs a reboot after cleaning.

With MDT 2013, a dirty environment detection with modal dialog was introduced:

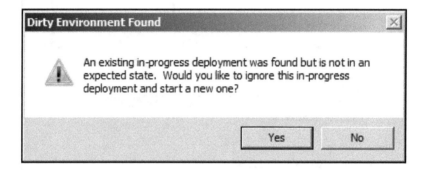

After clicking on **Yes**, Microsoft Deployment Toolkit will clean the old parts and start a new run.

Especially during the test lab phase, but possibly also later in the productive environment phase for highly automating the process (Zero Touch) you do not want to get stuck on this mentioned modal dialog. It is as well a good idea to automatically get rid of all old parts of a former task sequence before making a new installation attempt.

However, you cannot easily delete both folders every time you start the PE, as you will need it in the case of capturing the final image from PE. Here is a sample script to clean up with checking the condition of an applied PE for capturing phase. Hook this script to your Unattend.xml.

The sample cleanup script is as follows:

```
Option Explicit
Dim objWso,objFso
Set objWso = WScript.CreateObject("Wscript.Shell")
Set objFso = CreateObject("Scripting.FileSystemObject")
If objFso.FileExists("C:\Sources\boot.wim") Or
  objFso.FileExists("D:\Sources\boot.wim") Or
  objFso.FileExists("E:\Sources\boot.wim") Then
  ' We are running with integrated PE = WIM creating mode = do nothing
Else
  ' We are in deployment mode first boot = wipe MININT and _SMSTaskSequence
  If objFso.FolderExists("C:\MININT") Then
    On Error Resume Next
    objFso.DeleteFolder "C:\MININT", True
    On Error Goto 0
  End If
  If objFso.FolderExists("D:\MININT") Then
    On Error Resume Next
    objFso.DeleteFolder "D:\MININT", True
    On Error Goto 0
  End If
  If objFso.FolderExists("E:\MININT") Then
    On Error Resume Next
    objFso.DeleteFolder "E:\MININT", True
    On Error Goto 0
  End If
  If objFso.FolderExists("C:\_SMSTaskSequence") Then
    On Error Resume Next
    objFso.DeleteFolder "C:\_SMSTaskSequence", True
    On Error Goto 0
  End If
  If objFso.FolderExists("D:\_SMSTaskSequence") Then
    On Error Resume Next
    objFso.DeleteFolder "D:\_SMSTaskSequence", True
    On Error Goto 0
  End If
  If objFso.FolderExists("E:\_SMSTaskSequence") Then
    On Error Resume Next
    objFso.DeleteFolder "E:\_SMSTaskSequence", True
    On Error Goto 0
  End If
End If

Set objFso = Nothing
Set objWso = Nothing
```

Run this script every time you start up your PE environment by linking it to `Unattend.xml` in the root directory:

```
<RunSynchronousCommand wcm:action="add">
    <Description>Wipe MININT if needed</Description>
    <Order>1</Order>
    <Path>cscript.exe X:\WipeMININT.vbs</Path>
</RunSynchronousCommand>
<RunSynchronousCommand wcm:action="add">
    <Description>Lite Touch PE</Description>
    <Order>2</Order>
    <Path>wscript.exe X:\Deploy\Scripts\LiteTouch.wsf /Cleanstart</Path>
</RunSynchronousCommand>
```

Look up error codes

Error codes are numbers (or letter and number combinations) that are associated with more or less helpful error messages. Translating these error codes to useful error messages is sometimes tricky. Let's shed some light onto this area.

Converting error codes:
Many error codes in the log files are presented in a hexadecimal order (recognizable by the leading `0x`). If you get, for example, `0x80070040`, look at the last four digits. Converting `0x40` (trailing zeroes are dropped) to decimal will get a 64 Error. To translate the error code in a meaningful text, open a command prompt and type the following:
net helpmsg 64
This will get you the following extended help text:
The specified network name is no longer available.
If you don't want to translate the error code manually, you can use a command-line tool, Microsoft Exchange Server Error Code Look-up utility. You can find this utility in the Microsoft Download Center (`http:/ /www.microsoft.com/en-us/download/details.aspx?id=985`).

Beginning with Microsoft Deployment Toolkit 2013 Update 2, the rich documentation was changed to an online version. You will find `launch.htm` in the `Documentation` folder. This `launch.htm` is pointing to the corresponding TechNet pages. Within the Microsoft Deployment Toolkit documentation, there is a very detailed 56-page Troubleshooting Reference (`http://technet.microsoft.com/en-us/library/dn781088.aspx`) with multiple examples of problems with AutoLogon, BIOS, database connections, partitioning, PXE boot, and more and their solutions.

The MDT 2013 documentation can also be directly accessed at `https://technet.microso ft.com/en-us/library/dn781294.aspx`.

More than 40 common problems are described in detail and a possible solution is given.

The following is a sample from the Troubleshooting Reference document:

Lost Network Connections

- **Problem**: An installation may fail if it installs device drivers or alters device and network configurations. These changes may result in a lapse in network connectivity that causes the installation to fail.
- **Possible solution**: Implement the `ZTICacheUtil.vbs` script to enable download and execution for the installation. This script is designed to tweak the advertisement to enable download and execute. The download uses **Background Intelligent Transfer Service** (**BITS**) if the Configuration Manager distribution point is Web-based Distributed Authoring and Versioning and BITS enabled. At the same time, it modifies Configuration Manager to run the `ZTICache.vbs` script first, which makes sure the program does not delete itself during the deployment process.

It also includes a long table of error codes in numerical order and their description, but with no further information/help/solution.

To help with this issue, Michael Niehaus wrote a document called Troubleshooting Windows Deployments 2012-09-11.pdf in September 2012. Download from his blog at `http ://blogs.technet.com/b/mniehaus/archive/2012/09/11/troubleshooting-wind ows-deployments-take-2.aspx`. He also announces if there will be a newer version of this document on his blog. Even though this document was originally written for MDT 2012, most parts are still valid for 2013.

This document contains an approximately 40-page table with all return codes, the script that it is normally raising, the original error message, and troubleshooting suggestions. Additionally, each of these errors are rated on two categories on scales from 0 to 10, representing the Likelihood (where 0 stands for `highly unlikely`, up to 10 for `very common`) and Quality is the error that is self-explanatory or make little sense without further explanation (where 0 stands for `useless message` and 10 for `nothing to add, all explained`).

Although Michael Niehaus gave me permission to use/copy his troubleshooting document for this book, adding this table would not only blast the length of this chapter, but also not be very readable/searchable. Having it in digital PDF format makes it easier to look the return code very fast. So I'm adding only one sample to give you a teaser of what to expect from this document.

The following is a sample from Michael Niehaus' document:

Return code	Script	Error Message	Likely?	Quality	Troubleshooting Suggestions
5212	LiteTouch.wsf	Welcome wizard failed or was cancelled	10	5	This is normal if you cancel the LiteTouch welcome wizard (the initial wizard that shows up in Windows PE unless you set `SkipWizard=YES`). But it also might mean that the wizard crashed. You can't really tell the difference though. (The wizard sets a variable `WizardComplete` to `Y` when it succeeds. The error means `WizardComplete` wasn't set to `Y`.) You might also see this message show up in the log file for the next task sequence executed on the computer because of a left-over `BDD.log` found on the computer in the `C:\MININT` folder structure. This is harmless, but will result in a yellow summary screen at the end of the deployment.

Common errors and frequent pitfalls

Beside these two mentioned good troubleshooting documents (I'm sure there are more documents that are worth mentioning, but space is limited, and I want to share my findings with you), there are some more common errors to add.

Deployment stop during applying patches offline

During deployment task sequence at the Apply patches / Install Updates offline step, installation is failing and you get error message and deployment stops.

Possible solution: Some patches/hotfixes cannot be applied offline due to pending file actions. Identify the blocking patch by reviewing `dism.log` and `CBS.log`. Select/review first patch with error, as other error messages could be after effects. After applying such a pending action patch, following installations of patches can be prevented until the system is booted once.

To avoid this scenario, a `/PreventPending` option was introduced to `DISM.exe` to skip the installation of the package if the package or Windows image has pending online actions. This option can only be used when servicing Windows 8, Windows Server 2012, or Windows PE 4.0 and newer images. So there is no automatic prevention for Windows 7/Server 2008 R2 and older systems. If you identified the patch that caused the error, and you need this patch integrated into your image before first boot up, you need to create a patched reference image by running a full deployment, patching, Sysprep, and capture sequence. Otherwise, just remove the patch from offline apply folder and move it to the Windows Update step (use of WSUS recommended).

Dirty environment found during Windows Update before or after the application step

During deployment task sequence at the Windows Update step, you get the Dirty Environment found error message after reboot/applying patches.

Possible solution: Your deployment was possibly broken by a multi-reboot update. Microsoft is maintaining a regularly updated list (`https://support.microsoft.com/en-us/kb/2894518/`). Review your `WindowsUpdate.log` and `CBS.log` to identify the last patches installed before reboot. If one of these patches is mentioned in the KB, exclude this patch (it can only be done if controlled by WSUS) or apply it offline.

The Dirty Environment found error message during installation of software and the HideShell=YES option used

During deployment task sequence at the Installing Software step, you get the Dirty Environment found error message without seeing a reboot. The `HideShell=YES` option is used.

Possible solution: Your deployment was possibly broken by an installation routine that tried to restart `Explorer.exe`. The `HideShell=YES` parameter is preventing `UserInit` `/Explorer.exe` to start and presenting a desktop/Start menu. When the installation routine is trying to restart the Shell by killing and restarting `Explorer.exe`, it is triggering *Dirty Environment* as MDT does not expect a running `Explorer.exe`, execution of all startup scripts, and so on. As a quick workaround in Windows 7, you can try `HideShell=NO`, but it lacks the hidden desktop. For Windows 8 and 8.1, `HideShell=YES` is mandatory. Therefore, in this case or when you don't want to show desktop or give the user possibility to interact with the system before the installation is finished, you need to contact the vendor of the software to request a fixed/updated version of its product. (Also, restarting `Explorer.exe` is a quick and dirty solution and should be avoided.)

Your customized Windows PE image boots only from PXE/USB, but not from CD-ROM

Starting your Windows PE image by PXE/WDS server or from an USB drive works as expected. However, on the same hardware, the same Windows PE image hangs on boot when ISO is burned to a CD-R and started from a CD-ROM or DVD-ROM drive.

Possible solution: Your customized Windows PE image was broken by a faulty/conflicting chipset or storage driver. Also, this is very often seen when using an outdated driver not optimized for this OS version (for example, using a Windows 7 only driver on a Windows PE 5.0 = Windows 8.1). If you are building a PE 4.0 or higher version, try to remove all storage drivers as most of the actual hardware is already covered by Out-of-Box Drivers of these newer WinPE. If you still need your storage driver, try to only integrate one version of this driver (avoid integrating, for example, Intel RST 12.x and Intel RST 13.x, as they possibly use the same SYS driver filenames and get in conflict).

Your customized Windows PE image boots from USB but then fails to find scripts and/or content

Your customized Windows PE image boots from USB. As soon as it tries to access scripts, you see an error message similar to `Please reinsert the media (CD, DVD, or USB) needed to complete the deployment.` or `A connection to the deployment share xxxxxxxx could not be made.` The drive letter `X:` is missing.

Possible solution: This is very similar to PE 3.0, but in rare cases, is also seen on newer PE versions when using an USB 3.0 drive in an USB 3.0-capable USB port without adding suitable USB drivers to the PE image:

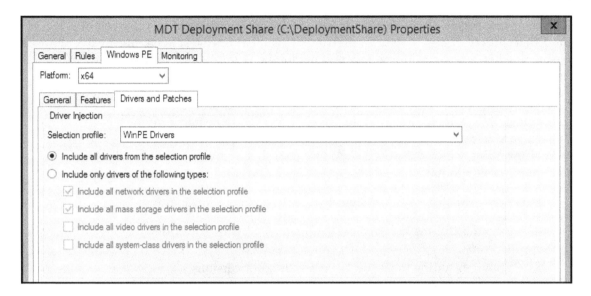

By default, only network drivers and **mass storage drivers** are included to PE. Even adding the **system class drivers** selection will not help in all cases. This is caused by different classification of USB 3.0 drivers depending on the vendor. So, even if you include the drivers in your example WinPE selection profile directories, the drivers are not considered by MDT as long as you do not select **Include all drivers from the selection profile**. Please do not use/change the default **All Drivers and Patches** selection profile before building your PE.

Be very careful with this setting, as it will try to include all the driver classes pointed to by the selection profile, also drivers known to break your PE due to incompatibility. Only add drivers that are absolutely needed to access the network share and your local drives. Don't add your example audio, modem, fingerprint, or similar drivers to your WinPE image.

After complete rebuild of Windows PE image, it is no longer loading correct driver or not working

During the integration of new hardware for faster creation of Windows PE, you have chosen only the default **Optimize the boot image updating process** option, maybe together with the **Compress the boot image contents to recover space used by removed or modified content** option. When transferring the content from test lab to productive share or next time when selecting **Completely regenerate the boot images**, your Windows PE is no longer working as expected and the drivers seem to malfunction.

Possible solution: When choosing the fast/optimized build process, only new files are added to the image. If you integrate multiple drivers using the same name for the SYS driver file, this will lead to problems, especially if you do not review the build warnings and ignore them. Depending which driver (version) was included first, this scenario will work or lead to unpredictable results.

To prevent this situation, you need to keep the following points in mind:

- Avoid including the driver if the device is already supported by Out-of-Box Drivers
- Avoid including the same driver in different versions
- Review not only build errors, but also build warnings carefully
- Periodically choose the **Completely regenerate the boot images** option, as shown in the following screenshot:

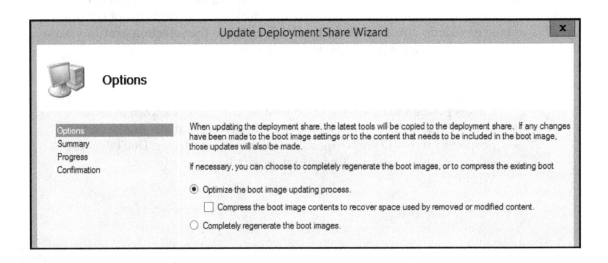

Task sequence Windows Update step cannot communicate with Windows Update Online due to the need of a proxy

When executing the task sequence Windows Update step, the update process comes back with the `8024402F` error. This is a very common error when the communication is blocked by proxy.

Possible solution: You need to set a proxy before executing the Windows Update step. This can easily be achieved by configuring the `ProxyServer (REG_SZ)`, `ProxyEnable (REG_DWORD)`, and `ProxyOverride (REG_SZ)` registry values under the `HKEY_CURRENT_USER\SOFTWARE\Microsoft\Windows\CurrentVersion\Internet Settings` hive. Don't forget to clean up the three values after successful patching/deployment. The Deployment Guys created a script back in the MDT 2010 times that is still usable and valid. You'll find the set and cleanup scripts at `http://blogs.tech net.com/b/deploymentguys/archive/2010/11/30/using-the-mdt-windows-updat e-tasks-in-image-engineering.aspx`.

Task sequence Windows Update step does not select minor updates, recommended updates, and trusted publisher certs

When executing the task sequence Windows Update step, the update process does not select minor updates, recommended updates, and trusted publisher certs.

Possible solution: You can force these updates by setting several regkeys under the `HKLM\SOFTWARE\Policies\Microsoft\Windows\WindowsUpdate\AU` hive. You need to activate `AutoInstallMinorUpdates`, `IncludeRecommendedUpdates`, and `AcceptTrustedPublisherCerts REG_DWORD`.

The following is a possible sample `LTIPrepareUpdates.wsf` script:

```
<job id="LTIPrepareUpdates">
  <script language="VBScript" src="ZTIUtility.vbs"/>
  <script language="VBScript" src="ZTIDataAccess.vbs"/>
  <script language="VBScript">
Option Explicit
RunNewInstance

Const SCRIPTVERSION = "1.0"

Class LTIPrepareUpdates

  Dim iRetVal,objWso,strSyscall

  Private Sub Class_Initialize
    Set objWso = WScript.CreateObject("WScript.Shell")
  End Sub

  Function Main
    oLogging.CreateEntry "Start LTIPrepareUpdates.wsf v" & _
      SCRIPTVERSION, LogTypeInfo

    ' Include Minor Updates
    oLogging.CreateEntry "Include Minor Updates", LogTypeInfo
    strSyscall = "cmd /c reg.exe add
      HKLM\SOFTWARE\Policies\Microsoft\Windows\WindowsUpdate\AU /v
        AutoInstallMinorUpdates /t REG_DWORD /d 1 /f"
    iRetVal = objWso.run(strSyscall,0,true)

    ' Include Recommended Updates
    oLogging.CreateEntry "Include Recommended Updates", LogTypeInfo
    strSyscall = "cmd /c reg.exe add
      HKLM\SOFTWARE\Policies\Microsoft\Windows\WindowsUpdate\AU /v
        IncludeRecommendedUpdates /t REG_DWORD /d 1 /f"
    iRetVal = objWso.run(strSyscall,0,true)

    ' Accept TrustedPublisher Certs
    oLogging.CreateEntry "Accept TrustedPublisher Certs", LogTypeInfo
    strSyscall = "cmd /c reg.exe add
      HKLM\SOFTWARE\Policies\Microsoft\Windows\WindowsUpdate /v
        AcceptTrustedPublisherCerts /t REG_DWORD /d 1 /f"
    iRetVal = objWso.run(strSyscall,0,true)

  End Function
End Class
    </script>
</job>
```

DiskPart fails with error – The parameter is incorrect

When partitioning DiskPart fails with the **DiskPart has encountered an error: The parameter is incorrect** error and deployment fails with 0x80004005:

Possible solution 1: This error can be caused by a faulty sector on drive. Run a complete disk check, including sector check by executing chkdsk /r.

Possible solution 2: A very common mistake is to use the same label twice during disk partitioning. Please check your DiskPart settings to have different labels for all partitions.

Getting a list of all available variables used in MDT / get all current values

When troubleshooting MDT issues, it is very helpful to get a list of all the available variables used / get all current values.

Possible solution: To get a list of all the available variables, you can use a SQL query when you connect your MDT environment to a SQL server. Click on the **Roles** subtab. Click on **New** and select **Details**. All the available variables will now be listed.

If you did not link your MDT environment to a SQL database, or you need current values of all the variables dumped, you need to use a small script. Michael Niehaus created two easy versions of the script: one in VBscript and the other in PowerShell: http://blogs.techne t.com/b/mniehaus/archive/2010/04/26/dumping-task-sequence-variables.asp x.

The following is a sample DumpVar.wsf script:

```
<job id="ZTIConnect">
  <script language="VBScript" src="ZTIUtility.vbs"/>
  <script language="VBScript">

  Set env = CreateObject("Microsoft.SMS.TSEnvironment")
  For each v in env.GetVariables
    oLogging.CreateEntry v & " = " & env(v), LogTypeInfo
  Next

  </script>
</job>
```

The following is a sample`DumpVar.ps1` script:

```
# Determine where to do the logging
$tsenv = New-Object -COMObject Microsoft.SMS.TSEnvironment
$logPath = $tsenv.Value("_SMSTSLogPath")
$logFile = "$logPath\$($myInvocation.MyCommand).log"

# Start the logging
Start-Transcript $logFile

# Write all the variables and their values
$tsenv.GetVariables() | % { Write-Host "$_ = $($tsenv.Value($_))" }

# Stop logging
Stop-Transcript
```

Further help

Now that you know how to locate more detailed error information in the logs, the following are some locations that you can use to search to find solutions for your issues:

- Ask the Core Team blogs on TechNet: `http://blogs.technet.com/b/askcore/`
- The Deployment Guys blogs on TechNet: `http://blogs.technet.com/b/deploymentguys/`
- The MDT Social Forums on TechNet: `http://social.technet.microsoft.com/Forums/en/mdt/threads`
- The Microsoft Deployment Toolkit homepage on TechNet: `https://technet.microsoft.com/en-us/windows/dn475741`

User state migration tool logs

To know more about user state migration tool logs you can refer to `Chapter 8`, *USMT – The User State Migration Tool*.

 Windows 10
All the concepts shown in this chapter are still valid for Windows 10. For errors during in-place upgrades, take a look at `C:\$Windows\~bt\sources\Panther`.

Summary

In this chapter, we gave you some insight and guidelines into troubleshooting, and helped you gather up as much experience as possible. This includes experiences around *standard* problems and specific problems and solutions, as well as techniques for getting to the root cause, even for uncommon issues that no one has seen before. Now it is up to you to get familiar with the logs and get trained in hunting down the root cause.

But most of us realize that "perfection" cannot be achieved. That means we will need to do troubleshooting. So how do you do this effectively? Well, there are really two ways:

- Learn through your own experiences.
- Learn through the experiences of others.

So which is the best? Neither, as you need to be able to do both. You want to leverage the experience of others while also learning how to investigate your own unique issues without depending on others to do it for you.

- Michael Niehaus in September 2012

However, don't become desperate with your problems; there is a very strong and powerful community around MDT with lots of helpful people. Additionally, as it is a fully supported product by Microsoft, you always have the possibility to open a case.

In the next chapter, we will discuss techniques for image validation in terms of quality gate, bad drivers, poor performance, and tools to use for this validation.

10
Validating the Image

In the previous chapter, we discussed how to troubleshoot deployment logs and deployment share operations:

- We looked at tools to decipher the MDT log files and error codes
- We discussed the locations of the log files and importance of the logs in general
- We also looked at a few common mistakes or errors that one might encounter in a standard MDT process

In this chapter, we will cover image validation scenarios:

- We will talk to different tools that can be used to validate the image
- We will check for bad drivers and poor performance and articulate the cost of purchasing lower-end hardware to the management
- We will determine the operational and performance costs of anti-malware, antivirus, and other security auditing software

While it is all well and good to have a universal hardware-agnostic image deployed by the task sequence that lays down applications based on input criteria, how do we know that once the image reaches the end user, it will perform well? Do we know that we have solid **Windows Hardware Quality Labs** (**WHQL**) drivers that don't have memory leaks or **Blue Screen of Death** (**BSOD**) scenarios in them? How do we know the antivirus and security software suite that we've chosen (or had mandated by the security team) isn't going to cause significant performance degradation; and if it did cause degradation, could we articulate it to the decision makers or vendor?

With the tools discussed in this chapter, you will be able to perform these tasks. First, we'll look at a built-in utility in Windows. Then we'll get into some free tools in the Windows ADK, namely, the **Windows Performance Toolkit** (**WPT**), **Windows Assessment Toolkit** (**WAT**), and the infrastructure-requiring **Windows Assessment Services** (**WAS**).

Driver Verifier

Driver Verifier (or `verifier.exe`) has been native to Windows since Vista and can be used to test particular drivers in Windows or test the entire image's hardware drivers for stability tests. It even inserts debugging information into the memory dumps that are generated by its tests to help pinpoint the root cause of a particular driver problem:

1. Driver Verifier is launched by simply typing `verifier` into an elevated command prompt:

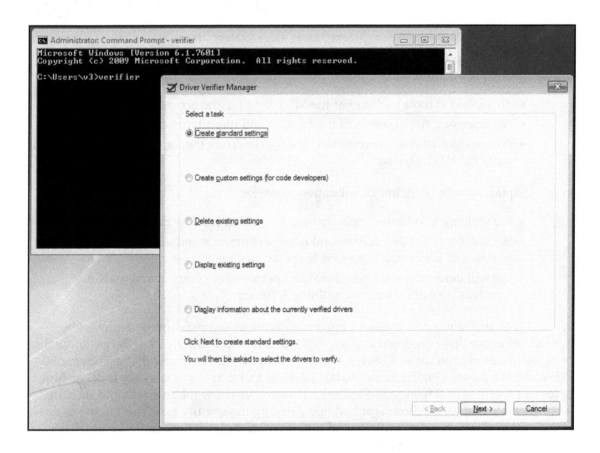

2. Testing a particular driver is as simple as selecting **Next** at **Create standard settings** and then setting the radio button to **Select driver names from a list**, as shown in the following screenshot:

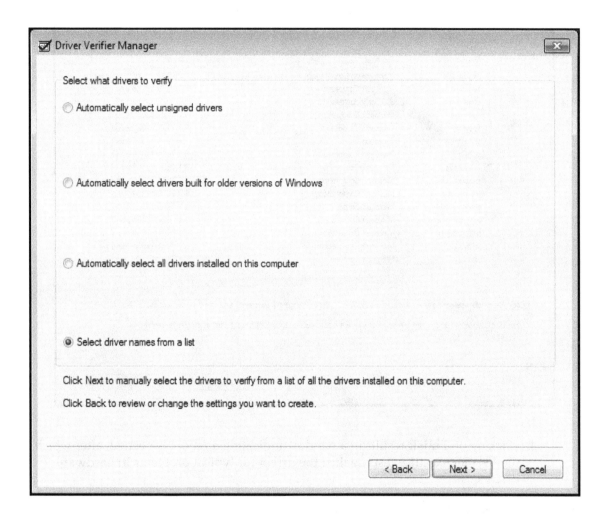

3. Then pick the driver(s) you want to test (in this case, **storport.sys**):

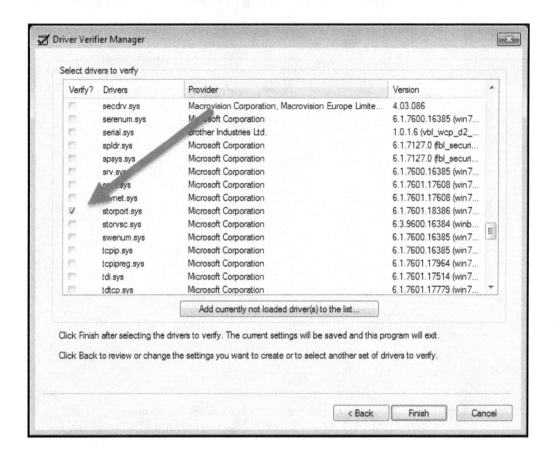

4. Clicking on **Finish** results in a window indicating a reboot is needed, after which, the Verifier executes tests against the driver for typical problems in hardware drivers.

If a dump is generated, `!verifier` in **Windows Debugger** (**WinDbg**) would be a starting point for debugging. Defrag Tools Episodes 16, 17, and 18 on `Channel9.msdn.com` cover Verifier data results extensively and get into debugging and code, which is beyond the scope of this work (`http://channel9.msdn.com/Shows/Defrag-Tools/Defrag-Tools -16-WinDbg-Driver-Verifier`).

Windows Performance Toolkit

WPT is a deep troubleshooting toolkit used to triage many scenarios in the Windows ecosystem. We can use it to troubleshoot power consumption problems, high CPU usage scenarios, heap leak analysis, and many other scenarios. This toolkit is covered in Clint Huffman's Windows Performance Analysis Field Guide, so I will not delve deeper into it here. Suffice it to say, the toolkit has a steep learning curve and requires a good knowledge of the Windows kernel and system architecture.

Michael Milirud gave a talk in 2011 in California on this subject and is on Channel 9 at `http` `://channel9.msdn.com/events/BUILD/BUILD2011/HW-59T`.

Windows Assessment Toolkit

WAT is essentially a WPT wizard. We can utilize the built-in templates to collect and measure a variety of performance test cases. It can even be used against domain-joined machines. It is unfortunate that the tool set isn't as documented as one might have hoped. Many of the links in the tool set for **More Information or Updates** simply point back to the same URL that you downloaded the tool set from:

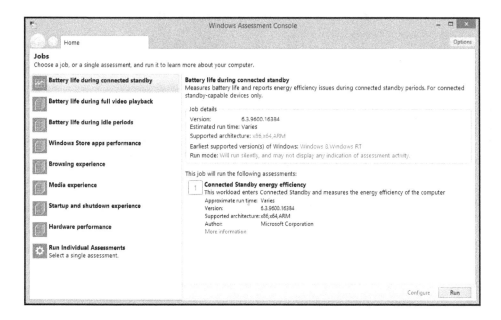

One of the interesting things with this tool set is that one can select individual assessments and create a custom package for troubleshooting purposes, as well as benchmarking:

Run Individual Assessments
Double-click an assessment from the list to continue.

Boot performance (Fast Startup)
Measures boot and shutdown times when using Fast Startup, and identifies components that might cause delays.

Approximate run time:	2 hours
Version:	6.3.9600.17029
Supported architecture:	x86,x64
Author:	Microsoft Corporation

More information

Boot performance (Full Boot)
Measures the overall duration of full boot and shutdown.

Driver verification
Identifies issues with devices and drivers.

File handling
Measures the duration of common file functions, such as copy, move, delete, and zip.

First boot performance
Identifies issues that affect the first startup boot performance.

Hibernate performance
Measures time to hibernate/resume, and identifies components that might cause delays.

Internet Explorer browsing performance
The Internet Explorer® browsing performance assessment measures the quality of the browsing experience and

Internet Explorer Security Software impact
The Internext Explorer Security Software impact assessment measures the primary performance attributes of Inter

Internet Explorer startup performance
Measures the time to launch the Internet Explorer process, when the Internet Explorer process has already been l

Media transcoding performance
Measures the process of changing a video file to a different format or bit rate.

Memory footprint
Measures overall system memory usage, focusing on driver allocations and dynamic allocations.

Minifilter diagnostic: Boot performance (Fast Startup)
Identifies performance issues with minifilter drivers during system boot.

Minifilter diagnostic: File handling
Identifies performance issues with minifilter drivers while performing common file functions, such as copy, move,

Minifilter diagnostic: Internet Explorer
Identifies performance issues with minifilter drivers during Internet Explorer launch.

Many of these tests require ETW providers from a particular version of Windows or higher. Therefore, if you are analyzing Windows 7, for instance, some of the tests won't work and will end in error. After the engineer has selected a set of individual assessments to run, the series of tests can be executed immediately or made into a container for easy portability to another system to be run by another person (say, for an end user's workstation having issues). The results of the test case can be analyzed back at the engineer's workstation after the end user captures the test data.

Windows Assessment Toolkit example 1 – verifying drivers

The first example that I'll provide on utilizing the WAT (also known as Windows Assessment Console) is to validate that the drivers provided to the Windows installation are good. It will also serve as a walkthrough of the UI in general:

1. Launching the Windows Assessment Console results in the following view. Click on **Run Individual Assessments**, and instead of picking an out-of-box test, click the **Configure** button in the bottom-right corner of the UI:

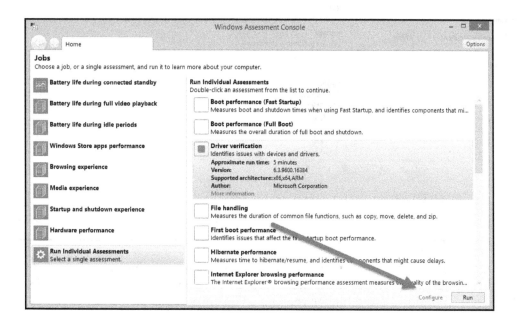

2. Once you've clicked **Configure**, the UI changes a little to give us options for job settings and assessments that we can add to the job. The pane on the right gives us a good description view of what we've selected on the left. A thing I'd recommend doing for all my tests is to check the **Stop this job if an error occurs** box as in this scenario, we are going to presumably be running this on a user's computer. We don't want to totally destroy it. We want the ability to restore the service if needed.

   Also, if you like, keep the temporary files around so you can learn what the tool set is doing and have records. If you don't do this, you'll have only report data, but no depth log data to go through if the tool set report doesn't go as deep as you'd like:

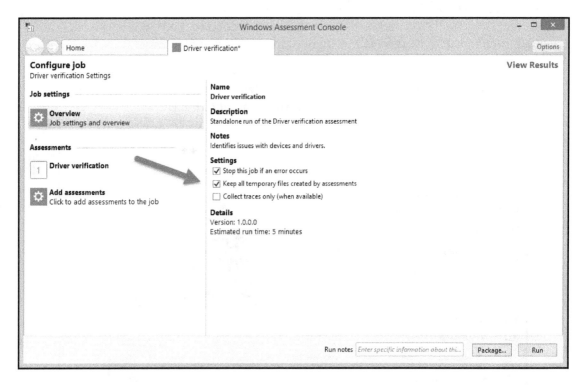

Typically, we see which operating system at a minimum is supported for the test case at hand in the display. In this case, we are okay to run this on Windows 7 and higher versions as no entry is listed.

We're perfectly fine to accept defaults in this area (and for most of the test runs, this is the case as well, not just for Driver Verifier).

Then click the **Package...** button in the bottom-right corner.

Give the custom job a friendly name. In this case, `Driver Verifier` seems apropos:

Next, you'll be prompted to select a package path and results path. The results path can be left as a default. For package path, I tend to place it on `Desktop` of the user I'm currently logged on as. Then click on **OK**:

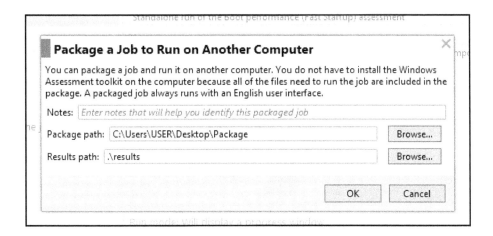

Now you get a Windows Explorer window in the package directory. Simply go up one directory and give the `Package` folder to the end user. They execute `runjob`, or you can call it as `psexec` or any other method for elevation if the end user doesn't have rights.

You can even run this task on a build where you've been given new video or NIC drivers and want to validate they are okay.

So, you run `runjob` and then get the following window. Simply click **Run job on this computer** to run the job:

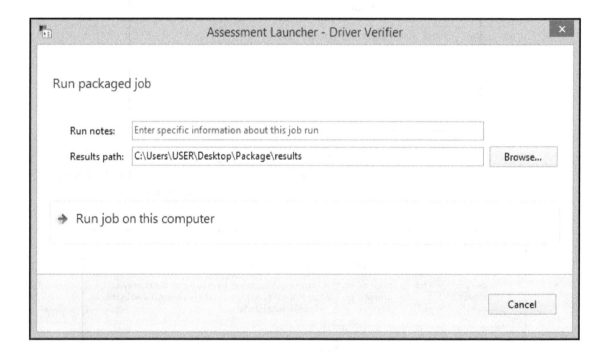

Once the job is done executing, you get an UI pop up, and the package directory has the results as well, for easy import on the **Windows Assessment Console** on another workstation:

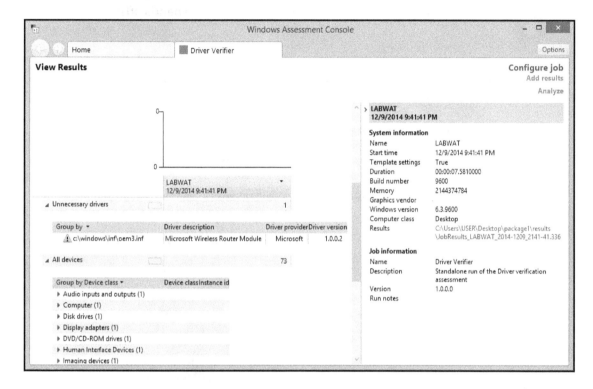

I personally was dissatisfied with the Driver Verifier run. Apparently, it doesn't reboot the box to perform full tests in an automated fashion anymore. However, it did perform a sanity check on them in a simple format.

The next test I'd like to highlight is browsing. It's the same drill, but instead of Driver Verifier, select **Internet Explorer browsing performance**.

 When you run `runjob`, you are told not to interact with the host during testing (it's essentially running a scripted macro, so hands off)!

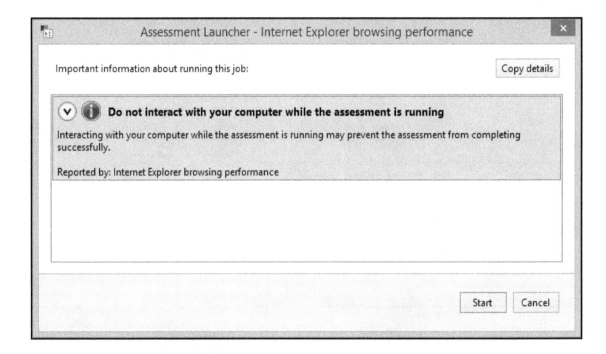

To perform browsing performance test, follow these steps:

1. The scripted tests are fairly amusing (the IE team had some fun here, especially with the speed reading test, also known as Wheel of Fortune):

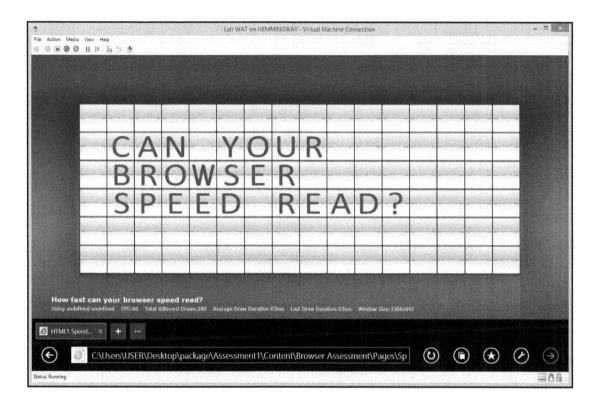

2. When the test is over, we get a scorecard of the test scenarios and how well the image and hardware did:

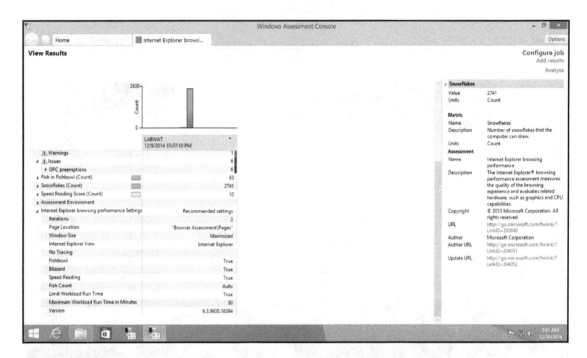

It should be a simple exercise to compare different models of hardware or builds with this tool at this point.

Windows Assessment Services

WAS will seem familiar if you've looked at the WAT. There are a few differences, though, that need to be understood. First, the WAS setup requires a SQL backend. It also requires more disk space, and cannot run in a domain-joined environment.

Installation is a fairly straightforward affair. Check the boxes as listed (the default):

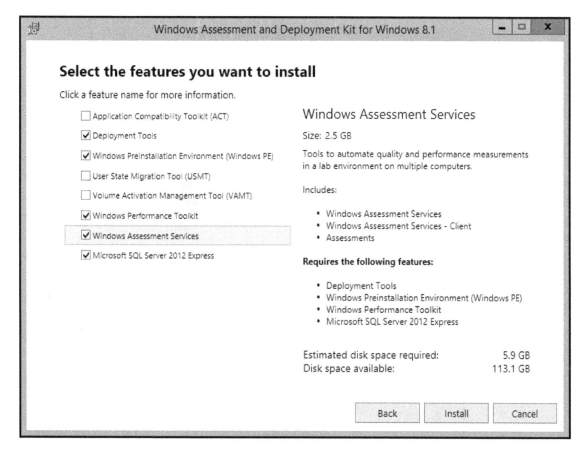

Note here that if you install WAS (really, if you run the ADK setup) on a domain controller, the **Windows Assessment Services** checkbox disappears. It cannot be installed in this scenario.

Running the WAS console post-install results in a prompt to initialize the server:

Part of the initialization is to create Win PE boot images, much like MDT shares have. You can observe this happening in the UI. Much like MDT, it is important to provide appropriate drivers if you intend to use the Win PE WIMs to do bare metal testing. In my example, these are not necessary:

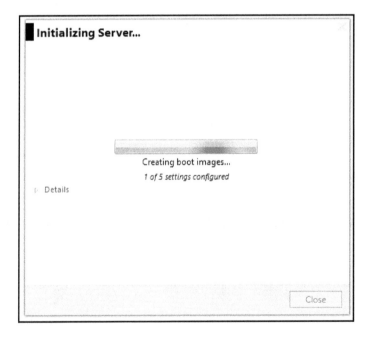

After the Win PE images are created, scripts are set up, and SQL DB is initialized, you receive the following prompt. It should take a few minutes to complete all this:

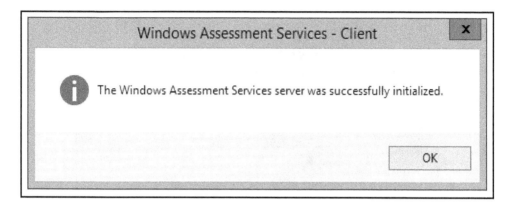

The console is a simple UI, which in places is not terribly intuitive. For example, the default screen gives you no real guide on how to get started without referring to the documentation and is not usable out-of-box, without following the procedures in these documents:

The first action to get this thing going is to connect your victim machines that you want to test up to the test harness in the console. This is a fairly straightforward operation. On the server, a share called **relax** was created and a user account called **localadmin** (which, despite the name, is not an admin of the WAS server; in fact, it has no group memberships when created). The password of this account is `Pass.word`.

The account is a local account on the WAS server. Changing the rights and trying to make this work in a domain-joined environment is a pretty daunting task and beyond the scope of this book (and unsupported by Microsoft as well):

Note the lack of any group memberships. The account is really a sort of orphaned execution account:

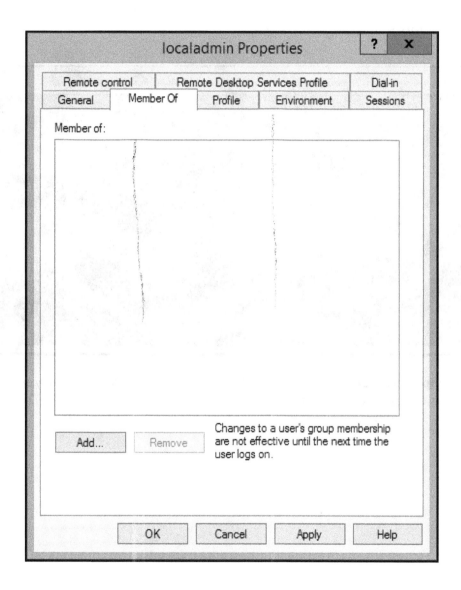

Armed with the local account knowledge, we can then go to each of our target hosts and perform an elevated CMD prompt to NET USE the `relax` share using the local account of the WAS server. Then run the `completedeployment.cmd` file to make the host a victim of the relax directory scripts and WAS engine:

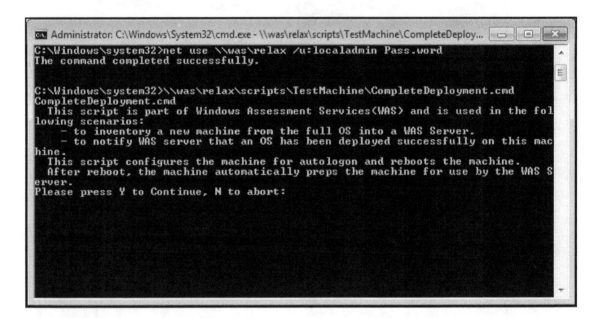

Once the script runs, it prompts for a Y or N to become a victim, enable autologon, and so on. Then it prompts for a group name if you wanted to group your machines. The default option is fine here and can be changed later if need be.

Once the script runs, a refresh of the console will reveal the victim is now registered with the WAS server and is a valid target for actions:

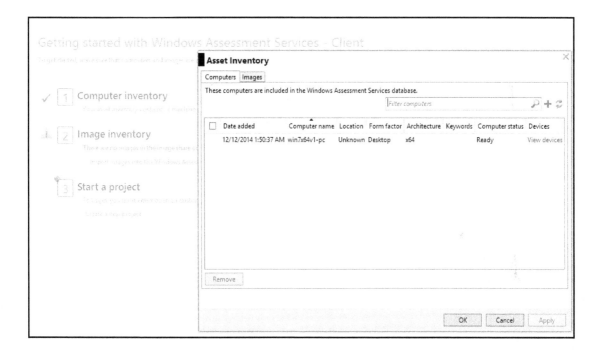

After we add an asset to the inventory, we are prompted for our next step, which is importing a WIM as our image. This step is actually discretionary, based on whether we are going to do bare metal testing or not:

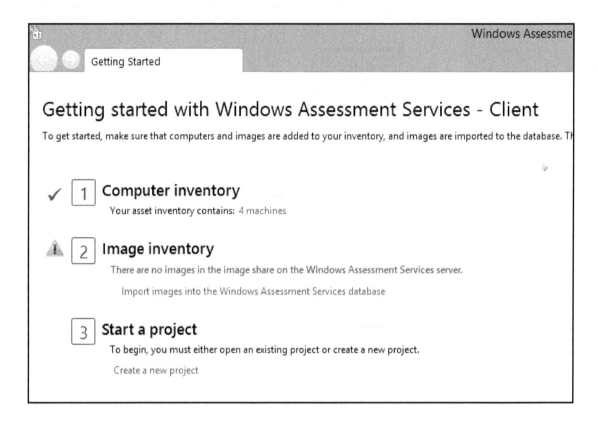

Here we will give the WAS server our WIM file, in case we want to deploy our image over Win PE in an automated test case fashion. In this walk-through, we don't need to do this, we're hooking up the existing hardware models or VMs to the WAS server instead. Therefore, this is optional, but it looks similar to the following screenshot if we give it an image (which must be placed in the `C:\relax\images` directory on the WAS server:

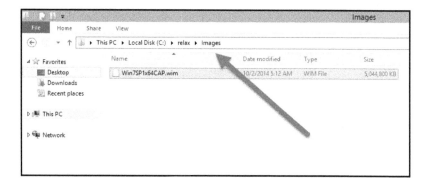

Double check the image to make sure that it's the correct architecture and version of `ntoskrnl` as a way to validate that you imported the correct one (using a WIM from your capture directory is completely appropriate here):

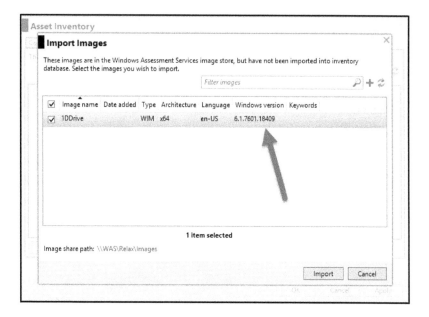

As we create our first project, we should give it a good logical name. Note that many tests can be run under a project. In this case, I am going to name mine `Windows 7 Image Test`. I will be using the same base WIM under different hardware conditions to test and confirm my image is performant in differing scenarios:

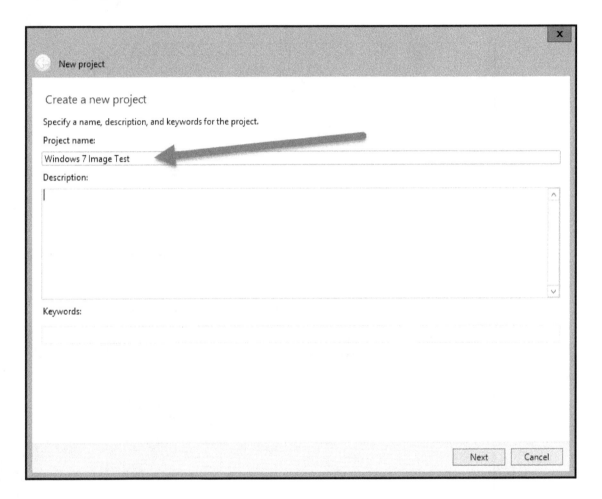

Next, you will add the victims (here, they are named assets) to the project. You can add additional victims to the project later without issue:

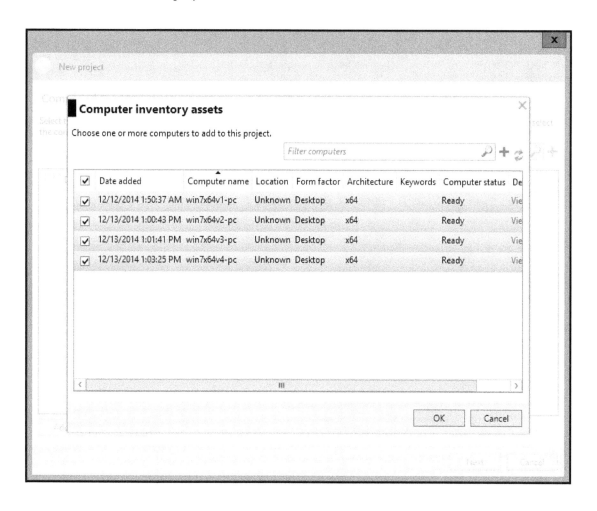

Next we are prompted to add an image to our project. Again this is an optional step, but since I added one to the WAS server, I'll also add it here:

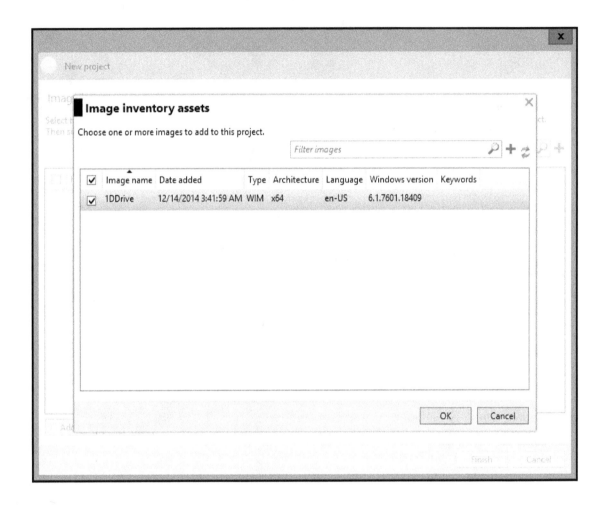

Note that as we create our job, we are connected to the **Windows 7 Image Test** project, and the server is actually running on port 8000 on the WAS host:

Now that we've created our project, let's create a job. The first job I'll create is a disk test (specifically, file operations). I'll name it `Hammer Disks`, as shown in the following image:

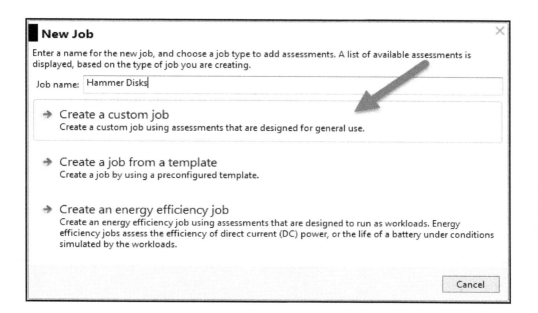

Now that there is a job wizard running to create a job named `Hammer Disks`, I need to specify the type of job (custom) and then give the job some victims to play with:

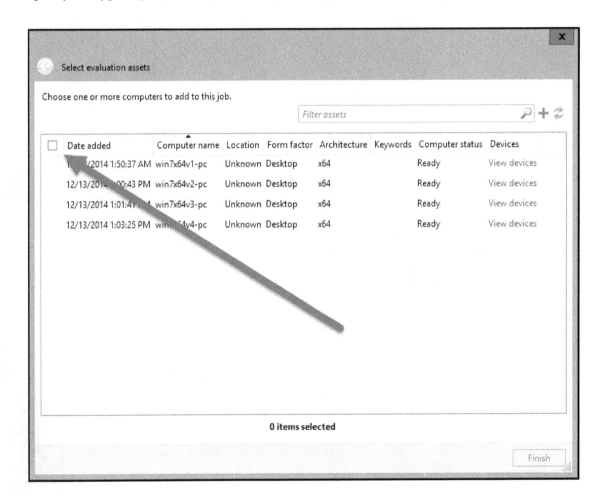

So I will check the box for all of them and click on **Finish**. After the barebones job is created, I will specify to continue on error and also to process results on the server (assuming the WAS machine is a beefy box here; if it isn't, processing locally may be a valid option):

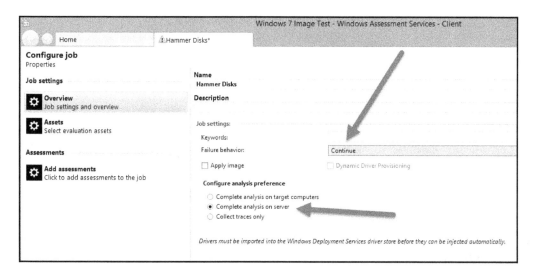

Then, I will pick the **File Handling** task. Note that you can't tell this job will run on Windows 7 until after you add it to the job. Why? I don't know. After this, simply click on **Run**, as shown in the following screenshot:

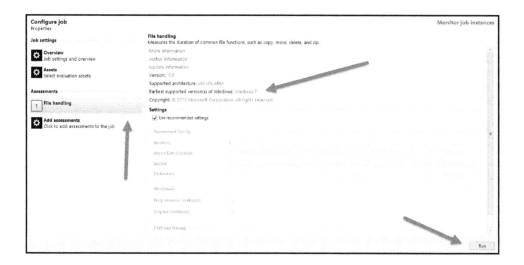

So, we see here the job is running, double-clicking on the job shows us the instances (per machine tests being run):

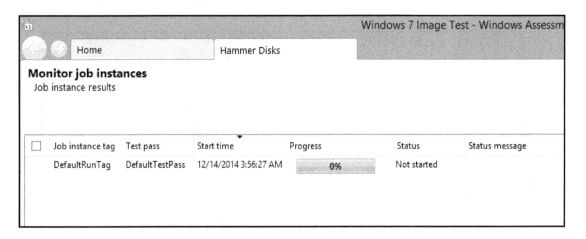

Note there are two actions. The first is to set up the environment and the second is to run the actual **File Handling** task, as shown in the following screenshot:

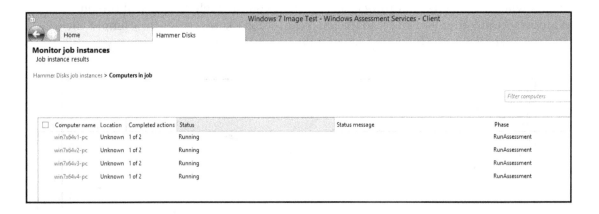

On our victims, the logged on instance shows a minimized command prompt running. This is the script engine executing the file handling test actions:

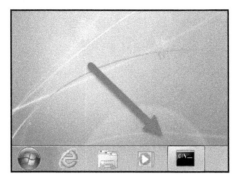

Note that on my host, I can see that the SSD is getting a bit of activity. All four victims are housed on the same SSD here:

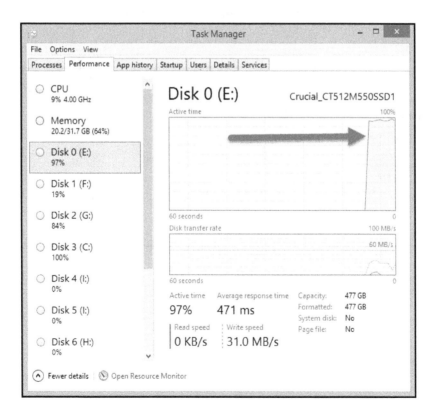

After the tasks finish, we can analyze the results by selecting the **View results** button:

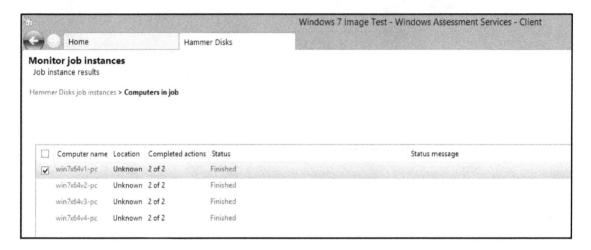

This rolls back to a job view versus a victim/target view, as shown in the following screenshot:

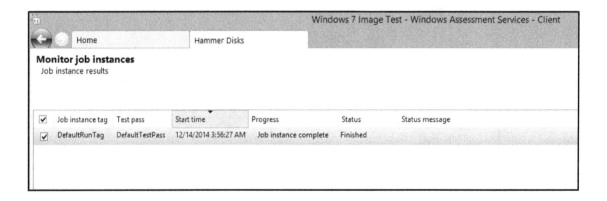

In the view, we can see the hardware of each host defined, along with the results in a graph format for easy comparison of results:

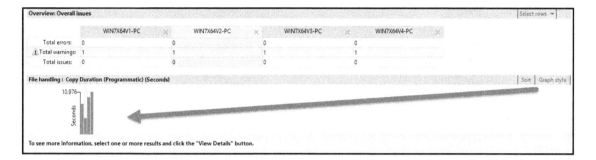

Now I'm going to move the VHDX files on my victims to different storage. This is an easy task in Hyper-V, where I simply select an individual VM and select **Move** and then only move the VHDX to a new drive:

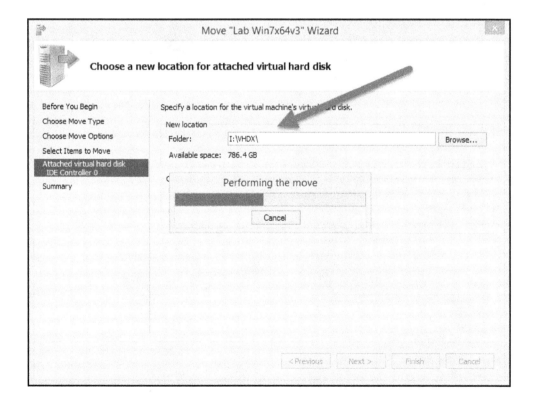

Now that I've rearranged the victim storage locations, I will rerun my test job:

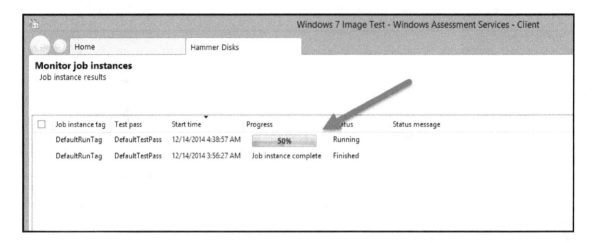

We can also see that one machine has finished (the one I left on SSD, naturally):

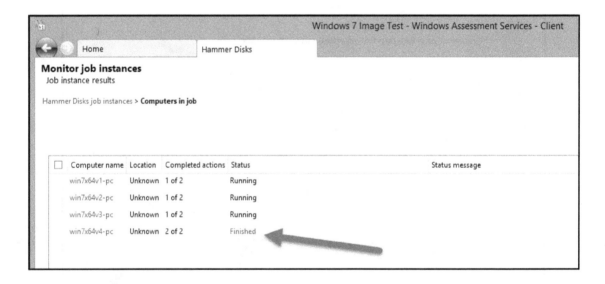

One is on much slower storage than the other three, and the test actually semi-times out here. We get a notice in the console that the test case is running long on this victim. I gave it some more time (simply waited) and the test finally completed:

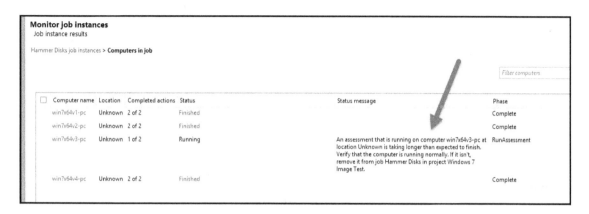

Now I am viewing the results, but only for this job; if I wanted to view the results for both runs of the job, I would just click on **Add results** and add the other test run:

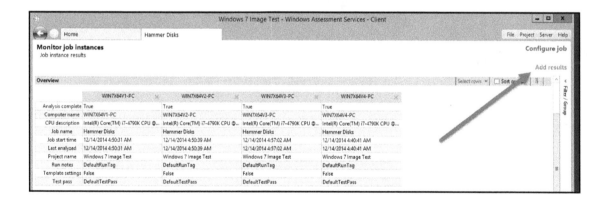

Now we can compare pure SSD storage versus a mixture of SSD, RAID 0, and RAID 1 storage, as shown in the following image:

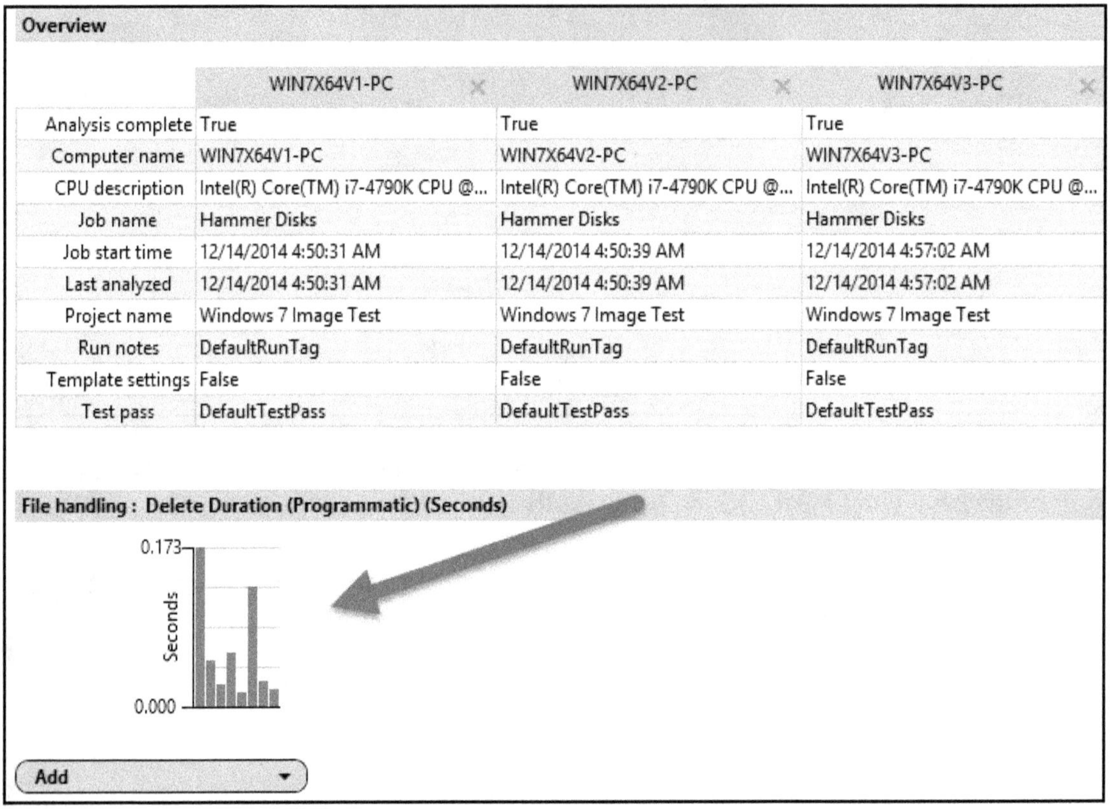

Overview

	WIN7X64V1-PC	WIN7X64V2-PC	WIN7X64V3-PC
Analysis complete	True	True	True
Computer name	WIN7X64V1-PC	WIN7X64V2-PC	WIN7X64V3-PC
CPU description	Intel(R) Core(TM) i7-4790K CPU @...	Intel(R) Core(TM) i7-4790K CPU @...	Intel(R) Core(TM) i7-4790K CPU @...
Job name	Hammer Disks	Hammer Disks	Hammer Disks
Job start time	12/14/2014 4:50:31 AM	12/14/2014 4:50:39 AM	12/14/2014 4:57:02 AM
Last analyzed	12/14/2014 4:50:31 AM	12/14/2014 4:50:39 AM	12/14/2014 4:57:02 AM
Project name	Windows 7 Image Test	Windows 7 Image Test	Windows 7 Image Test
Run notes	DefaultRunTag	DefaultRunTag	DefaultRunTag
Template settings	False	False	False
Test pass	DefaultTestPass	DefaultTestPass	DefaultTestPass

Considering what WAS brings to the table in terms of test cases, it's more robust than WAT; but again, it requires infrastructure:

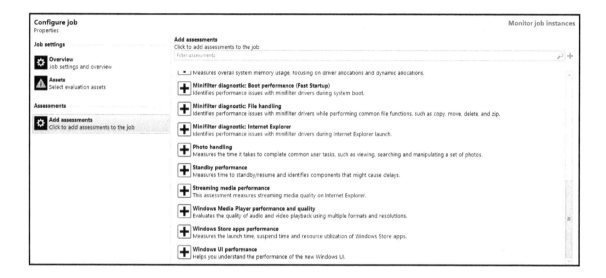

Windows 10

All the concepts shown in this chapter are still valid for Windows 10 image creation. Use the Windows 10 ADK according to your version of OS (v1507, v1511, v1607, and so on).

While the plan is definitely to enforce the new driver-signing model (signed by Microsoft directly), current builds (1507 and 1511) allow the legacy driver-signing model by default.

This was to work around upgrade challenges that will be removed in the Redstone timeframe.

Moving forward, the drivers will continue to be migrated and loaded successfully (even if they are not signed *properly*), but all new device drivers that are installed will require the new model.

Summary

In conclusion, there are several free tools available to the image builder to test for driver issues, boot time performance, browser performance, and many other scenarios. Therefore, you should not rely blindly on using your image on new hardware from an OEM, try your image and security stack with their hardware, and then test it out!

In our next chapter, we will examine UserExit scripts and some add-on packages from CodePlex that web-enable MDT to make it more of a self-service portal. We'll also take a look at the data configuration options available to us for advanced configuration.

11
Database, UserExit Scripts, and Web Services

In the previous chapter, we have learned techniques and tools to validate the image in terms of quality, performance, missing drivers, and finalization. We have also shown ways to automate these tests.

In this chapter, we will show the ability to web front-end the MDT implementation as well as how to utilize the configuration database capabilities of MDT for deeper deployment options. Also, we'll discuss UserExit scripts. We'll get into the whys and hows, what options are available, and when to use these UserExit scripts, by covering the following types:

- Database and the flexibility it brings
- Custom UserExit scripts
- Web services available for use

MDT Configuration Database step by step

The entire purpose of the MDT Configuration Database is to make your deployments more dynamic and your `CustomSettings.ini` less complex. As *dynamic* has many different meanings, let's define dynamic a little bit. When using `CustomSettings.ini` for configuration and selections of task sequence, you need to hardcode everything. And every change of `CustomSettings.ini` means in effect rebuilding your media or, if using PXE and share, updating all shares.

If you are using MDT just to build your golden image or in a small test lab scenario, this disadvantage can be small enough. But as soon as you think about productive use/rollout, you should think twice before using MDT without the SQL database.

With the MDT database you can apply different customizations for different groups of computers based on the computer's hardware, such as the MAC address, its physical location, or manufacturer and model.

Furthermore, a configuration database gives you the ability to assign settings based on the MAC address, **universally unique identifier** (**UUID**), serial number, computer manufacturer and model, default gateway, and grouping, in a very easy way.

Sure, coding all this into `CustomSettings.ini` is also possible, but you need to be very experienced in writing conditions in `CustomSettings.ini` and it will get very hard to read/understand for people not directly involved in coding.

We will give you an overview of how to set up your MDT environment for use with SQL and an introduction to the `Computers` / `Roles` / `Locations` / `Make` and `Model` options used in MDT.

Supported versions of SQL Server

MDT is, in terms of SQL version, very *SQL agnostic*. Support statements about which version of SQL server can be used are more like *not tested*, than like *not working*. For test lab installations, it is *OK* to use the newest SQL version, but for a production environment, please stay with the recommended versions to get full support.

Also, MDT does not incorporate a huge amount of data stored inside the database, so in many cases, like test lab and small productive environments, the limitations of SQL Server Express will not hurt us. If you have a standard or enterprise SQL server available in your environment you can use them; if not you can use, for example, the SQL Server Express 2012 included in the ADK.

Official supported SQL Server versions in MDT 2013 include:

- SQL Server 2008 R2 SP1 CU6 and newer
- SQL Server 2012 SP1 and newer
- SQL Server 2012 R2 and newer
- The corresponding Express versions

Even so, MDT *supports* lower versions of SP/CU; we recommend to upgrade to the latest SP/CU of the SQL Server available.

Installing SQL Server (Express) is very straightforward and there are many tutorials available on how to set up such a SQL Server Express. Please install SQL Server (Express) and install all needed Service Packs/Cumulative Updates. MDT does not need high performance of SQL, no special tuning of worker threads, or any special memory configuration of SQL, especially in test lab/small environments. So if unsure, leave SQL *out-of-the-box*. If you know what you are doing, feel free to tune your SQL Server. Afterwards, installing some basic configuration for communicating with SQL is needed. We will show how to configure SQL for use with MDT.

Configuring the SQL Server

To be able to communicate with MDT clients, it is important to open the needed firewall ports, enable the SQL Browser service and enable named pipe authentication. We will show how to do this:

1. First of all we need to configure the integrated Windows Firewall (if enabled). In a simple approach we can enable all communication of `sqlservr.exe` and `sqlbrowser.exe`.
2. Go to **Control Panel** | **System and Security** | **Windows Firewall**

3. Select **Allow an app or feature through Windows Firewall**:

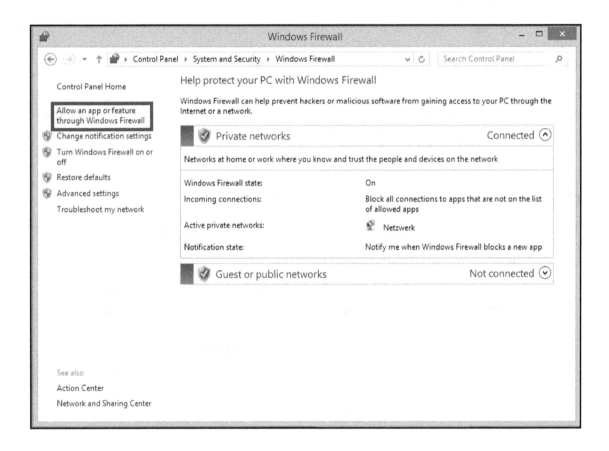

4. If **Allow another app...** is greyed out, please click on **Change settings** to enable editing:

5. Select **Allow another app…**:

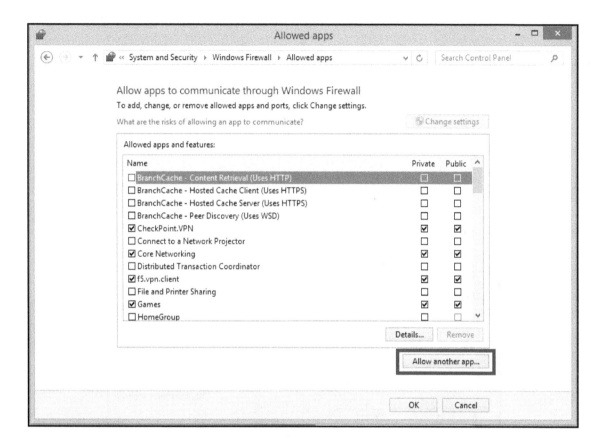

6. Click on **Browse…**, locate your `sqlservr.exe` (if you installed SQL Express 2012 from the ADK package, you will find it under `C:\Program Files (x86)\Microsoft SQL Server\MSSQL11.ADK\MSSQL\Binn\`) and click **Open**:

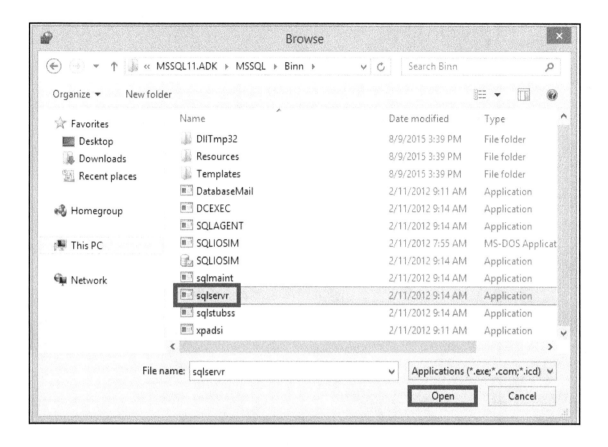

7. A new entry named **SQL Server Windows NT** will show up in the list. Select it and press **Add**:

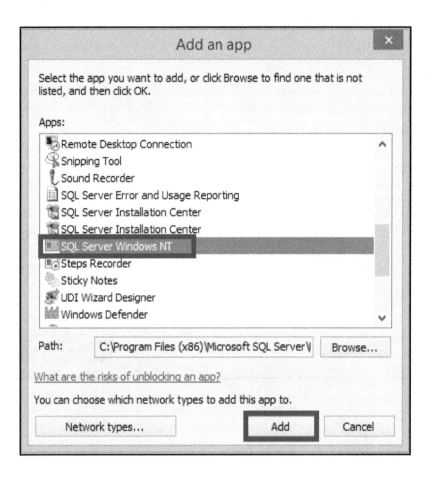

8. Repeat the steps beginning with **Allow another app...** to add `sqlbrowser.exe` (if you installed SQL Express 2012 from the ADK package, you will find it under `C:\Program Files (x86)\Microsoft SQL Server\90\Shared\`). It will be named **SQL Browser Service EXE**:

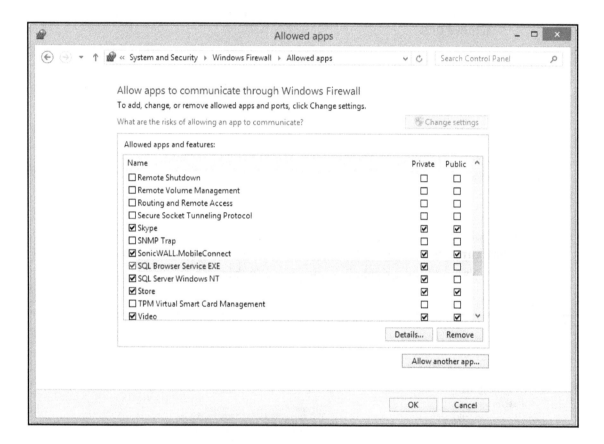

9. Allow communication in private networks. Additionally, you need to enable file sharing for using named pipes authentication.

   If you need a more sophisticated / reduced to the minimum ports solution, you need to open ports UDP 1434 and TCP 1434 for SQL and port TCP 445 for SMB/named pipe. You can use an administrative command prompt to achieve this:

   ```
   netsh advfirewall firewall add rule name="SQL Browser" dir=in
     action=allow protocol=udp localport=1434 profile=private
   netsh advfirewall firewall add rule name="SQL Server" dir=in
     action=allow protocol=tcp localport=1433 profile=private
   netsh advfirewall firewall add rule name="SMB" dir=in action=allow
     protocol=tcp localport=445 profile=private
   ```

If your computer is domain-joined, you need to replace profile=private with profile=domain.

10. Next we need to activate the named pipes protocol. Open **SQL Server Configuration Manager** and select **SQL Server Network Configuration**.
11. Select **Named Pipes**, right click and select **Enable**:

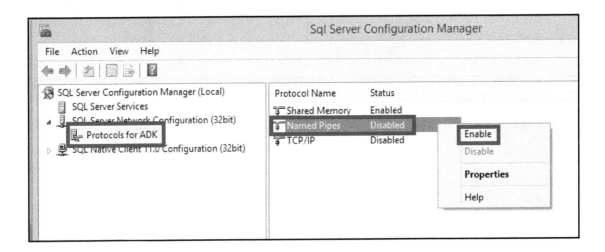

Unfortunately, Windows PE does not have the ability to use integrated security with TCP/IP sockets. If you want to use an **Active Directory** (**AD**) or Windows username and password to connect to the database, you must be using named pipes. You are connecting to a file share on the SQL Server and passing your credentials / authentication to SQL.
If you use TCP/IP sockets you will need a SQL user account and password, which we do not recommend.

12. Accept the warning that you need to restart the SQL Server:

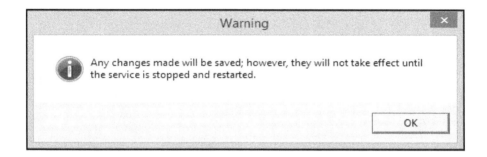

13. Go to **SQL Server Services** and select **SQL Server Browser**, right click and select **Properties**:

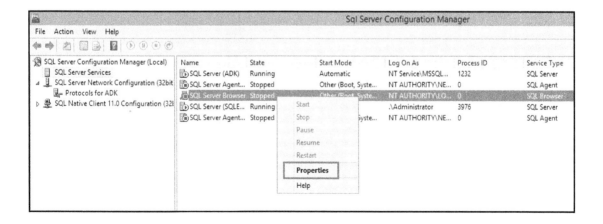

14. Go to the **Service** tab, select **Start Mode** from the drop-down list and select **Automatic**. Press **Apply/OK**:

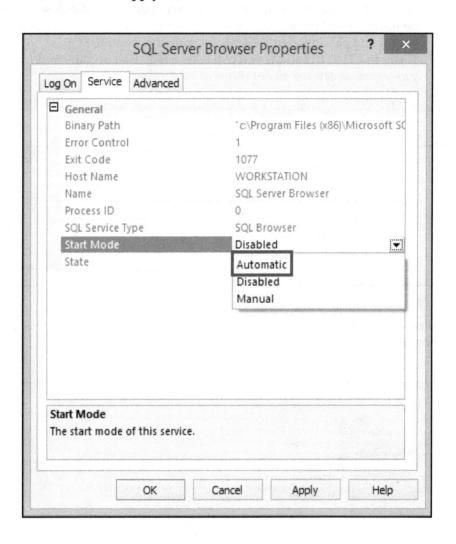

15. Now right-click on **SQL Server Browser** and select **Start**:

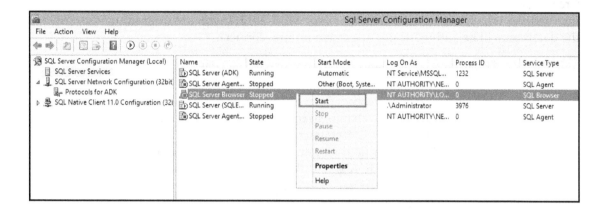

16. As a final step restart **SQL Server (ADK)**:

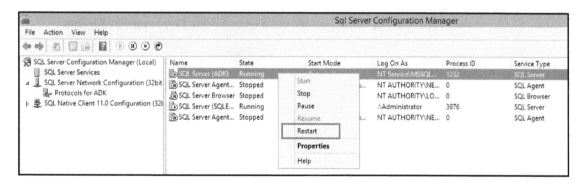

Congratulations, your SQL Server is now set up for its first communication with MDT and we can go on with the creation of the database.

Creating a MDT database

Creating a MDT database is really simple and fast, as you will see in the following instructions, which can be used with the older MDT 2012. If you are upgrading your MDT, the database will be automatically upgraded on first connect.

> Sometimes some manual steps are needed. Always look at the MDT release notes. For MDT 2013 you will find them at: `https://technet.mi` `crosoft.com/library/dn781277.aspx`.
>
> MDT 2013 includes a change to the database to extend the application name field from 50 to 255 characters. A new database in MDT 2013 will use the 255 character field length. An existing database upgraded from MDT 2012 Update 1 to MDT 2013 will retain the 50 character field length. Workaround: After upgrading to MDT 2013, manually alter the database table with the following SQL commands:
> ```
> ALTER TABLE [dbo].[Settings_Applications]
> ALTER COLUMN [Applications] [nvarchar] (256)
> ```

The following are the steps to create a MDT database:

1. Open the **Deployment Workbench** and expand your **Deployment Shares**.

2. Expand **Advanced Configuration**, right click on **Database**, and select **New Database**:

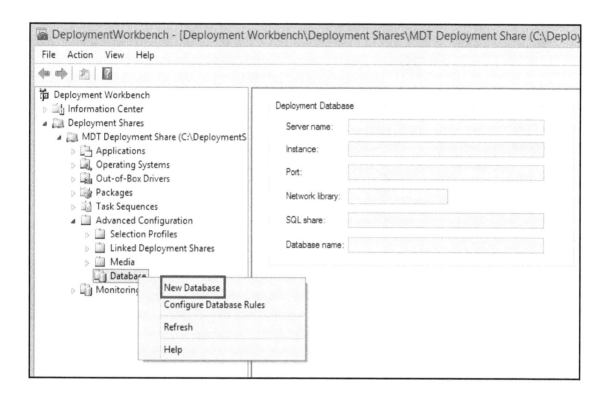

3. Enter the (FQDN) hostname of the server where you installed SQL Server (Express). Don't use `localhost` if you installed it locally; even so MDT will throw no error, as the PE environment will need to resolve the server name and cannot resolve the `localhost` correctly.

Enter the name of the instance. (Leave it empty for the default instance of the full SQL Server, type `SQLExpress` for the default instance of the Express SQL Server. In my case it is `ADK`, as I used SQL Express installation from the ADK setup.)

Choose **Named Pipes** under **Network Library** if not already selected.

If the information is correct and SQL Browser can be contacted, the wizard will continue. Otherwise, you will get an error message and will need to resolve connection problems:

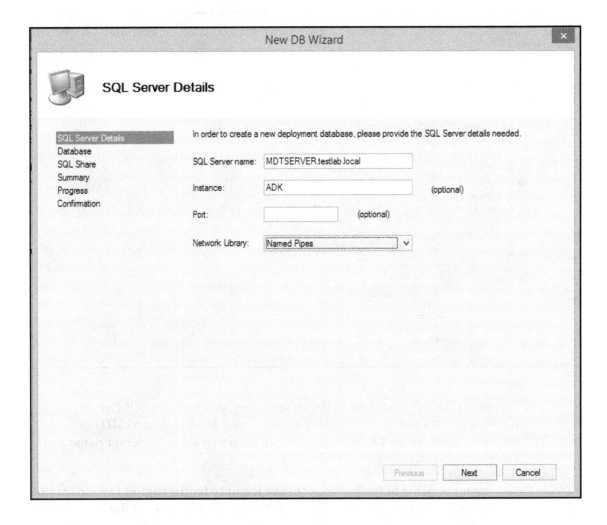

4. Select **Create a new database** and give your MDT database a name:

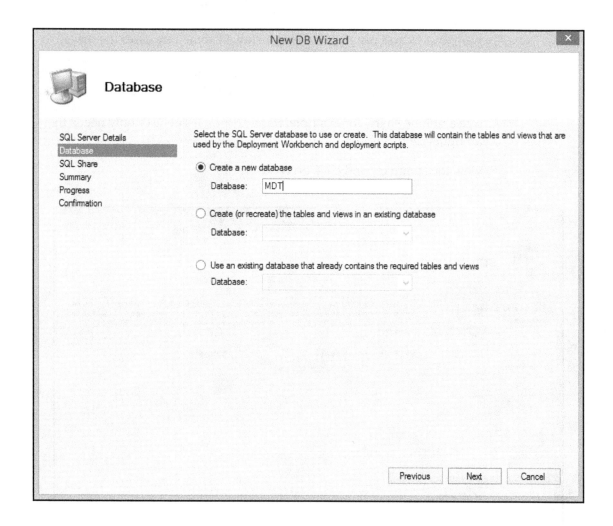

Use a neutral name. Don't use `MDT2013`, even if it may sound conducive.
When you later upgrade your MDT installation, the name of your
database will not change and so you could end up in a strange sounding
combination of, for example, MDT 2016 accessing a `MDT2013` database.
Changing the database name requires a lot of manual steps, so it is better
to choose `MDT` or `MDT_CompanyName` or `MDT_Testlab`, and so on.

5. Next you need to specify the share name on the SQL Server for named pipes authentication. Please don't use the example **DeploymentShare$**, as it will lead to several problems when using SQL together with MEDIA install. If you do use DeploymenShare$ and use MEDIA based install, in some rare cases the drive letter of this network mapping could be in front of the drive letter of the USB media. In this case, MDT would take configuration from the network and produce strange or paradox behavior, like drawing all content from the network.

Create a unique share, for example, NamedPipes$. The user only needs the Read rights for this folder.

Review the summary and click on **Next**:

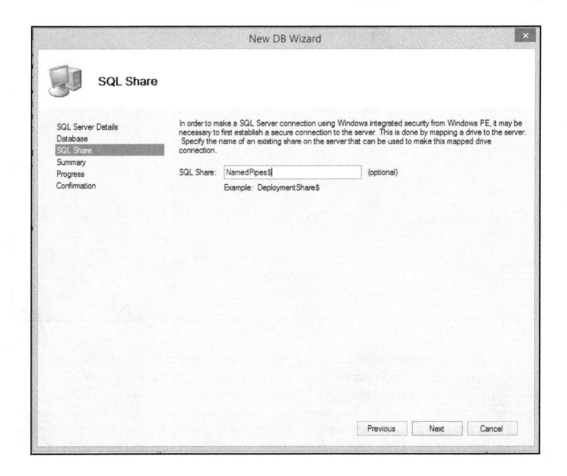

6. If everything completed successfully, click **Finish**:

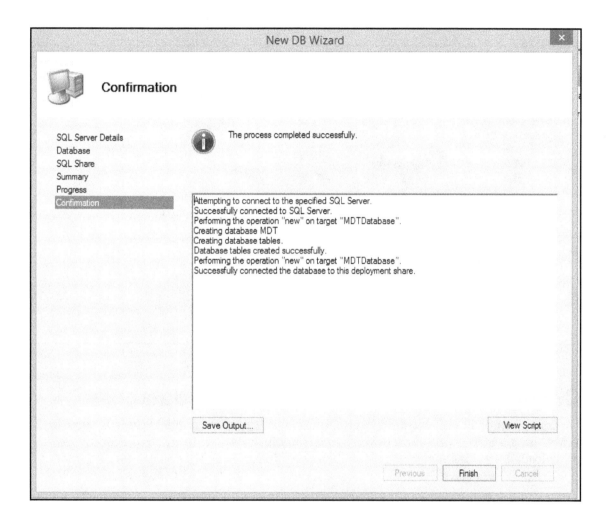

7. This is what the **Database** page should look like after successfully completing the wizard:

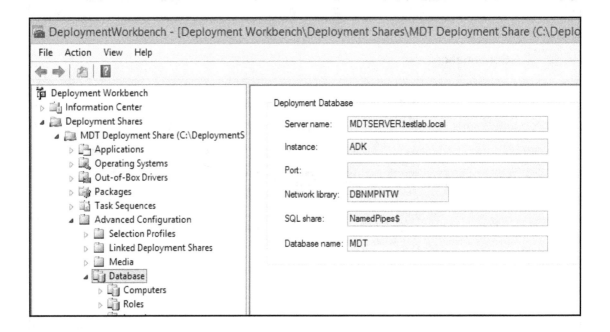

Configuring permission of the MDT database

For configuration of user accounts/user permissions, SQL Management Studio is needed. When using a SQL Express Server version, it is not included by default and needs to be downloaded/installed separately. For SQL Server 2012 from ADK, you can find it under `ht` `tps://www.microsoft.com/en-US/download/details.aspx?id=29062`.

When executing `SQLManagementStudio_x86_ENU.exe` or when running the SQL Server Installation Center of full server, select **Add Features** to existing SQL installation and select the following features:

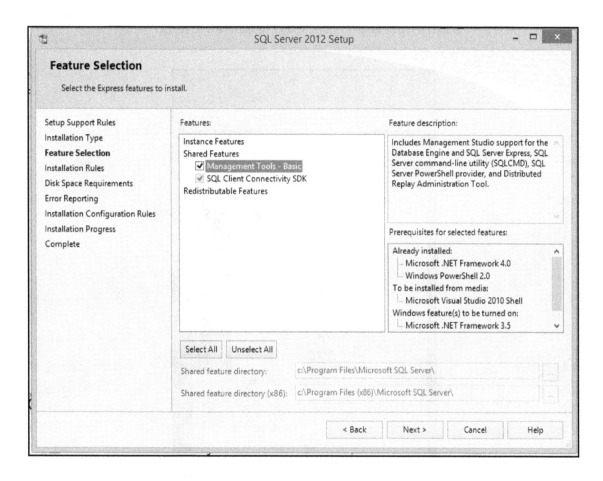

Installing Management Studio will take some time and will very likely require a restart.

The following are the steps for configuring permission of the MDT database:

1. Open the SQL Management Studio, log in to your SQL Server, open **Databases** |
   MDT | **Security** | **Users**. Right click and select **New User...**:

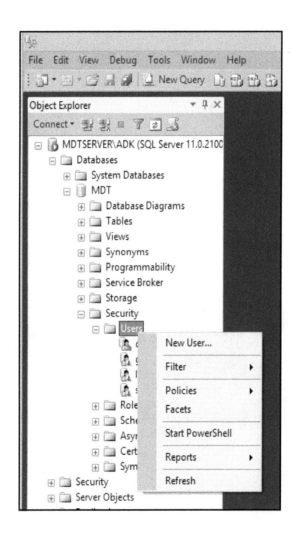

2. Switch to **User type** – **Windows user**:

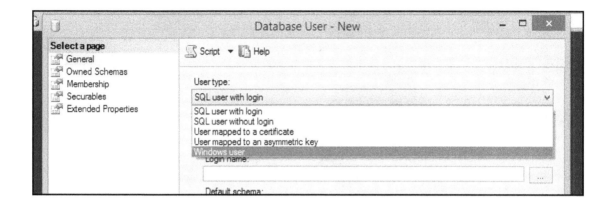

3. Browse or type in **User name** to add. Use the same user as connecting to `DeploymentShare$`:

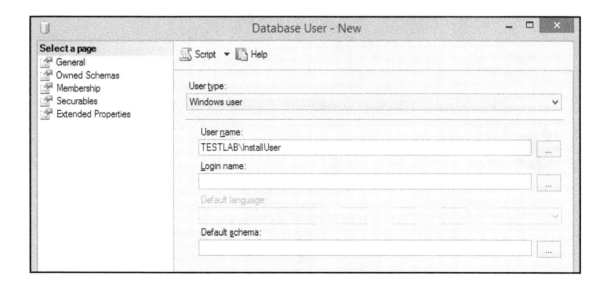

4. Select **Membership** and check the roles. For `InstallUser`, read permission is adequate. Don't grant too many rights:

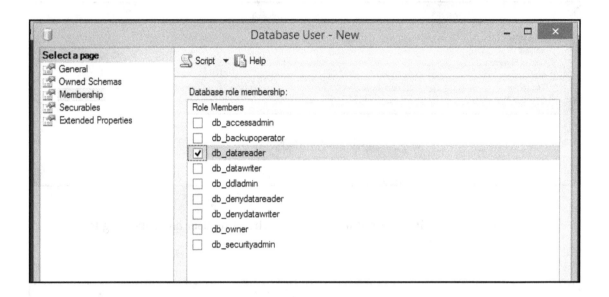

5. Press **OK** to accept the configuration changes.

If you are sharing SQL Server with other applications and want a fine granular permission control also for your MDT Deployment Workbench admin, you will need `sysadmin` or `db_creator` rights for the first creation of DB; later on, `db_ddladmin`, `db_datawriter` and `db_datareader` permission is enough for administration of the MDT database. For a more detailed overview of permissions, take a look at `http s://technet.microsoft.com/library/dn759415.aspx#Assigning theAppropriatePermissionstotheMDTDB`

After configuring and setting permissions to the database we have prepared everything for using the database.

Using the MDT database

The MDT database can handle different types of objects:

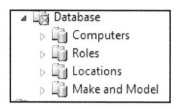

- **Computers**: Identified by Asset tag, UUID, serial number and/or MAC address. You need to specify at least one.
- **Roles**: Identified by role name.
- **Locations**: Identified by IPv4 default gateway(s) (IPv6 is currently not supported).
- **Make and Model**: Identified by computer manufacturer and computer model as represented by WMI query to CSProduct. (In the *UserExit script* section, we will discuss a mapping/trunking of names.)

Now, before we can use the MDT database to deploy our image based on the properties, intended roles, locations, or make/model of our target computers, we need to configure our `CustomSettings.ini` file so that it can use settings we choose to store in this database. To archive this, right-click on **Database** in the **Deployment Workbench** and select **Configure Database Rules**:

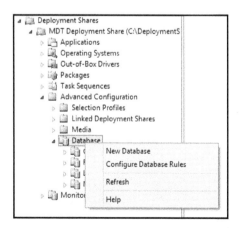

This launches the **Configure DB Wizard**, which is a bit misleading because it does not configure the database, but instead configures your `CustomSettings.ini` file by adding additional rules to it so that MDT can query the database during deployment.

Note that for each item selected in this wizard, MDT will use a script to perform the corresponding database query. That means the more items you select, the more queries will be performed and the longer it will take to perform the deployment. Also, you strain your SQL Server a bit more with each query.

In the first screen, **Computer Options**, you need to select which categories/information you want to store below your computer object:

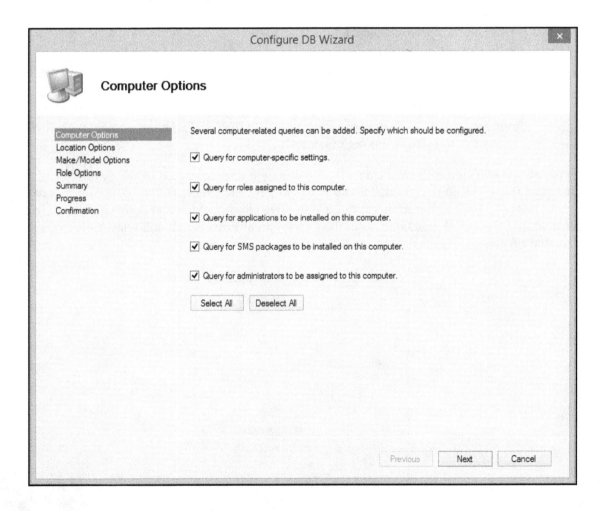

The following options are available:

- **Object specific settings**: You have the possibility to define one or more MDT values. All MDT values can be used, even if they are not computer-specific. Better wording would be *setting/value defined specific to this computer*.
- **Assigned roles**: You have the possibility to define one or more additional roles which should be included.
- **Applications**: You can specify MDT application packages which should be installed.
- **SMS packages**: (Only usable with `ConfigMgr`.) You can specify `ConfigMgr` packages which should be installed. Deselect if you did not integrate MDT into `ConfigMgr`.
- **Assigned administrators**: You can specify one or more administrators which should be created.

In the second screen, **Location Options**, you have all previous five options and additionally, an option to query the default gateway to resolve to location name. You should leave this option enabled:

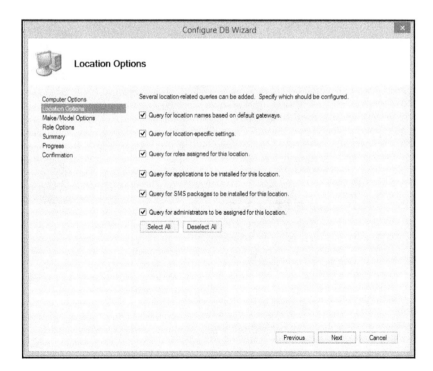

The third screen, **Make/Model Options**, has the same five options as computer objects:

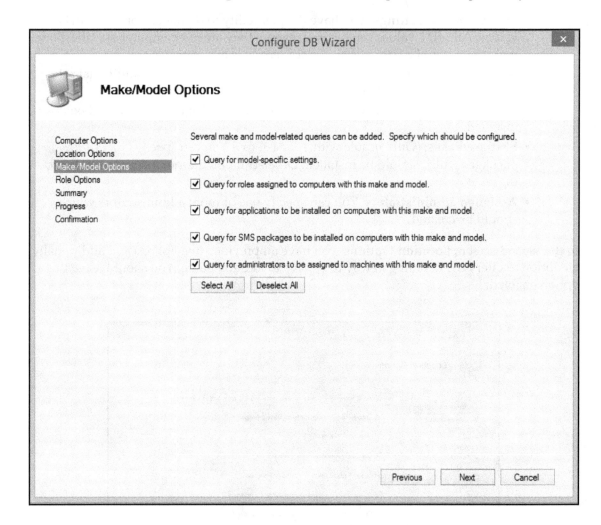

The last configuration screen, **Role Options**, has only four options. It is missing the query role option, as you cannot specify inherited/nested roles:

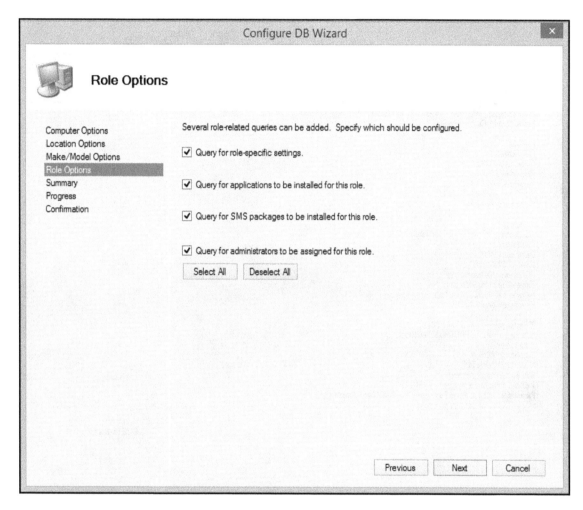

After going through all four configuration pages you get a **Summary** page, **Progress** page, and finally, a **Confirmation** page.

When selecting all available options this will result in 20 SQL queries/rules in
`CustomSettings.ini`, as shown in the following screenshot:

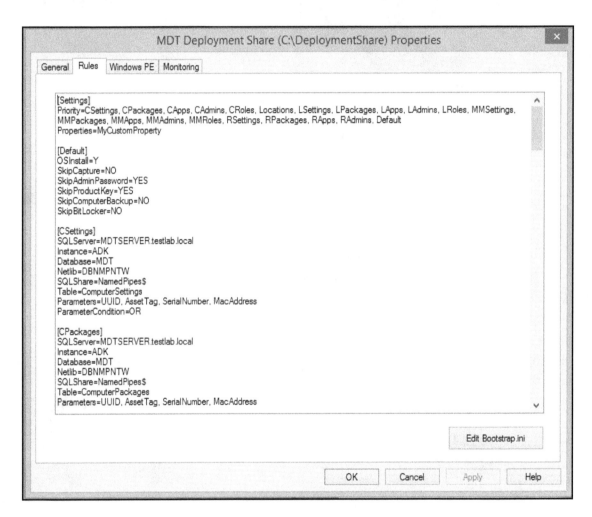

Now it is safe to modify the `CustomSettings.ini`, change the order/priority of rules,
and/or modify rules, for example, using `CustomMake` and `CustomModel` variables for
queries (see the *UserExit script* section). But be careful. Every time you execute the
Configure DB Wizard again it will overwrite your changes.

Applying customizations to individual computers

If you wanted to apply settings to specific computers in your environment, you need to create a **Computer** record in your MDT database and specify one or more of the following to uniquely identify the computers in question:

- Asset tag
- UUID
- Serial number
- MAC address

To create a **Computer** record in your MDT database, follow these steps:

1. First go to your workbench, expand the **Deployment Shares**, and navigate to and expand **Database** in the navigation pane:

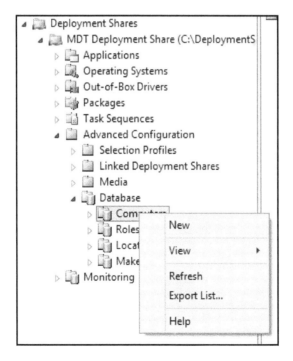

2. Right-click on **Computer** and select **New**, and you will see the following **Properties** window (without values):

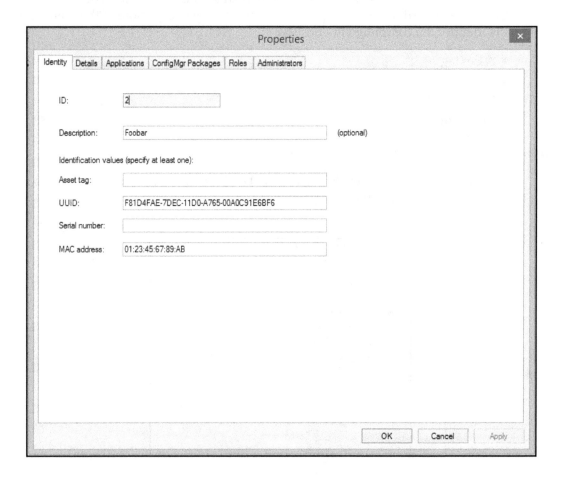

The **Description** is only for database usage; hostname needs to be specified as the `OSDComputerName` variable. You need to specify a minimum of one of the four required fields. All letters needs to be upper case notation. You can obtain this information from your target computer's BIOS.

Enter your choice of unique identifier along with a description of this particular computer in the **Identity** tab. MAC addresses must be separated by colons and UUIDs must be entered in the exact format.

Using a MAC address works well unless the target computer has two NICs, in which case it is safer to identify the computer using one of the other three unique identifiers.

 UUIDs are an octet string of 16 octets (128 bits). The 16 octets can be interpreted as an unsigned integer encoding, and the resulting integer value is more commonly represented with hexadecimal digits, with a hyphen separating the different fields within the 16-octet UUID. So, UUID is a set of 32 hexadecimal characters (36 if you count the dashes), noted as `12345678-1234-1234-1234-123456789012`. Be careful: some early BIOS implementations set the UUID to all (`0000-000`...).

The customization settings are entered in the **Details** tab. Any customization settings you enter here will be applied at the time of deployment to your specified target computer.

The computer name needs to be inserted into **OSDComputerName** (the old value **ComputerName** is now obsolete), as shown in the following screenshot:

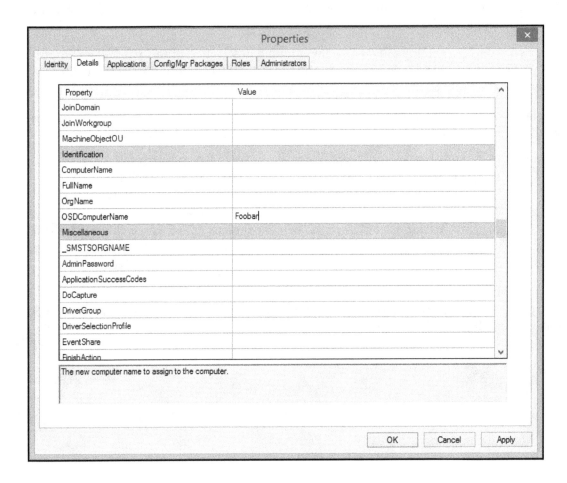

The deployment workbench does not provide an easy way to show all the values set on all computer objects in one view. You need to open each object individually.

Computer settings should be reduced to a minimum and be unique. More often/global used values are better stored in roles objects.

Use the **Role** tab to assign one or more roles assigned to this individual computer.

Editing all this information in GUI can be time consuming and prone to error. But you can use PowerShell to bulk import, for example, a prepared CSV file.

If you have, for example, a CSV file named `bulkimport.csv` with four columns (Description, MAC, Name, Roles), you can import it with the following easy code:

```
Import-Module -name .\MDTDB.psm1
Connect-MDTDatabase -sqlServer MDTSERVER.testlab.local -instance
  ADK -database MDT
$computers = Import-Csv .\bulkimport.csv
For ($i=1; $i -le $computers.count; $i++)
{
New-MDTComputer -macAddress $computers[$i-1].mac -description
  $computers[$i-1].description -settings @{
OSDComputerName=$computers[$i-1].name;
}
Get-MDTComputer -macAddress $computers[$i-1].mac ? Set-
  MDTComputerRole -roles
$computers[$i-1].roles
}
```

Other examples, like importing it directly from AD or from another asset DB are possible, depending on the source of your data.

Applying customizations to roles

If you wanted to apply settings to specific groups in your environment, you need to create a **Role** record in your MDT database and specify a unique role name.

1. Go to your workbench, expand the **Deployment Shares**, and navigate to and expand **Database** in the navigation pane:

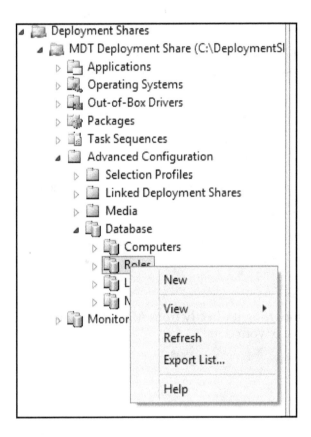

2. Right-click on **Roles** and select **New**, and you will see the following **Properties** window (without the **Role name**):

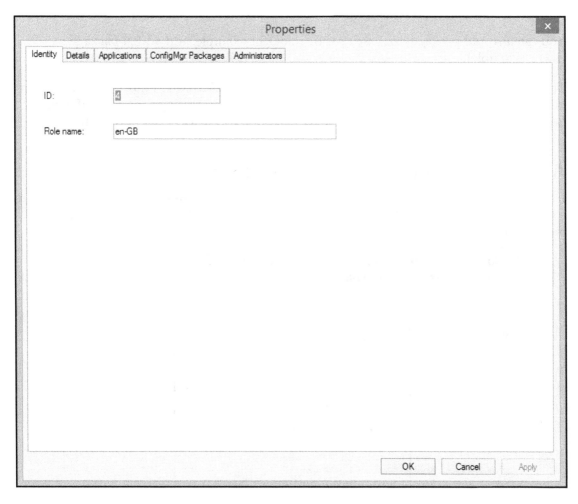

Enter a unique role name. GUI will not check if the name is unique. Spaces are allowed, but we recommend to exchange them with an underscore character.

The customization settings are entered in the **Details** tab. Any customization settings you enter here will be applied at the time of deployment if the role is targeted to your specific computer.

You can create roles for global settings (for example, Global), country-based settings (for example, United_Kingdom, Germany, USA, or en-GB, de-DE, en-US), department-specific settings (for example, HR, Finance), computer role-specific settings (for example, Laptop, Desktop, Workstation), and many more.

You can also add packages to these specific roles (for example, add a VPN package to the Laptop role).

Try to avoid defining the same setting with different values in two or more roles which can be assigned at the same time, as the order of role settings processing cannot be influenced easily and settings, once set, are no longer overwritten by the MDT environment.

Applying customizations to locations

If you wanted to apply settings to specific locations in your environment, you need to create a **Location** record in your MDT database and specify a unique location name and one or more unique IPv4 gateways for each location.

1. Go to your workbench, expand the **Deployment Shares** and navigate to and expand **Database** in the navigation pane:

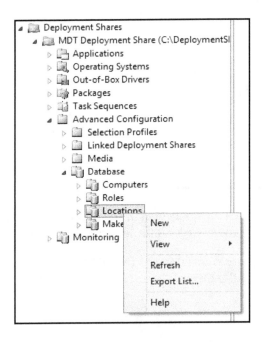

2. Right-click on **Locations** and select **New**, and you will see the following **Properties** window (without the values):

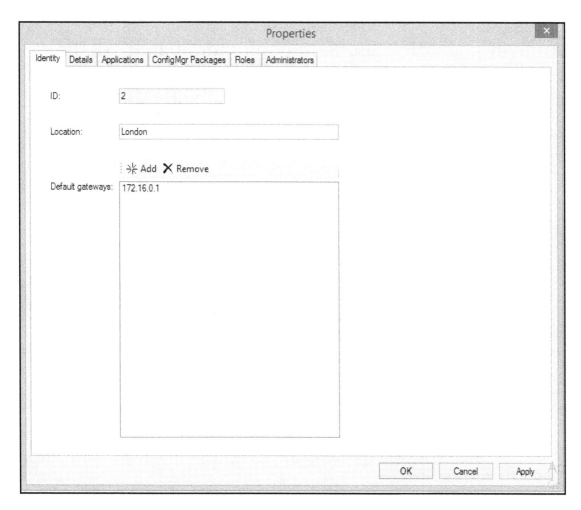

Enter a unique location name. GUI will not check if the name is unique. Spaces are allowed, but we recommend to exchange them with an underscore character.

Then click on **Add** and enter a unique IPv4 gateway address. If one location has multiple gateways, repeat this step accordingly. GUI will not check if the IP is unique.

The customization settings are entered in the **Details** tab. Any customization settings you enter here will be applied at the time of deployment if the default gateway of your computer during deployment matches one of the default gateways.

As already mentioned in individual computer settings, displaying all settings in MDT GUI is not very comfortable. It is better to think about creating roles and assigning roles to your locations.

Applying customizations to computers based on their manufacturer and model

If you wanted to apply settings targeted at a particular manufacturer and/or model of computer, you need to create a **Make and Model** record in the MDT database and provide the manufacturer and model name of the targeted computers:

1. Go to your workbench, expand the **Deployment Shares**, and navigate to and expand **Database** in the navigation pane:

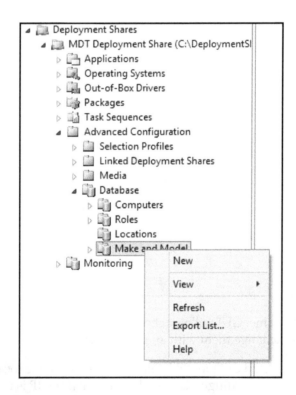

2. On the Deployment Workbench, right-click on **Make and Model** and select **New**. A **Properties** window will come up as shown here (without the values):

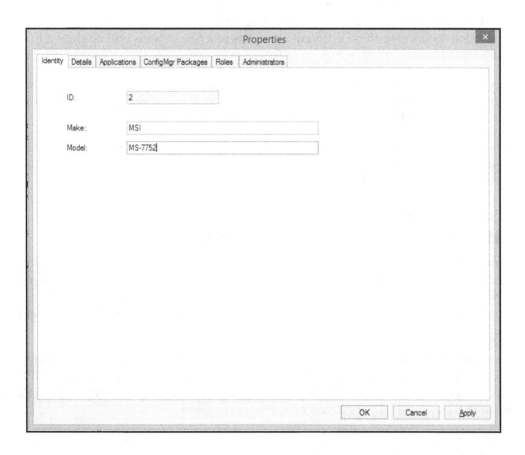

3. Enter the **Make** and **Model** fields in the **Identity** tab, making sure you copy the vendor and name values returned from the WMIC query on your target computer correctly:

The **Make** and **Model** fields do not support wildcards like asterisk (*) or question mark (?). You need to type in the **Make** and **Model** fields exactly as it will be returned by the WMI query. This can lead to many entries, as some manufacturers have different notations for their models (with or without brackets, including serials, including location coding, and so on). A solution to tail/map these different notations to a few models will be shown in the *UserExit script* section.

Again, you enter your customization settings in the **Details** tab. Any customization settings you enter here will be applied at the time of deployment if the **Make and Model** of your computer exactly match the database.

As already mentioned in individual computer settings, displaying all settings in MDT GUI is not very comfortable. It is better to think about creating roles and assigning roles to your locations.

Considerations on MDT database usage

Of course, this is only the basics of what's possible with the MDT database. The level of complexity and the customizations you choose to make will depend on your deployment environment. There is no one-fits-all master design which can be used for all MDT databases. But we will give you some hints, best practice, and experience from the field on how to configure/use these objects.

You can compare the MDT database model to the Group Policy data model. Information which is more general resides in a hierarchically higher **organizational unit** (**OU**). GPOs valid for all systems are stored in the topmost OU. GPOs valid only for some systems/users are stored in the nearest OU or filtered by the security group.

The same should be done in MDT. General values should be stored in Roles, Location specific / Model specific in their objects.

Individual information like computer name, static IP, or similar things, should be stored where they belong, in the computer object itself. Information which enters the same value several times, should be abstracted into a role object and instead the role object should be assigned.

By this abstraction, you only need to change one place (the role itself), and not several hundred computer objects, to change a value.

Depending on your company's infrastructure and geographical setup, there can be one or more roles defined. If your company resides only in one country with one language spoken, it could make sense to pack everything in a default configuration role object. If you have multiple countries, it could make sense to create country-specific configuration roles. If you have multiple domains, it could make sense to create a configuration role object for each domain, and so on.

By this model, you can always override default values of roles by setting a different value directly on the computer object itself if needed, as MDT won't change an already set value.

Always set the `SkipWizard` control in the object itself where you entered the information. So if you are creating a role with time zone information, set `SkipTimeZone=YES` directly inside this role. By this bundling, you mitigate the risk of an unhealthy installation due to skipping all wizards without entering the necessary information.

Role definitions need to be done before or during the gather process. It is not possible / has drawbacks to setting roles during the task sequence. We recommend to define all roles in the database directly or the latest inside `CustomSettings.ini` by adding `Role001=<Role name>`.

Editing the database in GUI can be time consuming. Take a closer look at Michael Niehaus' blog about editing data by PowerShell: `http://blogs.technet.com/b/mniehaus/archive/2009/05/15/manipulating-the-microsoft-deployment-toolkit-database-using-powershell.aspx`.

If plain data gathering is not enough and you need the ability to process data during gather, you need to have a closer look at UserExit scripts. We will show you how to create such script in the next section.

UserExit script

With all the rules, conditions and WMI queries, MDT is already a very powerful tool. But sometimes you hit limitations during the gather process.

What if the vendor of your PC hardware has three different model names of the same hardware and you need a model mapping or model alias? Your serial number contains unneeded characters and needs to be truncated? Or in short, you need the ability to execute a custom VBS script.

MDT gives you this opportunity. It is a little bit misleading calling it *UserExit script*. You can define one (or more) scripts, which will then share its functions inside `CustomSettings.ini`.

Let's open an editor and create a file called `MDTUserExit.vbs`. Copy the following code mentioned inside this VBS.

A UserExit script always needs the main function with name `UserExit()`:

```
Function UserExit(sType, sWhen, sDetail, bSkip)
  UserExit = Success
End Function
```

But this basic function does not provide any logging. So you never know if `UserExit()` was triggered and when. For better logging, you should extend the function, for example, as follows:

```
Function UserExit(sType, sWhen, sDetail, bSkip)
  oLogging.CreateEntry "USEREXIT:MDTUserExit.vbs v1.0 started: " &
    sType & " " & sWhen & " " & sDetail, LogTypeInfo
  UserExit = Success
End Function
```

Next you need to add your needed functionality as a separate function. We will implement a generic **Make** mapping, for example, with Dell and Panasonic and their different Make notations, as shown in the following code. You can add more cases if needed:

```
Function SetMakeAlias()
oLogging.CreateEntry "Init USEREXIT:MDTUserExit.vbs|SetMakeAlias",
  LogTypeInfo
  //Get Make from MDT environment
  sMake = oEnvironment.Item("Make")
    SetMakeAlias = ""
  Select Case UCase(sMake)
    Case "DELL COMPUTER CORPORATION", "DELL INC.", "DELL COMPUTER
      CORP."
      SetMakeAlias = "Dell Inc."
    Case "MATSUSHITA ELECTRIC INDUSTRIAL CO.,LTD.", "PANASONIC
      CORPORATION"
      SetMakeAlias = "Panasonic Corporation"
    Case Else
      SetMakeAlias = sMake
      oLogging.CreateEntry "USEREXIT:MDTUserExit.vbs |SetMakeAlias
        - Alias rule not found.  MakeAlias set to Make value.",
        LogTypeInfo
  End Select
  oLogging.CreateEntry "USEREXIT:MDTUserExit.vbs|SetMakeAlias -
```

```
MakeAlias has been set to " & SetMakeAlias, LogTypeInfo
  oLogging.CreateEntry "Exit
    USEREXIT:MDTUserExit.vbs|SetMakeAlias", LogTypeInfo
End Function
```

Save this script in your MDT environment under `DeploymentShare\Scripts`. Modify your `CustomSettings.ini` to include the following bold lines:

```
[Settings]
Priority=Default
Properties=MakeAlias

[Default]
OSInstall=YES
UserExit=MDTUserExit.vbs
MakeAlias=#SetMakeAlias()#
```

But a `MakeAlias` is worthless without a `ModelAlias`. So let's construct a suitable additional function. We will also reuse the `MakeAlias`:

```
Function SetModelAlias(sMakeAlias)
  oLogging.CreateEntry "Start
    USEREXIT:MDTUserExit.vbs|SetModelAlias", LogTypeInfo
  sModel = oEnvironment.Item("Model")
  SetModelAlias = ""
  ' Check by MakeAlias
  Select Case UCase(sMakeAlias)
    Case "DELL INC."
      If Instr(sModel, "(") > 2 Then
        SetModelAlias = Trim(Left(sModel, Instr(sModel, "(") - 2))
      Else
        SetModelAlias = sModel
      End If

    Case "PANASONIC CORPORATION"
      'Panasonic Toughbook models
      If Left(sModel,2) = "CF" Then
        SetModelAlias = Left(sModel,5)
      Else
        If Instr(sModel, "(") > 2 Then
          SetModelAlias = Trim(Left(sModel, Instr(sModel, "(") -
            2))
        Else
          SetModelAlias = sModel
        End If
      oLogging.CreateEntry "USEREXIT:MDTUserExit.vbs|SetModelAlias
        - Alias rule not found.  ModelAlias set to Model value.",
        LogTypeInfo
```

```
        End If

    Case Else
      If Instr(sModel, "(") > 2 Then
        SetModelAlias = Trim(Left(sModel, Instr(sModel, "(") - 2))
      Else
        SetModelAlias = sModel
        oLogging.CreateEntry
          "USEREXIT:MDTUserExit.vbs|SetModelAlias - Alias rule not
          found.  ModelAlias set to Model value.", LogTypeInfo
      End If
  End Select
  oLogging.CreateEntry "USEREXIT:MDTUserExit.vbs|SetModelAlias -
    ModelAlias has been set to " & SetModelAlias, LogTypeInfo
  oLogging.CreateEntry "Exit
    USEREXIT:MDTUserExit.vbs|SetModelAlias", LogTypeInfo
End Function
```

We need to extend `CustomSettings.ini` to look like the following:

```
[Settings]
Priority=Default
Properties=MakeAlias
[Default]
OSInstall=YES
UserExit=MDTUserExit.vbs
MakeAlias=#SetMakeAlias()#
ModelAlias=#SetModelAlias("%MakeAlias%")#
```

All function calls inside hashtags (#) will be looked up in the UserExit script. You can even parse values or variables when enclosed in quotes as shown for `SetModelAlias()`.

With this easy modification it is now possible to use this new `MakeAlias` and `ModelAlias`, for example, in the Make Model SQL query, as shown here:

```
[MMSettings]
SQLServer=MDTSERVER.testlab.local
Instance=ADK
Database=MDT
Netlib=DBNMPNTW
SQLShare=NamedPipes$
Table=MakeModelSettings
Parameters=MakeAlias, ModelAlias
```

This is only a small teaser to all the thinkable possibilities of such UserExit scripts.

Sometimes you will need to include more than one script. Deployment Guys have shown an easy way without creating several subsections: `http://blogs.technet.com/b/deploymentguys/archive/2013/09/13/loading-user-exit-scripts-with-vbscript-classes.aspx`.

MDT out-of-the-box does not provide the ability to write back information to the database. If you ever need this ability, you should have a closer look at the Deployment Guys blog on how to write data to a database during gather with the help of UserExit script: `http://blogs.technet.com/b/deploymentguys/archive/2015/07/01/writing-data-to-the-mdt-database-during-gather.aspx`.

And there are even more possibilities. You can use UserExit script, for example, to gather a web service. We will show in the next section how to achieve this.

Web services

If the MDT database and UserExit script are still not sufficient for customizations, you can further extend MDT with the use of web services.

Jase T. Wolfe wrote a good explanation of web service in his **QuickStart Guide to Using Web Services in MDT / SCCM** (`http://myitforum.com/myitforumwp/2013/03/07/a-quickstart-guide-to-using-web-services-in-mdt-sccm/`):

"For those not completely familiar with a web service (WS), the condensed and over simplified introduction is this: A WS is a middle man that simplifies obtaining information or performing a process on behalf of the client and returning some type of data to the client. As the name suggests, the WS is a web based process which is used (in this article) by having a source client make an HTML request to the WS server, and that server returning an XML response which can be used by the client.

For instance, the build process may need to know what the correct display resolution is for the hardware it is building. The build process sends the make and model of the local hardware to the WS, the WS performs a lookup based on that information, the WS returns the resolution information to the client, and finally the build process uses that information to configure the local environment. Using that methodology, the build process doesn't need to have been developed with all the configuration information locally and doesn't require any modification when new hardware is introduced to the environment. This obviously simplifies the build process and reduces administrative time when making environmental changes.

[…]

That said, implementing a WS in MDT isn't completely straightforward. MDT provides the framework for WS calls, but neither provides a ready to use WS interface nor crystal clear documentation on how to implement and use one on your own. In this article I've condensed the how-to in the hopes that your implementation and usage is quick and fully understood."

Jase T. Wolfe incorporates the web service application of Maik Koster and shows in an easy way how to build a web service. The QuickStart Guide was written for MDT 2012, but is still valid for MDT 2013. Be careful with guides and tutorials written for web services in MDT 2010, as some important parts have changed.

Beside this QuickStart Guide, we recommend the following links for further information about web services for you:

- `http://mdtwebfrontend.codeplex.com/` is currently a bit outdated, but Maik Koster announced in November 2014 that an updated MDT web front-end would be coming soon (`http://maikkoster.com/time-for-a-new-start-time-for-a-new-blog/`)

- `https://mdtcustomizations.codeplex.com/` contains a collection of web services and web front-ends written for MDT. A good source for review and inspiration.

Windows 10
All the concepts shown in this chapter are still valid for Windows 10.

Summary

In this chapter, we showed you how easily MDT can be extended by a SQL database and how this benefits and brings flexibility to your deployment, especially when using at larger scales. With UserExit scripts, you can extend and modify MDT in nearly every way. You can use these scripts, for example, to build a Wrapper for your own GUI instead of the MDT wizard, you can use these scripts to easily merge different models/makes, WMI data, and so on. Last but not least, the web services bring you a lot of comfort features to query AD, IP ranges, and lots of other information, without the need to expose critical AD user account information into scripts. All these features would surely fill an entire book for themselves, so this chapter only introduces you to these topics. Read the mentioned blogs and links to learn more about these features. Additionally, you will find a lot of information in the rich MDT community.

Additional Enterprise Configuration Items

In this appendix, we will cover some supplementary information for reference VM configuration and how to secure the MDT process by limiting access rights to your deployment share. Additionally, we will discuss the new Windows Imaging and Configuration Designer and why you should be careful when using this tool with MDT.

Reference VM configuration

A common problem that system administrators will run into is the installed memory of your VM and Windows PE's requirement of 768 MB. Hyper-V, by default, will give a VM only 512 MB and the dynamic memory driver will not service Windows PE either.

Currently, this manifests in my lab, as shown in the following screenshot:

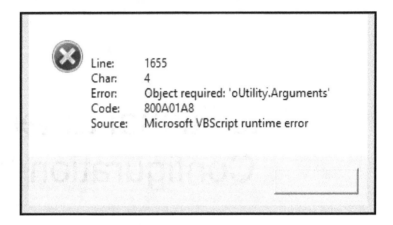

Simply increasing the system-installed memory in your VM to over 768 MB should remediate the memory problem, and Windows PE from your MDT share will function properly. To avoid this, I'd just set it to 1 GB or more.

Securing the MDT process

In some environments, security concerns are a primary driver, and thus the following questions come up: what can we do to secure the share, and what can we do to validate that the image is not tampered with?

For the first question about securing the share, the following rights are needed to allow MDT to work properly:

1. `\\path\deploymentshare$` rights:

- In Sharing, remove EVERYONE and add the user account specified specifically in your `Bootstrap.ini` and `CustomSettings.ini` file for READ access only
- NTFS rights would be the following:

   Creator Owner: Full control of subfolders and files only

   Administrators: Full control of this folder, subfolders and files

   System: Full control of this folder, subfolders, and files

Users: Check the following check boxes:

- **Read and Execute**
- **List Folder Contents**
- **Read**

2. \\path\referenceshare$ rights:

- In Sharing, again remove EVERYONE and add your user account used in the capture process for READ and CHANGE rights
- NTFS no changes needed

For the second part, how do we validate the image integrity?

The simplest way is to use PowerShell to generate a file hash of your WIM file. Use the PowerShell cmdlet get-filehash. The following command is simple enough to add to your process:

```
Get-FileHash .\install.wim | format-list
```

You can then validate the returned value by checking the deployment time or in audit processes in same way as the security requires.

Windows Imaging and Configuration Designer

The new **Windows Imaging and Configuration Designer (WICD)** is part of the Windows 10 ADK. It will be updated/enhanced with next releases of ADK.

WICD is described on MSDN as a tool that can do the following tasks:

- View all of the configurable settings and policies for a Windows 10 image or provisioning package
- Create Windows provisioning answer files
- Add third-party drivers, apps, or other assets to an answer file
- Create variants and specify the settings that apply to each variant
- Build and flash a Windows image
- Build a provisioning package

The source of this information is `https://msdn.microsoft.com/en-us/library/wind ows/hardware/dn916113(v=vs.85).aspx`.

Not only does it have the possibility to create configuration packages, but it is also able to switch the SKU of your Windows 10 installation. This was previously not possible. You still cannot move to **Long-Term Servicing Branch** (**LTSB**) via this mechanism, as this is a completely different build. At this stage of the process, you cannot downgrade. Currently, only an upgrade from Pro to Enterprise is possible (except for the Education SKU, which allows an upgrade from Home to Education).

The WICD can be used to create packages that implement any **mobile device management** (**MDM**)-based setting. Alternatively, you can run external scripts to set most MDM settings.

For some actions, such as pre-provisioning Windows 10 Mobile or switching to Windows 10 Mobile Enterprise, WICD is the only available tool to the enterprise.

WICD has a wide range of functionality in addition to script support. All in all, it sounds like a very mighty and powerful tool. However, it is currently not directly supported inside the MDT 2013 Update 2 GUI; this is subject to change in future releases. You can integrate a command line as a workaround, but this has a major drawback.

Currently, there is no way to fully automate or silently install the provisioning package. You can sign the `ppkg` to remove some prompts, but not in all circumstances. You also need to embed it in an image so that it gets installed during the OOBE process to get no prompts. However, this takes away a lot of flexibility.

If you hit the Windows key five times during OOBE, you can put in a provisioning package!

It has been our field experience that certain functions WICD can perform or try will break the MDT deployment process. Therefore, it should be tested and care should be taken while including this tool in your work (at the time of writing).

Some issues found at the time of writing (1511 release) include the following:

- Changing the SKU inducts a non-interruptible reboot that will break the MDT task sequence engine.
- Currently, you can only set what is shown through the UI. It is not possible to enter extra OMA-URI-based CSP policies.
- Removal of preinstalled applications does not work properly at this time.
- Most policies configured are MDM-related, so some options are only available in this toolset for customization.

With all these required workarounds, caveats, and limitations, we decided to move WICD here for supplementary information purposes. This tool is likely to be improved in future releases of the ADK. Also, future releases of MDT will likely support WICD directly in the deployment workbench, so keep an eye out for release notes changes and expansion of the tool's capabilities.

Index

A

access control lists (ACL) 160
Active Directory (AD) 267
ADK 8.1
  using, with Windows XP 180
application bundle, reference image
  application bundle object, creating 68, 69
  creating 65, 66, 67
  installing 70
  modifying 70
  updates, managing 71
applications 10
Assessment and Deployment Kit (ADK) 8
audit mode
  reference link 83

B

Background Intelligent Transfer Service (BITS)
  207
Business Desktop Deployment (BDD) 9

C

Client Log files
  about 197
  CBS.log 197
  dism.log 198
  netsetup.log 198
  setupact.log 197
  setupapi.app.log 198
  setupapi.dev.log 198
  setuperr.log 197
  WindowsUpdate.log 198
  wpeinit.log 198
CMTrace
  obtaining 202, 203
CustomSettings.ini file

  comparing, with Unattend.xml file 106
  dynamic modification 106
  structure 95, 96, 97, 98, 99, 100

D

Deployment Image Servicing and Management
  (DISM) 8
deployment network
  about 153
  configuring 154
deployment share
  about 147
  boot media, creating 32, 33
  confirmation 22, 23
  creating 148, 149, 150, 151, 152
  deployment options, modifying 20, 21
  descriptive name, specifying 20
  geographical considerations 154
  hotfix, including 45
  network considerations 153
  setting up 18, 19
  summary 22, 23
  updating 30, 31
driver detection 118, 119
driver injection 118, 119
driver installation
  controlling, with model variable 123, 124, 125,
  126
Driver Verifier
  about 220, 221, 222
  URL 222
drivers
  about 10
  as applications 126, 127

E

encrypting file system (EFS) 182
Error Code Look-up utility
  URL 206
error codes
  converting 206
error handling
  about 208, 209, 211, 212, 213, 215, 216
  references 216

F

file copy
  versus hard-link 179

G

globally unique identifier (GUD) 8
golden image 9

H

hard-link
  versus file copy 179
hotfix
  deployment share, updating 45
  downloading 42, 43
hybrid image 10, 135
Hyper-V drivers
  importing 40, 41

I

image customization
  about 75
  Audit mode, leveraging 83, 84, 85
  changes, analyzing 82
  documentation, checking 76
  games, adding to Enterprise image 78, 79, 80,
    81, 82
  Local Group Policy Object (LGPO) 86, 87
  reference link 88
  Security Compliance Manager (SCM) 86, 87
  Windows System Information Manager (WSIM),
    accessing 76, 77
image
  hybrid image 10

thick image 9
thin image 10
validating 219
imaging tools
  about 11
  MDT 11
  task sequence 11
  task sequencer 11
  variables.dat file 11
imaging
  concepts 9, 10
  history 7, 8, 9
ITNinja
  about 47
  URL 47

L

LoadState
  executing 167
  syntax 168
Local Group Policy Object (LGPO) 86, 87

M

mass storage drivers 211
MDT database, uses
  customizations, applying to computer based on
    manufacturer and model 296, 297, 298
  customizations, applying to individual computers
    287, 289
  customizations, applying to locations 294, 295
  customizations, applying to roles 292, 294
MDT database
  about 258
  creating 270, 271, 273, 274, 276
  objects, types 281
  permission, configuring 276, 277, 278, 279,
    280
  SQL Server, configuring 259, 260, 262, 266,
    267, 269
  SQL Server, supported versions 258, 259
  usage, considerations 298, 299
  using 281, 283, 285, 286
MDT installer
  downloading 15, 16
  URL 15

MDT logs
  about 199, 200, 201
  CMTrace, obtaining 202, 203
  error codes 206, 207, 208
  failed MDT deployment, clearing 204, 205, 206
MDT Monitoring 114
MDT Task Sequence Editor
  URL 84
Microsoft Deployment Toolkit (MDT)
  about 7, 11, 13
  deployment share, setting up 18
  installing 18
  process, securing 308
  reference share, setting up 18, 19
  setting up 13
  virtual machine, setting up 14, 15
Microsoft Management Console (MMC) 19
migration options
  about 176
  file copy, versus hard-link 179, 180
  offline migration 179
  online migration 179
  PC Refresh scenario 176
  PC Replacement scenario 177, 178
model variable
  used, for controlling driver installation 123, 124,
    125, 126
Multilingual User Interfaces (MUIs) 159

N

Network Basic Input/Output System (NetBIOS) 97
network drivers 211

O

offline migration 179
offline servicing 118
online migration 179
Operating System (OS)
  image properties, viewing 39
  importing 34, 35
  importing, from DVD media 37, 38
  selecting 36
organizational unit (OU) 12, 298
Out-of-Box Drivers node
  populating 119, 120, 121, 122, 123

out-of-box experience (OOBE) 75

P

packages 10
patches
  deployment share, updating 45
  hotfix, downloading 42, 43
  importing 41
  packaged import, setting up 43, 44
Plug and Play (PnP) 10, 111, 118

R

reference image creation
  about 56
  application bundle, creating 65, 66, 67
  entries, summarizing 60
  general settings, specifying 56
  OS settings, specifying 58, 59
  OS, selecting 57, 58
  password, specifying 59
  product key, specifying 58, 59
  security, specifying 59
  task sequence configuration, modifying 64, 65
  task sequence, finalizing 60, 61, 62
  task sequence, observing 63
  template, selecting 57, 58
reference image deployment
  about 134
  hybrid image 135
  thick image 134
  thin image 135
reference image
  .msi file, placing 47
  .msi files, searching with ITNinja 47
  .msi source directory, searching 50
  application details, specifying 49
  application, setting up 48
  applications, adding 46
  command details, inserting 52, 53
  destination directory, specifying 51
  image updates, automating 46
reference share
  exploring 23, 24, 25
  ISO-generated files, naming 29
  properties, setting 25, 26

scratch space, increasing 28
setting up 18, 19
share name, specifying 20
task sequence, setting up 27, 28
trace files, including in boot WIM 28, 29
reference task sequence
boot media, creating 73

S

ScanState
executing 165, 166
syntax 168
Security Compliance Manager (SCM) 86
about 87
Server Log file
about 199
wdsserver.log 199
Server Message Block (SMB) 14
Shell customization
about 88
Windows 7 background, customizing 90, 91
Windows 7 logon screen, customizing 90, 91
Windows 7 Start menu, customizing 88, 89, 90
Windows 7 taskbar, customizing 88, 89, 90
Windows 7 user tiles, customizing 90, 91
Windows 8, customizing 92, 93
Single Instance Storage (SIS) technology 123
SQL Server
configuring 259, 261, 264, 266, 267, 269
supported versions 258, 259
Sysprep
about 71
limitations 72
URL 72
System Center Configuration Manager (SCCM) 28
system class drivers 211

T

task sequence
about 11
initialization 108
install 112
logging 113, 114
postinstall 113
preinstall 110, 111

state capture 109
state restore 113
structure 107
validation 108
task sequencer 11, 200
task sequencer logs 199, 201
thick image 9, 134
thin image 10, 135
Toolkit Reference document
URL 26

U

Unattend.xml file
comparing, with CustomSettings.ini file 106
dynamic modification 106
structure 101, 102, 104
universally unique identifier (UUID) 258
UpdateDP 73
user interface (UI) 25
User State Migration Tool (USMT) 109, 154
about 157
applications, migrating 161
best practices 181, 182, 183, 184, 185
capabilities 160
components 163, 164, 165
downloading 163
GUI wrappers 192
history 157, 158
limitations 160
LoadState process 167
logs 216
requisites 159, 160
ScanState process 165, 166
troubleshooting 185, 186
URL 163
working with 163
UserExit scripts
about 12, 106, 299, 300, 301, 303
URL 106
USMTGUI
about 192
URL 192
UsmtUtils tool
about 171
compressed migration store, verifying 171, 172

files, recovering from compressed migration store 172
hard-link migration stores, deleting 171
supported cryptographic algorithms 173

V

variables.dat file
  about 11
  structure 104
virtual machine
  creating 136, 137, 138, 139, 140, 141
  deployment 142, 143, 144, 145, 146, 147
  setting up 14
VM configuration
  reference 307

W

Webservices
  about 303, 304
  URL 303
Windows 7
  background, customizing 90, 91
  logon screen, customizing 90, 91
  Start menu, customizing 88, 89, 90
  taskbar, customizing 88, 89, 90
  user tiles, customizing 90, 91
Windows 8
  customization 92, 93
Windows Assessment and Deployment Kit (Windows ADK)
  about 13
  installing 17
  URL 15
Windows Assessment and Deploytment Kit (Windows ADK) 163
Windows Assessment Services (WAS) 219
Windows Assessment Toolkit (WAT)
  about 219, 223, 224
  example 225, 226, 227, 228, 229, 230, 231

Windows Assessment Services (WAS) 232, 233, 235, 236, 238, 239, 241, 244, 246, 247, 248, 249, 251, 252, 253
Windows Automated Installation Kit (WAIK) 158, 163
Windows Deployment Services (WDS) 199
Windows Imaging and Configuration Designer (WICD) 309, 310
Windows Imaging Format (WIM) 8
Windows logs 196, 199
Windows Performance Toolkit (WPT)
  about 219, 223
  URL 223
Windows Preinstallation Environment (Win PE) 134, 165
Windows Recovery Environment (WinRE) 113
Windows Server Update Services (WSUS) 71, 111
Windows System Image Manager (WSIM) 75, 102
Windows XP
  using, with ADK 8.1 180
Windows
  setup process 11, 12
WinPE drivers
  about 128
  injecting 128, 129, 130, 131
Workstation Migration Assistant
  about 192
  URL 192

X

xcopy 93
XML files, customization
  about 173
  folder, migrating 174
  folder, migrating with subdirectories 174
  folder, migrating without subdirectories 175
  registry keys, migrating 174

www.ingramcontent.com/pod-product-compliance
Lightning Source LLC
Chambersburg PA
CBHW062102050326
40690CB00016B/3180

* 9 7 8 1 7 8 2 1 7 2 4 9 9 *